WISDOM *and*
IMAGINATION

Three important questions arise for people of religious faith today. What are you asking me to imagine? Where did that imagination originate? How does that imagination resonate with what I know about reality today? For anyone wanting to engage those questions, *Wisdom and Imagination*, provides solid ground on which to rebuild faith that withstands the most critical scrutiny.

Michael Morwood
Kirkridge Retreat Centre, and Author of "In Memory of Jesus".

With an outstanding collection of authors, this book offers some of the finest thinking on where religion and spiritually are today and a vision of where they may be headed in the future. A great contribution to the important conversation.

Fred Plumer
President, ProgressiveChristianity.Org USA

Drawing on the insights of modern, critical scholarship combined with experiences from the grassroots, this fine collection of essays directs the reader to serious questions about religion and its future. Emphasizing the wisdom that religion has to offer without ignoring the problems of extremism, we find in these pages an expression of hope, a commitment to honesty, and a sigh of relief that humanity might well find a way forward with, if not beyond, its shared cultural heritage embedded in the world of religion. The contributors of these essays are to be congratulated.

David Galston
Westar Institute Academic Program Director and Author of
"Embracing the Human Jesus"

Thank you from one who found it difficult to enter the church. This book will be a gift to those who want to have their questions and deepest yearnings honoured.

The Very Rev'd Dr Peter Catt
Dean, St John's Anglican Cathedral, Brisbane

WISDOM *and*
IMAGINATION

Religious Progressives **and** the Search for Meaning

Edited by
Rex A. E. Hunt and Gregory C. Jenks

WIPF & STOCK · Eugene, Oregon

Wipf and Stock Publishers
199 W 8th Ave, Suite 3
Eugene, OR 97401

Wisdom and Imagination
Religious Progressives and the Search for Meaning
By Hunt, Rex A. E. and Jenks, Gregory C.
Copyright©2014 Morning Star Publishing
ISBN 13: 978-1-4982-3051-3
Publication date 5/11/2015
Previously published by Morning Star Publishing, 2014

CONTENTS

Foreword

The test of a first-rate intelligence is the ability to hold two opposing ideas in mind at the same time and still retain the ability to function.

— *F. Scott Fitzgerald*

Some might suggest that the qualities that define *wisdom* and the characteristics from which spring the creativity of *imagination* are mutually exclusive, opposing ideas. After all, wisdom is acquired over the course of years of experience and carries with it the weight of hard-won integrity. On the other hand, imagination is often associated with one's ability to launch into previously unknown realms of possibilities that are often seen as a threat to those who are uncomfortable with anything other than the status quo.

In *Wisdom and Imagination,* the reader will find the inspiring results of a kind of theological alchemy. From the intersection of both wisdom *and* imagination, Rex Hunt and Greg Jenks have distilled a rich sampling of spiritual possibilities that spring from the combined efforts of the organisers of the first three Common Dreams conferences in Australia. Bringing together the understandings of some of the most insightful leaders of Australia and New Zealand's progressive religious movement, Common Dreams has sought to move beyond the musings of the ivory tower and provide a platform for the reality-based observations of those who have been in the trenches of what is essentially a post-Christian society for most, if not all, of their adult lives.

When I take stock of my own spiritual journey, I see that I owe much of its direction—not to mention the inspiration for Jeff Procter-Murphy and my curriculum series, *Living the Questions*—to Aussie and Kiwi influences. As a Rotary graduate scholar attending Perth Theological Hall in 1989, I was fortunate to be mentored by the likes of Bill Loader and inspired by conversations with Dorothy McRae-McMahon. In my role as a United Methodist pastor in Arizona, hardly a week goes by that I don't refer online to the non-theistic and progressive liturgies on offer from Rex Hunt, the lyrics of George Stuart, and through their writings and online resources, enjoy the theological camaraderie of many of the authors represented in this volume.

As one who has been privileged to participate in several of the Common Dreams conferences, I am thrilled to see much of the spirit of these gatherings captured here in print. Yet the reader will find more than just a snapshot of the proceedings of a conference or a disjointed collection of essays. *Wisdom and Imagination* presents a cache of insights that have grown out of the real-life experience of the hardscrabble reality of being a progressive religious thinker in Australia and New Zealand. It's an outstanding example of the richness and depth of the kind of collaborative effort that is often necessitated in standing for and voicing a minority report.

In his book, *Against the Stream: Progressive Christianity Between Pulpit and Pew*, Rex Hunt suggests that "we can start by acknowledging that none of us will ever have all the 'truth,'" and continues with asking, "has what we've been following made us a blessing or a curse to others".[1] As he notes, another way of asking that second question is to whether our efforts have increased or decreased the amount of compassion and understanding in the world?

The thoughts and examples laid out in *Wisdom and Imagination* make no claim to be the whole truth, but neither are they just a collection of tentative musings or unspecific conclusions addressing the great questions of life. What is on offer is a catalogue of hopes to be realized and causes to be furthered in the name of a world that is hungry for what progressive religious thought can contribute to the healing of the world.

The observations and methods you'll find expounded in this volume will stir in different readers a variety of directions that are possible in the progressive future. Val Webb appeals to the *Te Tao Ching* as she encourages religious progressives to function as midwives of change:

> You are a midwife, assisting at someone else's birth. Do good without show or fuss. Facilitate what is happening rather than what you think ought to be happening …

Drawing on a different tradition, Rabbi Aviva Kipen challenges us to get some *chutzpah* and see how we can emulate the midwives of Exodus by sabotaging the decree of the Pharaoh.

With both practical examples and an appeal to embrace what some might say are the impractical consequences of dissent, Glynn Cardy affirms

---

1   Hunt, *Against the Stream*, 87.

that 'prayer' is a big word, encompassing everything from thoughts and words to making love and being arrested. Jenny Te Paa Daniel addresses a predominantly white (and male!) movement with the challenge to engage a broader cultural and social base in the mutual task of critiquing, confronting, and correcting the injustices that cripple our secular and faith communities.

Lorraine Parkinson and Lloyd Geering explore what is—to some—the still scary and blasphemous but utterly essential contributions of John A.T. Robinson's *Honest to God*. They acknowledge that "negotiating with the previously non-negotiable" won't be easy, but remains a crucial element of moving forward with theological integrity.

From preaching Jesus and imagining a new future for the Bible to Eco-Theology and a call to reclaim Islam, *Wisdom and Imagination* hums with a sense of the possibilities when those of a progressive theological mindset embrace their common dreams. Pierre Teilhard de Chardin wrote that, "The whole future of the earth, as of religion, seems to me to depend on the awakening of our faith in the future."[2] The collaboration of ideas in *Wisdom and Imagination* is just the kind of catalyst one needs in awakening one's faith in the quest for more depth, breadth, and integrity in our collective spiritual future.

As economic and cultural realities conspire to demand hard decisions about the purpose of the church and the future of religion all around the world, those with a stake in whatever the church and religion will look like in the future would do well to recognize the importance of the progressive religious voice in Australia and New Zealand. The contributors to *Wisdom and Imagination* not only offer ideas toward transforming thought, practice, and faith. The developing networks and connections created through Common Dreams offer companionship along the journey as religious progressives challenge one another to broaden and deepen the search for meaning and relevance in the twenty-first century.

Revd. David M. Felten
Co-author of *Living the Questions: the Wisdom of Progressive Christianity*
Fountain Hills, Arizona, USA
Easter, 2014

---

2   Teilhard de Chardin, *The Future of Man* (Epigraph: "Letters to Mme George-Marie Haardt").

Introduction

Progressive religious thought is not new to either Australia or New Zealand. In one form or another it has been around for 170 years or so, often practised by individuals but not exclusively.

Various historical resources tell us, for instance, the first Unitarian church in Australia was established in Sydney in 1850 by a Rev. Stanley. The Melbourne Unitarian Church was founded two years later, in 1852, while English settlers commenced the church in Adelaide in 1855. In New Zealand the story is similar: the first Unitarian congregation was formed in Auckland in 1863.

Efforts at establishing progressive Jewish synagogues in both Melbourne and Sydney date from 1882 and 1932 respectively, with the first enduring Liberal or Progressive congregation being founded in Melbourne in 1930, and Sydney's Temple Emanuel founded eight years later.

Perhaps the most daring effort at church-planting occurred in 1885 in Melbourne, when former Presbyterian minister, Charles Strong (1844–1942) assisted in founding the Australian Church—a free, non-sectarian, undogmatically-based religious fellowship. The underlying idea of the Australian Church was that it should:

> attempt to provide a favourable climate and a home for those who were convinced of the significance and importance of religion, but who were unable to accept the traditional formulae of the churches and a theology derived from the past.[1]

The Australian Church continued to be part of the Victorian landscape from 1885 through to 1955. While it appears to have been the hope of some of the original founders of the Australian Church that it might become a truly national church, attempts at founding branches in Sydney, Newcastle and Brisbane were not successful.

A notable and more recent effort occurred in Sydney when the NSW Methodist Conference in 1963 asked Ted Noffs to establish a mission in Kings Cross to be run out of some property it owned. It became known

---

1   C. R. Badger, The Reverend Charles Strong and the Australian Church, 106.

as the Wayside Chapel. Writing of Noffs in her book, *Men Ahead of Their Time*, Winifred Ward said:

Noffs' ministry has been arguably the most extreme, most public and most sustained expression within the NSW Methodist Church [and later, the Uniting Church] of a ministry which rejected significant areas of traditional Christian dogma and doctrine. At the same time, the wide popular approval of his ministry from outside the established church institution warranted [a] description of the ministry as one which related religion to the daily needs of the people it served.[2]

Noffs consistently maintained that an authentic Christianity must be involved with the world. It is reported that on several occasions he publically urged church people "to get up out of the pews and look for human needs".[3]

Like Strong before him, Noffs was accused of heresy, usually presented as 'unfaithfulness to the doctrines of the Church'. The charges against both Strong and Noffs related to the doctrine of Atonement. Strong resigned just before his case was decided. The charge against Noffs was 'dismissed'.

A colleague of Noffs at the Wayside Chapel was Professor Charles Birch, a lay theologian and biologist from the University of New South Wales. A significant interpreter of process theology, Birch was also a prominent adviser within the World Council of Churches.

What seems new about the current progressive religious expression, is that this open and pluralistic faith is 'coming out' or resurfacing in many congregations in mainline/old-line churches, despite—or in spite of— Archbishops, Moderators and 'religious right' lobby groups. Progressive religious thought is giving sustenance and support to thousands of disillusioned individuals—often called 'the church alumni' or post-Christians—who now meet in informal, safe, discussion/nurturing groups in a dynamic and broad grassroots movement.

Over the past ten years several important books have been published from within this movement that detail both the shape and the story of this growth. Four from a much wider number are worth mentioning, even just briefly.

In 2006 New Testament scholar and founding member of the Jesus Seminar, Hal Taussig, published *A New Spiritual Home*.[4] It was the result of two years of research in the USA and documented "literally thousands"

---

2   Winifred Ward, Men Ahead of Their Time, 82.
3   Ibid., 99.
4   Taussig, *A New Spiritual Home*.

of local groups and communities "celebrating a lively, open-minded, and openhearted Christianity ... emerging at the grassroots across America".[5] Taussig demonstrated that these new communities were not the result of some national program or initiative from above.

> Although they exist clearly within all denominations, including Catholicism, their emergence is not in response to an overarching collaboration among the various religious bureaucracies. Nor are they a product of some popular and charismatic national leader. Rather... they come from an unorganized but broad-ranging kind of Christian response to felt needs for vital spirituality, intellectual integrity, new ways of expressing gender, an alternative to Christian sense of superiority, and a desire to act more justly in relationship to the marginalized.[6]

Five years later, Australian biblical scholar Greg Jenks published *The Once and Future Bible*.[7] It quickly became a study book within the Australian progressive communities as a way "to engage with the Bible as a set of sacred texts that can serve as a hymnal for believers in exile [and] a song sheet for the church alumni association".[8]

This was followed 12 months later when fellow Australians, Rex A. E. Hunt and John W. H. Smith, edited a collection of articles, cameo essays, and progressive resources under the title *Why Weren't We Told?*[9] More than thirty international writers, practitioners, and scholars contributed to this handbook on progressive Christianity. However, it was during the collection and editing of this book that other individual stories began to emerge. So within nine months the editors published a second collection, titled *New Life: Rediscovering Faith*.[10] Twenty-five lay people from both New Zealand and Australia shared their journeys out of fundamentalist or conservative religion into a more open-minded and openhearted progressive religion perspective. Together they were saying: (i) we don't want our religion in the old way, (ii) we cannot give up our minds for it, and (iii) we cannot become pre-modern people.

---

5   Ibid., 2.

6   Ibid., 2–3.

7   Jenks, *The Once and Future Bible*.

8   Ibid., xvi.

9   Hunt and Smith, *Why Weren't We Told?*.

10   Smith and Hunt, *New Life*.

Common Dreams

Now, all this is by way of an introduction to the series of international conferences called *Common Dreams Conference of Religious Progressives in Australia, New Zealand, and the South Pacific*.

It all started in 2005. Rex Hunt was in Canberra and Jonathan Rea in Sydney. Both were members of the growing Australian progressive religion/progressive Christianity movements. Both were members of The Centre for Progressive Religious Thought, based at St James Uniting Church in Canberra, while Jonathan was also an executive member of CPRT Sydney.

During one of their lunchtime meetings around the Hunt dining room table in Canberra, Jonathan proposed 'we should stage a national progressive conference'. To that end, Jonathan talked with Ian Pearson—then minister at the celebrated Pitt Street Uniting Church, Sydney—and a meeting was arranged for January 2006. Present by invitation were: Rex Hunt (Canberra), Jonathan Rea, Ian Pearson, Eric Stevenson and Valerie Worswick (all from Sydney), Greg Jenks and Scott McKenzie (both from Brisbane), and John Smith (Melbourne). Jim Veitch (New Zealand) was unable to attend but participated in part of the discussion by telephone.

Discussion centred on establishing a national progressive religion network, using The Centre for Progressive Religious Thought Canberra as a model, which could then stage a national Conference. The meeting adopted an aim and set of objectives for the proposed national network …

> The AIM of the national network is to be a forum that explores progressive religion and spirituality, in a way that provides a safe place for those who have found organized religion irrelevant, unresponsive or damaging.

The OBJECTIVES of the National network are to:

- Build a network of support for those who seek to discover and live by a progressive faith, sharing ideas and pursuing questions and answers.
- Create an open and welcoming community that respects the faith position of all participants, and encourages authentic interfaith engagement.
- Promote progressive religious thought as an agent of change and renewal in faith communities and society.
- Link with other groups and Centres of progressive religious thought.

While both CPRT Canberra and CPRT Sydney adopted the aim and objectives, progressive communities in other states began to shape themselves differently. Many identified more with progressive Christianity than progressive religion. Hence, when a network was established in Melbourne in June 2006 they adopted the name 'Progressive Christian Network of Victoria'. A group in Brisbane adopted the name, 'Progressive Spirituality Network'.

The 2006 meeting also discussed the need for a national conference of religious progressives. After agreeing to support such a conference, a theme was suggested: "Common Dreams: Progressive Religion as a Transforming Agent". The theme was a direct response to the race riots in Cronulla, south of Sydney, and the commentary of some fundamentalist/conservative Christians.

As Greg Jenks has since written:

> Common Dreams … is intended to be an interfaith and ecumenical project to promote, protect and expand the role of reasonable and tolerant religion in the public space. As such, I have an investment in the success of Common Dreams as a Christian progressive and also as a citizen. The significance of 'Common Dreams' as a name for this movement is its potential to invite us beyond differences derived from culture, ethnicity and religion, and into a shared space where we have common dreams for a better future.[11]

Principal international speakers suggested for such an event included: Bishop John Shelby Spong, Brandon Scott, and Joseph Bessler—with all of them eventually attending CD1. A tentative date was set for August 2007 in Pitt Street Uniting Church, Sydney. Local Australian and New Zealand speakers were also identified, including theologian Val Webb, interfaith minister Stephanie Dowrick, educator Michael Morwood, and ethicist Noel Preston.

The projected progressive network did not eventuate at that stage, but a continuing series of international conferences did. Towards the end of the 2007 conference, chair Rex Hunt approached Richard Carter, president of the Progressive Christian Network of Victoria and invited them to consider holding a second conference in Melbourne. Richard Carter accepted, giving

---

11   Email to the CD4 local arrangements planning team dated 19 August 2013.

birth to the Common Dreams alliance, and the adoption of the name, with 'Common Dreams' becoming official, and continuing.

Common Dreams 2 Conference was held in St Kilda in 2010 with the theme: "Living the 'progressive' Dream". The keynote international presenter was Gretta Vosper, founding chair of the Canadian Centre for Progressive Christianity, and she was supported by Fred Plumer of ProgressiveChristianity.Org (USA).

A feature of the CD2 Conference was the inaugural 'Francis Macnab Progressive Religion Lecture', honouring Rev. Dr Francis Macnab, minister of St Michael's Uniting Church, Melbourne. Francis is an outspoken progressive who has ministered at St Michael's for nearly 40 years, often standing alone in the 'courts' of the Church.

Three years later, Canberra—in its centennial year—was the host city of the Common Dreams 3 Conference, held within the Australian National University. The international keynote presenters included Marcus Borg (USA), Bruce Sanguin (Canada) and David Felten (USA). For the first time, participants from the Progressive Christian Network in Britain were in attendance. The theme of the conference was: "Midwives of Change: Progressives Shaping Religious Communities". Again, these international presenters were supported by leading Australian and New Zealand progressives, including Margaret Mayman, Lorraine Parkinson, Glynn Cardy, Val Webb, Greg Jenks, Nigel Leaves, and Steven Ogden, along with other international speakers from Britain and Canada. The Common Dreams 4 conference will be held in Brisbane in 2016.

At each of the Common Dreams conferences there has been active involvement of some progressive Jews, and—at CD1 and CD2—progressive Muslims. Of those who identify as progressive Christian the largest number are affiliated with the Uniting Church in Australia.

Since that first international conference in 2007 there has been a further development: the introduction of 'Common Dreams on the Road' (CDoR) events. Such events are held between the conferences and feature one keynote presenter who either travels around Australia or has an extended stay in one centre. In 2014 this will be extended to New Zealand. CDoR guests have included Brandon Scott (2008 and 2014), Margaret Mayman (2011) and John Dominic Crossan (2010 and 2012).

Wisdom and Imagination

Now to this published collection. All but one of the authors in this volume has presented or led a workshop at a Common Dreams Conference. They were included on a Common Dreams program because it was felt they had something important to say on progressive religion. Other participants were keen to learn from them and share their experiences with them. While the object of this collection is not to publish a set of proceedings from the Common Dreams meetings, it is our hope that the volume might assist in giving wider exposure to the wisdom and imagination associated with Common Dreams.

Val Webb's opening chapter is in direct response to the theme of the Common Dreams 3 Conference: Midwives of Change. Webb says a midwife is one who assists at someone else's birth. So the midwife's role is to facilitate what *is* happening rather than what you think *ought* to be happening. Touching the personal experiences of those who have discovered and shared in the 'progressive journey', Webb suggests there is a real "thrill" experienced when contact is made with another and there was a discovery "that others had asked the same questions … Then we found that theologians who studied the traditions in depth had also asked the questions, allowing us to walk away from traditional doctrines minus a load of guilt". This process was a long "pregnancy of chipping away layers of old truths", and it "needed a gentle midwifery." A midwifery that was provided by the increasing number of study and support groups being established around the globe.

Like progressive religion more generally, the Common Dreams Conferences are about more than just a revisioning of 'Christianity'. *Aviva Kipen,* a progressive rabbi from Melbourne, raises the question of change within communities and asks: who are the heroines and heroes, and who are the saboteurs of change, in our sacred communities? Indeed, do we automatically understand heroes and heroines as positive and saboteurs as negative? By exploring the polarity between those two concepts of heroism and sabotage, Kipen invites us to measure ourselves against both ideas. "No matter how uncomfortable," she says, "we must at least admit to ourselves which is our preferred or perhaps our default stance. But then again, do we have to occupy the either/or? Is there a better alternative?"

2013 was the fiftieth anniversary of the publication of John A. T. Robinson's classic book, *Honest to God.* Two of the chapters in this volume are devoted to the importance and impact of Robinson's book. Well known New Zealand theologian, **Lloyd Geering,** sets out to explain why *Honest to God*, which was not a particularly easy book to read, "blew the roof off the Church and let in some fresh air"—becoming a runaway bestseller. One reason, suggests Geering, is that Robinson was pulling together the thoughts of a number of theologians—Bonhoeffer, Bultmann and Tillich—who were then at the leading edge of Christian thought. Another was the public impression created from the very beginning that Robinson was making a break with Christian orthodoxy on the basic issue of the reality of God. Geering claims Robinson was not denying the reality of God, but calling for 'a restating of traditional orthodoxy in modern terms'.

Australian **Lorraine Parkinson** focuses on the 'grassroots' pastoral and evangelistic concerns which motivated *Honest to God*, and how these continue to be relevant, or not. Parkinson also addresses Robinson's remarks about what he called 'The End of Theism' and argues that those ideas "have opened up for lay people a priceless opportunity to express openly their already changing understandings of God and Jesus". Such ongoing conversations, involving both lay and ordained people about issues of faith and belief, "represent an essential and pervasive evolution of Christianity".

John Smith looks back over the emergence of progressive Christianity and offers some reflections from the edge of the progressive "flood plain" in Australia and New Zealand. These reflections include the influence of historical Jesus research in recent decades, and particularly the Jesus Seminar project sponsored by Westar Institute; the formation of mutually supportive lay groups eager to explore their own individual spirituality stimulated by materials such as 'Living the Questions' and 'Exploring Open Christianity'; and tracing how all these influences may shape the future of Christianity.

Towards the end of his life, Westar Institute founder Robert Funk, issued a 'call to arms' on the Sunday morning experience: "throw the old forms out and start over [again] ... design a new Sunday Morning experience from the ground up ... new music, new liturgy, new scriptures, new ceremonies, new rites of passage". **Rex Hunt** takes up that challenge by Funk and addresses not only the *shape* of progressive/evolving liturgy but also explores some progressive liturgical models for Baptism, the Jesus Banquet/Holy Communion, and Words of Committal at a Funeral Service.

Greg Jenks asks an important and challenging question: What if the 'open table' of Jesus and his first followers was paired with an 'open Scripture' rather than a closed canon? After noting that the Bible is already more diverse than most Christian communities care to admit, Jenks then explores some future possibilities of a 'once and future Bible', and imagines an inclusive set of Scriptures that speak from and to the heart of religious progressives.

Brisbane theologian, **Nigel Leaves,** addresses the iconic question that St Mark attributes to Jesus—'Who do you say that I am?' (Mark 8:29). According to Leaves, this is as relevant today as it was two thousand years ago, especially for those who in some way or another are still 'followers of Jesus'. In his chapter he sets out to answer Mark's question with reference to four recent books about Jesus that reflect the agenda for what he terms 'today's Jesus context'. "These texts", he writes, "both encapsulate the current debate about Jesus and provide appropriate source material from which to formulate a tentative answer to how we might preach Jesus today." In particular, they show how these books bring into sharp relief four important 'Jesus themes' that preachers must deal with whenever they undertake either a personal or a homiletic answer to 'Who do you say that I am?'

Glynn Cardy suggests there are many ways to understand prayer. For a number of progressive Christians, prayer is living into and embodying a vision of mutuality and compassion. Beginning with examples from the Jewish tradition, the author describes his own journey of prayer and theological discovery away from a male dominating God to a God of mutuality and compassion. This understanding of God as compassionate mutuality, Cardy claims, can lead progressive Christians to change from and discard traditional forms of spoken prayers. "New words and ways of praying can emerge, as can new images/metaphors for God". But as the author points out, to pray/live a vision of mutuality can lead some people to politically confront the status quo. Cardy concludes his chapter by suggesting that to believe in a power of mutuality and compassion, to name that power as God, and to politically work for the expression of that power in both church and state, "will lead to conflict with the God and worshippers of domination and control".

Ethicist **Noel Preston**, drawing on process theology, re-examines traditional Christian theological themes from an eco-centric perspective, outlining an orthopraxis approach that is a firm basis not only for interfaith dialogue but also for spiritual engagement with those of no faith. He argues that eco-theology is now the 'main game' for religious progressives.

As an indigenous Aotearoa-New Zealand lay leader and a woman, **Jenny Te Paa Daniel** raises her concerns that 'white fellas' dominate the current religious progressive movements. "I was and still am hoping," she writes, "that among religious progressives there might just be a far more profoundly empathetic and informed sense of the broader geographic and thus socio-political context within which all in the South Pacific neighbourhood are constantly 'searching for meaning'". And then this challenge: "It would seem therefore timely for religious progressives to witness to a radically new apprehension of just who is who in the Pacific neighbourhood and how might we collectively imagine afresh ways of being God's good Pacific peoples together in the ongoing struggle for justice and opportunities for flourishing for all and not just for some."

Progressive Muslims the world over are calling for a revival of Islamic teachings that underpin universal values such as gender equality and reconciliation. These Muslims offer a striking vision of a new Muslim identity, one that rejects the stereotype that Islam must be defined in opposition to the West. Australian Muslim leader **Sherene Hassan** debunks some of the myths associated with Islam and explores the issues of *sharia* law, Muslim women, and violence.

But what of those who have attended rather than presented at a Common Dreams Conference? **Heather Carter**, a retired judge of the Family Court of Australia, was invited by the editors to offer a personal perspective on the impact of these progressive religious movements. While expressing gratitude for all she has now learned, Carter remains resentful that much of the thinking and teaching of students of theology, seminarians and the like did not find its way—as often as it should have done—into the sermons delivered by many of the clergy she encountered. There was, and sometimes still is, a division between what the ministers learnt and what they told their congregations.

> Through … Common Dreams conferences, I have been able to meet many leading Australian and international progressive thinkers and writers. It is one thing to read the writings of the progressive thinkers. It is even better to see and hear them speak. Connecting with others who are on the same journey and engaging with the leading progressive religion thinkers has been important to me.

Carter goes on to claim she is convinced that the decline of attendance at traditional churches "can be traced to the lack of relevance which people not only experienced in what they were told from the pulpit", but what they were told and how they were treated when they commenced to challenge. "Many people appear to have left in frustration."

Two international guests were also invited to offer their thoughts—bookend thoughts actually—to this collection. American David Felten, co-founder of the progressive 'Living the Questions' series of educational resources was asked to write the Foreword, while Canadian author and evolutionary theologian, Bruce Sanguin, was invited to contribute an Afterword. Their observations place the progressive religion agenda from Australia and New Zealand in a wider context, inviting us to be confident of our capacity to contribute to the larger movement and also reminding us of the global significance of our Common Dreams.

Irish theologian and poet, John O'Donohue, has observed:

> The imagination is the great friend of possibility. Where the imagination is awake and alive fact never hardens or closes but remains open, inviting you to new thresholds of possibility and creativity.[12]

We hope that you find this collection of work by religious progressives from Australia and New Zealand assists you to plumb the depths of your own creativity, encourages you to remain alive to new possibilities, and invites you to imagine the new expressions that our Common Dreams will take in the years ahead. The best is yet to come, and we look forward to sharing the journey with you.

As editors we wish to express our thanks and appreciation to all our contributors. While some were working under extreme pressure to meet our deadlines all were eager to participate in this collaborative project. Thank you one and all. Finally, we want to acknowledge Robyn Smith whose careful 'eye' helped remove some of our obvious errors of style, as well as Hugh McGinlay and the creative staff at Morning Star Publications for their professional assistance and guidance as this book has taken shape.

Rex A. E. Hunt
Gregory C. Jenks
May 2014

---

12   O'Donohue, *Anam Cara*, 183.

1. Midwives of change: Progressives shaping religious communities

Val Webb

"Midwives of Change: progressives shaping religious communities" was the theme of the 2013 Common Dreams Conference. When I was invited to address the conference topic, I submitted as my abstract something from the *Tao Te Ching*, the Chinese sacred text known as "The Way", written six centuries before Jesus also pointed out a way.

> You are a midwife, assisting at someone else's birth. Do good without show or fuss. Facilitate what is happening rather than what you think ought to be happening. If you must take the lead, lead so that the mother is helped, yet still free and in charge. When the baby is born, the mother will rightly say: "We did it ourselves!"[1]

"You are the midwife, assisting at someone else's birth." This is not about the convictions of the midwife. Midwives are neither the ones giving birth to something new, nor the ideas birthed - they are merely assistants of change. "Do good without show or fuss". Progressives as midwives are not called to create a new systematic theology and badger everyone into believing their creation. Instead, they offer good common sense from their experiences that might speak for itself in another situation. "Facilitate what is happening rather than what you think ought to be happening". It is about the mother and child doing what they need to do according to their natural instincts, not following someone else's prescriptions. "If you must take the lead, lead so that the mother is helped, yet still free and in charge". Midwives assist someone else's transformation without imposing control on the final result. What is the goal? "When the baby is born, the mother will rightly say: 'We did it ourselves!'" There are so many good lessons for midwife progressives in this gentle statement!

What changes do progressives wish for? While other lists may appear in this book for what John Smith calls the progressive trinity of doubt, deconstruction and discovery, I loosely describe them as follows:

---

1   *Tao To Ching*, 51.

- Progressives recognize that new scholarship, changes in our contemporary world, and personal experiences are challenging understandings of the universe, God, Jesus, the Bible, Church and humanity, challenges to be investigated with honesty.
- Jesus is recovered as a Jewish sage advocating a non-violent alternative empire to that of the Roman Caesar.
- God or the Sacred is re-imaged within our interconnected universe, rather than an interventionist Being controlling from outside.
- Personal intellectual integrity is emphasized, using human reason and experience in conversation with traditional teachings and contemporary scholarship.
- Religious communities where belonging and obedience are valued more highly than honesty and critical reflection are challenged.
- Christianity is not claimed as the only or best religion and interfaith connections are seen as an avenue to peace, global understanding and spiritual transformation.
- Full participation of women, gay-lesbian-bisexual-transgender people and other marginalized groups is required in all avenues of life
- Progressives show a strong commitment to social justice and the care of the planet.
- Creative worship and spiritual vitality are sought beyond limits imposed or ordered by the traditional church and its dogmas.
- Religious traditions are not static but living entities and vast reservoirs of potential interpretations. New eras have new questions needing new answers.

There have been similar movements down the centuries but this current global momentum is in relative infancy. Anthropologist Victor Turner coined a term that is applicable to the place I believe progressives currently stand. Researching initiation rites in indigenous cultures, he described a *liminal* period as the transition stage from a previous state—childhood—to a post-initiation state where people are "expected to behave in accordance with certain customary norms and ethical standards." In this liminal period, people are "at once no longer classified and not yet classified".[2] I am convinced that any premature attempts to systematize or formalize progressive thought

---

2   Turner, *The Forest of Symbols*, 94–97.

will truncate it and produce shallow roots. It took four centuries for creeds to be laid down in the early church and, once declared, they dampened creative thought rather than assisted its continuing evolution.

While some progressive groups have drafted affirmations, there is worthy resistance to universal statements creating new belief boundaries, however elastic. Many progressive groups began as lay-led, lay-energized gatherings formed because of an inability or refusal of church leaders to engage their questions. They provided places for laity to read and discuss without censure. According to John Bodycomb, such groups rest on three propositions, "No question is off limits; no literature, institution or professional caste is above criticism; and no formulation of the faith can be considered definitive". [3] These groups are not homogenous within themselves or across the progressive label. Some focus on historical Jesus research, others concentrate on living out Jesus' vision, others explore new liturgies, others work on social justice and eco-theology and others pursue interfaith conversations.

A general agreement about what they reject has held progressives together to this point more than uniformity about what they are. Since I move mostly in progressive groups these days, I become comfortable with discussions where no bounds are set in terms of belief, until I stumble across something that reminds me of where so many people *still* sit, exemplified by this recent note from a missionary to his supporters:

> These are dark and evil times in which many of our political leaders happily go along with homosexual "marriage" and the mass murder of unborn babies, while vigorously protecting flying foxes!! Floods, cyclones, volcanoes, fires and earthquakes fail to awaken them to the fact that God could open his fingers a little and *really* let such natural disasters rip rather than restraining them as He does! How much does God need to allow or make happen to get the attention of our nation? [4]

Many of you may have held these attitudes in your youth but have moved beyond this and encouraged friends and family on the progressive journey. Whenever I speak, the usual question comes up—"We have failed the next generation because our children no longer attend church, but what will we tell our grandchildren?" At a recent presentation, however, as murmurs of agreement went around the elderly hall, one young person spoke up,

---

3   Bodycomb, *Aware and Attentive*, 28.
4   Personal correspondence.

"You didn't fail us. You gave us what we needed—permission to think for ourselves—and we did!"

If these are changes progressives seek, in what way are progressives the midwives of change? Throughout history, midwives have cared for women during pregnancy and labour—and in between pregnancies—working in partnership with the woman. Midwives have been accorded different status and treatment at different times in history, from highly-trained professionals to village women using herbal remedies. In the Middle Ages, medical professionals and the church forced many midwives out of their craft, accusing them of witchcraft, in league with the devil, hence the horrifying murders of millions of women across Europe informed by the fifteenth century *Malleus Maleficarum* (Witches' Hammer), a manual for witch-hunting produced by Dominican inquisitors. Later in history, midwifery became more structured and professional and, by the early twentieth century, more regulated. Today, training, status and duties of midwives vary significantly in different countries, but in some tribal areas, midwives are still seen as shamans with a divine calling to perform varied rituals to keep patients safe.

Obviously there are many directions in which this midwife metaphor for progressives can go. I will focus on the *variety* of midwives. Undeniably, early midwives were the biblical scholars, in particular the Jesus Seminar, who made their findings available to lay people, not in barely coherent academic phrases but in language lay people could understand. Discovering more about the historical Jesus required new understandings of God and other doctrines and, once progressives could wriggle free of an infallible church, a literal, inspired Bible, a supernatural Jesus as cosmic pawn for our salvation, and other time-warped dogmas, they began to trust their own reason and experience. Once an external Being no longer intervened in the world, manipulating and judging every move, progressives could imagine sacred activity *within* the universe, whether called Life, Presence, Love or simply personal conscience.

There is variety amongst progressives as to how they imagine the Sacred. While almost all would reject an external interventionist God, the majority use terms such as the Sacred, Mystery, Something More or Creativity to name the reality behind them. Others have moved beyond a reality, talking instead about an ethical way to live. Some of these variations may be more about language than concrete divisions. In trying to describe something more, we suffocate amid words in liturgies and theologies, using them easily rather than remembering, as theologian Paul Knitter says, that "the unknown part of whatever we describe is much, much larger than the known part we are expressing ... Words are not only always inadequate... but they can be actual impediments to experiencing the Divine Mystery".[5]

Some progressives who do not see any reality behind ideas of the Sacred still hold Jesus and his teachings as their inspiration, but a few have moved beyond Jesus, working out their own ethics and actions simply by responding to life with justice and kindness—yet calling themselves Christian. However, Marcus Borg says, "The question of whether we make Jesus (and the Bible) central is a question of what community we wish to belong to and address. Can we bring insights from Ken Wilber [and others] into Christian community? Of course. Can we be Christian and shape Christianity without making Jesus and the Bible central (though not as exclusive revelations)? Probably not".[6]

Although progressives rightly celebrate this diversity as honouring peoples' autonomy of thought, it does create difficulties. For example, articles have appeared in popular and academic journals dismissing progressive Christianity by assuming that these more radical stances about the Sacred are what *all* progressives think. I have found it a minefield to speak to some progressive groups who have established firm walls of correctness about what language and imagery one can and cannot use about the Sacred. I also struggle with issues of hospitality in progressive communities when more radical positions are championed as what progressives *must* think, because these positions do not attract or make sense to people still in churches or to those taking first tentative steps into progressive groups. I am also not convinced they represent the majority of progressives. Do we *have* to abandon a rumour of God, however we might describe that term? Do we *have* to progress to a single conclusion, closing the conversation rather than opening it up, or will we, in time, separate out into different denominations according to our theologies? For myself, I find it over-confident, in light of ever-expanding knowledge of our universe and the assurance from scientists that we have not seen anything yet, to make definite claims about what is *not*, rather than living with the ever-emerging mystery.

5   Knitter, *Without Buddha*, 136.
6   Personal email communication.

Any resistance movement that knows what it rejects but is not unified as to what sort of a community it wishes to become faces such heterogeneity. The Reformation was united around theological and ecclesiastical abuses in a powerful church. As various reformers articulated the principles around which their emerging communities would rally, an increasing number of denominations emerged, even engaging in wars and executions over who was right. When feminist challenges emerged in the sixties, woman scholars were united around exposing theological and practical abuses of women by a patriarchal culture validated by the Bible. As different women articulated their experiences within particular settings, whether Hispanic, lesbian or indigenous women, separate groups emerged, often with conflicting positions on the cause and nature of the problems. However, while Reformation debates were about the *church* and feminist challenges were about *women*, this progressive discussion is about foundational elements of a God-reality and the importance of Jesus—hardly nit-picking stuff in a community calling itself Christian. It is about whether the baby handed to the mother by the midwife contains any of the mother's DNA (our heritage of Jesus and his vision of God) or whether it will be a baby by adoption, taking the mother's Christian name without any of the family genes. Are we birthing something in continuity with our heritage, or simply creating a baby from some contemporary dust mixed with water that could equally have its heritage in AA or Rotary? What fun metaphors are!

Paul Knitter's wonderful book, *Without Buddha I could not be a Christian*, tells how his conversations with Buddhism have helped him re-interpret problematic aspects of Christianity. In this process, he is careful that the theological genes he is passing on are still Christian and that his reinterpretations, though very different, are not totally different from what went before. "All good theology," he says "is a matter of discontinuity in continuity, creating something new that is rooted in and nourished by the old". [7] Since Christianity is an *ekklesia* or community, Knitter says, there has to be some degree of community affirmation for new insights to be received by the community. Of course, the question arises as to what we call "church". Is it the institution, our local church, our small study or working group, the church alumni or even a network across a city or the world?

---

7   Ibid., xiv.

Progressives celebrate *autonomy*, the independence of mind that nominates *ourselves* as our final authority in matters of faith and belief based on our reason and experience. While we receive input from many sources, we claim the right to choose what we believe amongst authoritative claims. The opposite, *heteronomy*, means passive surrender of authority to external rule, whether scripture, tradition, clergy or family, something we have done for centuries in the church. Remember the thrill of our first contacts with progressive thinking, the discovery that others had asked the same questions? Then we found that theologians who studied the traditions in depth had also asked the questions, allowing us to walk away from traditional doctrines minus a load of guilt. This process is rarely a sudden "once I was blind but now I see" experience, but rather a long pregnancy of chipping away layers of old truths, with recurring moments of uncertainty and fear as so much we once treasured is discarded. Such a pregnancy needs gentle midwifery.

In progressive communities, however, once such exploration begins, something like the Tour de France can happen. Some members burst from the starting block with enthusiasm and freedom to throw off everything and anything that gives them problems. All caution is swept away as they peddle off, not even looking behind to see if anyone else is coming. Such people have often long been struggling internally with doubts and only needed space and permission to speak. They include many clergy and theologically trained folk who may not have voiced their doubts within their institutions. Now in a progressive space, they can forge ahead, sometimes dragging other members along with their particular convictions and even unconsciously despising those not keeping up—the "you don't still think *that*, do you?" syndrome. Although many progressive groups began with faithful lay people helping each other struggle in the absence of clergy support, some of the theologically educated now in progressive groups assume they will work out for all the others what they should think. Peer pressure can make lay people follow a guru to an end point, even if they do not feel comfortable with the conclusions, and this can become reverse orthodoxy, albeit *progressive* orthodoxy, if certain new 'truths' silence others.

Progressive midwives in communities need to be careful that those taking their first scary steps out of traditional boxes are not stunned or obliterated by powerful voices wanting to jump forward to some definitive end. New seekers should not be evicted at the first exit if they can't ride with the dominant crowd. We need to think carefully about what sort of hospitable communities we wish to be. I feel this acutely as a laywoman who struggled much of my life against doctrines that left me full of doubts and without a safe place where these could be examined. I began theological studies, not as a career (I already had a few of those) but to sort out my own questions. Later, when I couldn't leave theology alone, I resolved to help others free themselves from the terrors of correct belief while not suggesting an end point they must reach. Gary Bouma has defined social cohesion as "the capacity of a society or group to so organize its resources and people to produce what it needs to sustain and reproduce itself". [8] Internal conflict undermines the capacity to do this. Progressives have to find ways to maintain social cohesion without denying people the freedom to hold beliefs important to them. We need ways to say who we are and what we think, to acknowledge our need for each other, yet gently confront those who insist on one correct stance or attempt to eliminate or trivialize others. Perhaps our title should be, instead of progressives, "Christians without borders".

Having discussed some positives and negatives of theological diversity, let me go in a different direction on the variety of midwives. Progressives seem fairly insistent on emphasizing a way of life rather than a set of beliefs, with the Sacred as something we make happen in the world whenever we enact love, justice, mercy, joy and goodness. Bishop Jack Spong's mantra is about living fully, loving wastefully and being all that we are meant to be. [9] Others talk, not of an experience *of* Something, but about "experiencing"— imagery that moves us beyond the dualism of describing Mystery in relation to ourselves, to simply experiencing life, the known and that beyond our comprehension. If, then, the focus is about being and becoming fully human and acting within this world, whether we acknowledge something working within us or not, there are many, many midwives, both within religious traditions and with no links to religion.

Many midwives of change work within Christianity for the same goals as progressives, yet do not label themselves thus. In fact, labelling ourselves often separates us from others who also struggle for peace and justice, albeit with different theological understandings. In my past life, I was a microbiologist researching new ways to classify bacteria. Prior to that, all bacteria were first classified as gram positive or negative, with other tests following, but our research asked why this one test had priority over all

---

8   Bouma, *Being Faithful in Diversity*, 48.
9   Spong, *Why Christianity Must Change or Die*, 226.

other differences. We applied a battery of tests with no favouring, classifying bacteria on their overall number of similarities. In the same way, some classify themselves as progressives *first*, the primary box in which they sit, but the question of overall similarities arise. Should I sit in a box with those working for justice and ecology, regardless of their Christology, or in the progressive box, regardless of their concern for justice and ecology? Should I sit with interfaith dialogue midwives, despite different understandings of God, or with progressives who may or may not wish to engage other religious traditions?

It is also important to recognize the range of progressive organizations beyond our horizon. If you type "progressive" into a search engine, a host of groups come up. While they may not all agree on your particular progressive formula, they too are challenging the status quo and offer great resources as midwives of change. For instance, Frank Schaeffer helped his father Frank Schaeffer Snr. (from L'Abri in Switzerland) initiate what became the USA Religious Right. Frank has left all that now and is a member of the Orthodox Church, but is equally challenging the traditions, though not in all the ways you might. All these midwives are partners and the more we link together and encourage each other in moving Christianity into the twenty-first century, the better.

There are many midwives who may not yet have found their voice. Many active clergy speak of opposition to progressive stances, both from institutional hierarchies and conservative lay members, such that they avoid public expression of progressive views. When a recent questionnaire was circulated to Uniting Church in Australia clergy prior to an upcoming book, they were asked to what extent they followed progressive theologies. Almost half said often or always, while over half said progressive theologians were important or very important to the church. In ranking their educational needs and interests across nine categories, progressive and emerging theologies ranked the third highest after general theology and biblical study. It would seem clergy *are* paying attention to progressive thought, regardless of whether they publicly support progressive groups or feel supported in this by their institutions.

And what of midwives beyond the church? Science, more than any midwife of change, has encouraged us a to ponder our lives on a bigger drawing-board by showing us a universe far greater and mysterious than the universe of religion, the cosmos of our creeds, or a heaven of golden streets. This amazing glimpse into mystery and wonder pushes us to imagine a Sacred large enough to contain such grandeur, or else re-imagine our religious claims altogether. Science also offers us hints on how to assess our claims. Science is not about immutable laws but about provisional explanations open to revision when better information comes along. Such revision is seen as strength not weakness, whereas in religion it has been touted as weakness and lack of faith. We need to ingest the challenges of science, not just as a sub-theme of progressive interests, but as a stunning midwife in its own right that must inform all our religious deliberations.

Many atheist midwives create spaces for challenges to established 'truth'. The rise of new atheists, with their public annunciation of many of our own stifled doubts, has been a wake-up call as they invite us to explore beyond our religious borders. New atheism has given us the ability to step into their arguments as a place from which we can re-evaluate our own claims. It has provided dialogue partners with whom many progressives have closer links than with fundamentalist Christians. Politics is also a midwife of change if our goal is to reflect theologically from the context and circumstances in which we live. Politics is a public discourse where many midwives of change meet—ethics, economics, social justice, global action—in order to bring to birth changes in this world in which we live and move and have our being.

Literature, poetry, art and music are also midwives of change, whether with religious content or not, if we are to live fully as human beings. I am constantly amazed at how novels and biographies call me to theological reflection through the inspiring lives of both real people and fictional characters. I have notebooks of quotes from novels that offer more life skills than many theological tomes. Thus I enjoyed Gary Bouma's comment about *Star Wars*. Apparently 75,000 Australians put "Jedi Knight" or some related term in a census response for religion. When some people expressed offence at this, Bouma said:

> Have you seen one of the movies? You get three sermons. The injunction to 'trust the force' and the blessing 'may the force be with you'; a well developed moral frame, a theological orientation, and a basis for hope all packed up in some whiz-bang kind of visual stuff. Pretty impressive and rather more engaging than the average sermon … or Sunday School platitudes.[10]

After centuries of church resistance to natural theology, we are again reading from its leafy pages. Natural theology argues a knowledge of the

---

10   Bouma, *Being Faithful*, 28.

Sacred through human ability to interpret evidence within the universe and human nature. The traditional Christian argument against natural theology hinged on the fear that, if God could be known through nature, what was the need for a revelation in Jesus Christ? Theologian Karl Barth's opposition to knowledge of God as creator divorced from knowledge of God as redeemer set the tone for the twentieth century. When theologian Sallie McFague began her career in Barthian theology, she learned that "only the Word that reached my ears conveyed the presence of God, never the sights before my eyes". [11] Later she became a champion of natural theology, reminding us that any theological constructions are simply "houses to live in for a while, with windows open and doors ajar. They become prisons when they no longer allow us to come and go, to add a room or take one away or, if necessary, to move out and build a new house".[12] While neo-Barthian views are still strong in many Australian theological colleges, the progressive reimagining of divine creativity *within* the universe has both given permission and justified theologically our need to see the planet as something sacred. Such awe and wonder is not limited to a religious experience, however. Philosopher Sam Keen says:

> To wonder is to perceive with reverence and love ... and in wondering we come close to the feeling that the earth is holy. Historically, the notion of wonder has been closely bound up with a religious mode of being in the world ... Whether we continue to talk about God is not so important as whether we retain the sense of wonder which keeps us aware that ours is a holy place. [13]

Teilhard de Chardin, Jesuit priest and scientist whose writings were suppressed during his lifetime by his religious order, grew up with an irrepressible sense of the beauty and wonder of nature from childhood experiences immersed in woods, rocks, trees and sea. As a budding scientist, he scrutinized everything he could find, weighing, measuring and dissecting. These experiences set him pondering the inner aspects of life as well, forming a holistic philosophy of the universe that could accommodate his experience of the Sacred about which he wrote, "You came down into me by means of a tiny scrap of created reality [the objects of nature]; and then suddenly, you unfurled your immensity before my eyes and displayed

---

11   McFague, *The Body of God,* 94.
12   Ibid., 16.
13   Keen, *Apology for Wonder,* 15 & 211.

yourself to me". [14] People ask me at every progressive presentation, "What do we teach our grandchildren?" I say to all grandparents—midwife them into a passionate love for nature that can, in turn, midwife them into their own experience of what they will call sacred. There is a wonderful poem by Stephen Dunn about post-Christian parents sending their daughter to an Arts and Craft week at the local church. When she came home wearing a "Jesus saves" button and singing, "Jesus loves me", it was time to talk. They had assumed that Jesus, while a good man, was sufficiently dead in their lives—like Lincoln or Jefferson—that their children would not pay attention, but:

> … you can't teach disbelief
> To a child,
> Only wonderful stories, and we hadn't a story
> nearly as good.
> Evolution is magical but devoid of heroes.
> You can't say to your child
> "Evolution loves you." The story stinks
> of extinction and nothing
> exciting happens for centuries. I didn't have
> a wonderful story for my child
> and she was beaming. [15]

Evolution does not have to be dry and boring. Tell the grandchildren the history of our world, not through the usual trinity of conquests, wars and human inventions, but through the great book of nature—about forests, rivers, insects, trees and seasonal transformations. Stop feeling guilty about which religious stories to teach them and which to avoid. Anchor them deeply in this earth and let their wonder and awe lead to deeper reflection, with you as midwife rather than religious instructor with a bundle of information to transmit. As Norman Habel says, we need to act as earth beings in solidarity with earth, not God-like beings who happen to be sojourners on earth. In his beautiful book *Rainbow of Mysteries*, Habel calls ecology *his* midwife: "Instead of being another science that let me view nature with detachment

---

14   Quoted in King, *Spirit of Fire*, 77.
15   Stephen Dunn, "At the Smithville Methodist Church", quoted in Huston Smith, *Why Religion Matters*, 57–58.

because I was a superior intellectual being with a mandate to dominate creation, ecology revealed to me who I was: an Earth being!" [16]

Progressives recognise that Christianity is not the only way, neither can we claim it is universally the *best* way because how can one person objectively judge this and on what criteria? This opens us to interreligious dialogue, but it goes further than dialogue. If the world's religions are on a similar human quest, albeit in different contexts, surely they are midwives with something to offer us? Must we always arrogantly reinvent the wheel? Paul Knitter's passing over into Buddhism, as mentioned earlier, showed him new ways to return and remain in his own tradition. Buddhist understanding of the interconnectedness of all things helped him move beyond the dualistic Christian teaching of an infinite distance between God and the world. Enlightenment as 'emptiness' at the centre—not nothingness, but empty as able to receive new connections and new possibilities in this changing, relating worldly existence—returned him to his Catholic mystical tradition. [17] John's gospel says "God is *love*", not "God is the *father* who loves". Love as a verb is "the emptying, connecting energy that in its power originates new connections and new life ... an energy field that pervades and influences us all, calling us to relationships of knowing and loving each other ..." [18] As for describing God as personal, Buddhist imagery of connecting energy allowed Knitter to imagine, not a personal relating being but a personal "sense of groundedness that produces peace within myself, and a sense of connectedness that produces caring for others".[19] Since Buddhism does not feature a concept of God, emphasising instead one's own work towards transformation, its language and imagery can assist both those who see a reality behind the Sacred and those who do not.

Buddhists see enlightenment as waking up to wisdom or understanding. Knitter experiences this in ordinary human moments where "something extraordinary can happen as we feel ourselves connected or grounded and held by a peace that can endure even after the hype of the experience is gone". [20] On a personal note, the morning I admitted my mother into an aged care facility after she lived with us for six months, I was emotionally

---

16   Habel, *Rainbow of Mysteries*, 72.
17   Knitter, *Without Buddha*, 15.
18   Ibid., 18, 20.
19   Ibid., 42.
20   Ibid., 43.

distraught, even though this move had become necessary. I was sitting at my computer when two impeccably white cockatoos landed on the bird feeder outside my window. They are my favourite birds despite the damage they do to vegetation—a childhood dream was to have a pet cockatoo. I had not seen them on my feeder before. It was as if they had finally found the place they belonged. I would never call this a miracle or an act of God—in fact, calling it such takes away from the randomness and delight of being a part of this natural world—but the incident warmed my grieving heart.

This search for midwives of change that impact our lives at any moment, let alone a lifetime, is endless. *Everything* midwives us towards being fully human, not just the narrow limits of theology and scholarship. In every changing moment we are bombarded by a plethora of impulses—emotional, informational, psychological, physical—all of which influence our next moment. Within this bombardment is what we imagine as Sacred. We need to acknowledge this diversity of splendid import and pay attention to it all. As Philip Clayton says:

> On the one hand, theology is a never-ending quest; it calls one continually to respond in novel ways to new "horizons of interpretation", whether they come from science, philosophy, culture or society. On the other hand, theology harkens continually back to its past—its scripture, classic figures and its traditional themes or loci—in an ongoing process of retrieval and renewal.[21]

We have benefitted from people in our past through liberation theology, historical Jesus study, feminist studies, eco-theological awareness, to name a few. These are our own progressive apostolic succession, as it were. In any era, the outspoken and the outsiders do the groundwork for change that may not be established until a few decades later. As today's Christians without borders, we must

> ... continue to be the leaven in the bread, the salt in the soup and the light in the darkness [and the midwives of change] when it comes to living with authenticity in our time and place. Such people are usually in the minority and in the margins of institutions, but they crystallize their thinking on the perimeter such that, when authorities are finally ready to embrace new thinking, the paperwork is done.[22]

---

21 Clayton, *All That Is*, xi.
22 Webb, *Stepping Out with the Sacred*, 261.

2. Sabotage at the birthing stool: Heroines and heroes or saboteurs of change in our sacred communities?

Rabbi Aviva Kipen

This written contribution attempts to capture something of the verbal exchanges of a conference session in which hundreds of listeners from a different faith to my own went on a spiritual journey together. At the time, I described it as "mass individual theological reflection speed dating!"— but no one had to reveal anything about him or herself to anyone else. As the returning Rabbi to the 2013 Common Dreams conference, I could not speak about the challenges that lie ahead for a "Second Reformation", a re-birthing of Christianity in a progressive form of content, belief or action. But, standing on the Jewish ground of my own tradition, my session presented what I hoped would be a contribution to the journeys of progressive Christians, by means of text and the chance to rejoice in the opportunity of studying it together. The session asked participants "to journey towards the personal", towards insights into their personal response to being 'heroines and heroes, midwives—or the more gender neutral "birthing assistants"— of change and also saboteurs of change in sacred communities.'

Our vehicle was Torah study. We would use the biblical text of the midwives Shifrah and Puah to serve our context in learning about ourselves as change makers. Torah, the generic word for Jewish teaching, is also the name for the handwritten parchment scrolls from which Jews continue to read to tell the ancient Jewish stories of our unfolding religious experiences of the first five books, Pentateuch. From the verb, to show, *l'har'ot*, the cognate that provides the Hebrew word for teacher, *moreh (m)* or *morah (f)*, Torah is the "teaching". We began the journey. I recited the blessing for Torah study. Anticipating an experience of 'Torah enlightenment' we readied ourselves to receive some 'Torah radiance'. By singing with me or replying with the *Halleluyah*s in a short catchy tune, we came together in a potentially dangerous and heroic encounter: *Torah orah, Halleluyah.*

Transition into shared experience across the faith divide

What do readers make of the session title "Sabotage at the Birthing Stool: Heroines and Heroes, or Saboteurs of Change our Sacred Communities"? What does this level of language signal to you? Do you automatically understand heroes and heroines as positive, and saboteurs as negative? By providing the polarity between those two concepts of heroism and sabotage, the title implicitly asks that we measure ourselves against both ideas. Who thinks of themselves as a builder, a helper, a contributor? Who is energy-charged by opening themselves to new challenges? Who loves rekindling even the smallest flames of congregational involvement despite the toil of years of communal struggle? Who is at least a little bit of a hero? Who thinks of themselves—or knows that others think of them—as a blocker, a destroyer, a knocker, a saboteur? Who is over teamwork, could get things done quicker of they did them alone and without interruptions? Who is getting tired, has seen it all before, been there, done it, got the tee shirt! And those young people, no respect for the old ways, the tradition, the previous heroes! And who likes to paint the world into constructs this *or* that, black *or* white, to keep things apart, because let's face it, opposition is often the easier road. You know where *you* stand and sometimes that is comfort enough. Another pause. No matter how uncomfortable, we must at least admit to ourselves which is our preferred or perhaps our default stance. But then again, do we have to occupy the either/or? Is there a better alternative?

The less easy to enact, sometimes the more confronting and definitely the more complex, is the attempt to integrate seemingly separate—and sometimes even opposing—concepts. Who can accept that both qualities emerge within themselves from time to time? Who loves congregational work *despite* 'compassion fatigue'? Who continues to be tempted by the pull of usefulness, *anticipating from long experience* that they will be opposed and even subverted by 'George' and objected to on the Parish Council by 'Hattie'? Who is good at tolerating, even needs the challenge of the difficulty of working through others to get the communal outcome? On the other hand, who is so endlessly enthusiastic, that they see and admit into their emotions only the good, the positive, the means to each 'correct' end, without calculating and re-experiencing the hurts caused to others along the path to 'the right way'? Or who is so unforgiving that they see only the outcome and not the benefits of interaction and attempts along the way, no matter how time consuming, how intensive of volunteer time? We have to grapple with our own emotional responses to change in order to be honest within as drivers change. As assistants at the births of new forms, new ideas, new music, new teams, at the very least we owe ourselves and our communities an honest assessment of our own styles and strengths, so we know how best to help and which other helpers to bring on board. It is not always a comfortable process. But then again, the assessment must also steer away from the all good/all bad approach. Even harder to assess is the murky grey of interpersonal relations and the impact we are making upon them and the relationships of others towards us.

Speaking from across the faith divide, the realm of emotions may reflect lessons learned as to what is appropriate for one faith group and inappropriate for another. From inside Judaism I cannot know in detail what those of you who identify as progressive Christians experience of that additional range of emotional demands. There may be gaps between what is traditionally acceptable for the young with regard to the old, the traditionally learned as opposed to those without deep level knowledge, those who occupy official positions with titles and those who neither seek or would be declined membership of that group, women as opposed to men. For some Christian denominations, as for many sectors of the Jewish world, even the vocabulary for gay and lesbian, transgendered and inter-gendered, bisexual and queer congregants is missing, with the result that those people are frequently missing, or not recognised in their true identities. No-go zones come in all shapes and sizes, have all kinds of cultural and idiosyncratic histories and represent all kinds of insecurities and affirmations. Where there is need for progress, there may be a need to demand that these traditional boundary lines be moved or obliterated. But who will be the 'bringers of the new birth' and who, despite creating wonderful change opportunities, will always be identified simply as the wreckers of old traditions past?

From my Jewish point of view, the notion of being a change agent through the birthing metaphor focuses this paper on the story of the arrival of Jesus the babe, a human infant whose miraculous arrival in the byre of Bethlehem is treated always as appearance rather than birth. Having herself been conceived without the alleged taint of original sin, to enable her to be an immaculate vessel within which to carry the gestating foetus that has been created without sexual intervention, Mary appears in biblical texts and art works without any reference to a physical labour, delivery of an infant and afterbirth, or post-natal recovery.

Matthew 1:25 notes that Joseph had no sexual relations with Mary "until she had borne a son; and he named him Jesus." (NRSV). The son was simply "borne" without any story of Mary's birthing. It may have taken the Three Wise Men a day or two to arrive after being commissioned and following the star to the "newborn king", and that would have provided recovery time. But the sometimes noisy, painful, messy, long, confusing stages of physical birth are off the record. Whilst the carol honours their journey, its final stage was additionally commissioned by King Herod, who had clearly not learned from the earlier Exodus story. When the wise men arrived from the East via Jerusalem, they gave their tribute to the babe and then failed to advise Herod, leaving by another route, presumably to safety. Mark's Gospel solves the problem by beginning his Gospel with Jesus in adulthood (Mark 1:9). Jesus came from Nazareth of Galilee and was baptized by John. The Gospel of Luke provides a parallel story of infertility resolved—mirroring many such earlier Torah episodes—by recounting the story of Elizabeth and Zechariah, and tethering Mary's pregnancy six months later to Elizabeth's. Neither birth is recounted. Subsequently, Luke 2 narrates, "While they were there [Bethlehem], the time came for her to deliver her child. And she gave birth to her firstborn son and wrapped him in bands of cloth, and laid him in a manger, because there was no place for them in the inn (vss. 6–7) ... After eight days had passed, it was time to circumcise the child; and he was called Jesus" (vs. 21). Another emotionally and physically significant moment is noted but the details are left without even a hint. John's Gospel skips the entire story of Jesus's conception and birth, referring to the fact that the arrival of God in human form is a theological rather than a physiological process. "The Word became flesh, he lived among us, and we saw his glory, the glory that he has from the Father as only Son of the Father, full of grace and truth" (John 1:14).

What is significant here, in the context of the metaphor of birth as vehicle for Progressive change, is that the preparations from gestation period to delivery and the learning of skills to make physical birthing as gentle and enriching as possible, as confident and loving as possible, are missed by the male writers of the Gospels. The realities of physical birthing details are removed from the relived experience of the readers of the Gospels, even if those physical details were known to the four original writers.

The demands of birthing are not provided in the biblical texts as a means by which readers in each generation may remind themselves that it was the physical birth of the human-formed infant Jesus which provided the vehicle of "Word made flesh". Not only was Mary accepting of the startling gift of the virgin-conceived pregnancy, but also contributed the gift of the physical delivery by which the babe would emerge for the world. Looking towards that missing piece of the puzzle from a twenty-first century position requires that, while none of the Torah annunciation and eventual birthing stories contained labour or delivery details, we at least notice that the Mother of Jesus—as recounted by male scribes—was not able to leave behind the legacy of the birthing story as a gift by which others might follow her example through birthing for later generations. While nothing could equate with the birthing of the actual Jesus as a process or legacy, in the context of making progressive change, each Christian change-maker has the opportunity to identify with the birthing Mother of Jesus and those who attended her at the delivery, not one of whom is named. Being a stranger in town, Mary would not have had her own friends around. Perhaps the unique arrangements of conception required a unique birth without witnesses? But as a metaphor for being alone when a new idea or process is ready to be delivered to others, of being abandoned by friends or deprived of sufficient support in the demanding change-making situation, the Bethlehem story reminds present day readers to notice their roles as 'birthers' of new ideas and the birth assistants to others who are 'delivering' the goods.

Bible stories invite us to apply their constructs in our own times, to locate ourselves reflectively when we re-enact them in our own lives. The Exodus story of the biblical midwives invites us to test that proposition. But before we go to the text, let us pause for a personal, emotional moment. Whenever we speak of midwives, even metaphorically, we cannot obliterate from our psyches actual births that are close to us for a variety of reasons. We recall that the biblical midwives were commissioned for ill. Theirs was to have been a life-giving role for female newborns but a life-taking role for the males. It was to have been a role of entirely mixed blessing. So we feel the tension between life and death: the command that the midwives collude with the rule of law in Egypt or sabotage and outwit the decree of the Pharaoh, break the law, and cheat death.

Sadly, there are many dangers in the business of conceiving, carrying, birthing and surviving to bring a new baby to the world. Death cannot always be cheated. Consciously or not, as we read the story of the Exodus midwives and their ability to bring life, we also carry near the surface of awareness, our own brushes with losses in connection with pregnancy and birth. I invite you to the sacred place of grief and its companion, memory, in retrieving your own sense of sorrow in this regard. Take a moment, if you wish and take yourself to a sorrow associated with a birthing. I won't know whether that sorrow belongs to you, your extended family, or someone further afield. I won't know whether it is the sorrow of infertility or a miscarriage or spontaneous abortion pre-term, whether it is the death of a fetus *in utero*, or at birth, or the death of the pregnant or delivering mother. As you dwell for a moment on each such loss, I acknowledge that whilst we are presently in the realm of metaphor, we each have a reality that will be conjured as we journey into the book of Exodus with the biblical midwives. As we return to the moment of study through the healing balm of Bible wisdom, we bring our emotions with us, many individuals on a shared journey.

A systems approach: Stimulus, action and response in Exodus 1:1–22

Life in the Bible is a bit like life for us. Each episode has a structure which impacts on the next stage of the story. We can identify the stages of the structure as

- Preamble: problem, challenge or opportunity i.e. stimulus
- Planning i.e. action in thought and taking action in deed
- Results follow i.e. response
- The cycle begins again in response to those results i.e. stimulus.

Bible stories invite us to apply their constructs, to locate ourselves reflectively when we re-enact them, to break them down into cause and effect and then identify where *we* may situate ourselves in each story. The reading of the text presented in the conference session was a Jewish reading, delivered in the sure knowledge that listeners were inserting their own overlay as they heard it and studied together with the rabbi with whom they do not share a faith. By locating ourselves in the same old story, from the vantage point of our current contexts, we then have a useful tool for spiritual reflection; to make clearer in our analytically and religiously informed thinking how to be better [Christians], to get better [progressive] outcomes, to dare to aspire to more [change and progress], to achieve what we hope to do [in our home church and in the progressive network], to become more fully what we dream of becoming.[1]

---

1   Note for those using a Hebrew Bible text to follow this commentary: if choosing to read

Exod 1:1–6 The preamble is all about offspring, succession, past generations and the extended family of Jacob. The structure is signalling continuity through each individual and his house (*bayit shelo* = "*bay'to*") and the additional sense that each tribe is its own house within the extended family structure. While Jacob dies, his descendants number 70 men and women. They and the children of others in Jacob's generation are left with maintaining the families who have been settled in Egypt since the famine in Canaan.

Exod 1:7–8 They do such a good job of being prolific that when a new king comes to the throne, he is easily persuaded that there is a threat posed by so many outsiders. He doesn't have the depth of background to have known about Joseph, to be convinced of the loyalty of these sojourners who are monotheists and don't follow the cult of the living Pharaoh and his sister as gods over the land. The set-up is now in place for plans to be made. The off-stage voices are not recorded; it appears that the king comes to the realisation that a plan is called for without the input of others. He speaks to his nation (*amo*) but not of a unified household beyond the palace, which provides greatness to the whole kingdom. Pharaoh has no "*bayit*".

Exod 1:9–10 A well developed paranoia is on display as the peaceable shepherds from Goshen are characterized as taking sides with Egypt's enemies in some future time of war.

Exod 1:11–12 By now an enslavement plan, not previously announced, is already in place over the children of Israel (of Jacob, the one who struggled with/for/against God, Gen 35:1–7) who must create store cities. Perplexingly, the result of Plan A is that the slaves do well and multiply despite increasing rigor (**Exod 1:13–14**). The response is that the Egyptians feel they really have something to fear. This acts as a new stimulus and prompts a new round of actions, even harder labours and added afflictions.

Exod 1: 15–16 begin without the observation that previous attempts to shrink the Israelite population have failed. We can only guess at the length of time that must have elapsed before the king devised this appalling new strategy of infanticide for male newborns. The text is silent, as if there

a facsimile Torah text in Hebrew alongside your translation, do not imagine that the "p" letters between paragraphs refer to the Priestly source. They are a scribal indicator of an open spacing between paragraphs. When following translations, try to have a Jewish translation alongside your chosen Christian translation to check for variances in understanding and nuances.

was a break for a TV commercial and then a return to the program. Two new actors are drawn into the narrative, "The Hebrew midwives, of whom the name of the first is Shifrah and the name of the second Puah." Were they already collaborators somehow? Or were they quiet of demeanour, seemingly biddable, apparently submissive? Or perhaps there were off-camera vulnerabilities that meant they were susceptible to blackmail, that there would be some additional consequences if they did not comply? Or were they just 'usual suspects'? We simply don't know from the text. But in asking these and similar questions, we 'read' our projections into the story. We are already interpreting.

The midwives were preselected, but we do not know why these two in particular, although there must surely have been many midwives from whom to choose. Were they a team or two independents? Did they know each other? Were they related? Known allies or competitors? Brought to the palace, they had to tough it out and at least appear to submit to something horrendous: "*U'r'i'ten al ha'ava'nim*" literally, "look on the stones."

Translators are coy here: "Look upon the birth stool … If it be a son you shall kill him!" There are many suggestions about the primitive equipment available to women for childbirth. I suggest that the stones are not blocks of stone for birth mothers to stand or sit on, but rather the visible "pebbles" which distinguish whether the child is male or female. In other words, 'see whether the child has testicles and then you will know whether to save or slaughter!'

How did the women hold their tongues and their tempers? The text is unemotional; this is how it is to be, no room for negotiation. Their reactions are not recorded! They didn't get to reply, because there could have been no thought of dissent! Some Jewish commentators (*Exodus Rabba* 1:13) suggest that the two women were Yocheved and Miriam, the mother and sister of the as-yet-unborn Moses, whose wiliness would be proved in their scheme to save him. Rabbi Jonathan Sacks's essay on women in leadership during the final Egyptian years leaves the midwives as characters in their own right.[2] Either way, it would have been instructive to know their innermost reactions.

---

2   "Women as Leaders" (16 December 2013): http://www.rabbisacks.org/shemot-5774-women-leaders/

After another length of time, when it was becoming clear that the infanticide policy was not working, the silent midwives were recalled to the palace. This time they had a lot to say! When questioned as to why they were not following orders, they replied (**Exod 1:19**) that the Jewish women were swift at their labours. By the time the midwives arrived, the babes were well beyond the confines of the birthing stools and protected by the women around the mother. Now the roles are reversed, the midwives speak and the Pharaoh is silent. Imagine their speech, a cockney accent perhaps; "*Well, it's like this, your honour! Our women aren't like your Egyptian ones! They are "lively!" By the time we get there, the baby is already born, so it's too late to do anyfing!*" Given enough time, the systematic removal of Hebrew sperm donors would have ultimately ended the population of the Hebrews in Egypt. Yet now Pharaoh doesn't protest aloud, perhaps stunned by their level of insolence and exceptional defiance.

The midwives' awe (**Exod 1:17**) was directed to God and they appeared not to fear Egypt's earthly alternative. 'The midwives were in awe of God and they did not do as the king of *Mitzrayim* spoke to them; and the male children they saved and enlivened ... they allowed/caused to live.' We don't know the time frame; we don't know how the babies were checked up on. But is there not for Christians hearing this story, an anticipation of a future story in which the birth of a male baby was going to rock the Roman boat and thus all male babes would have to be slaughtered?

So time passed and the enslaved Hebrew people became even more numerous (**Exod 1:20**) and the midwives continued their work. Verse 21 recounts the result, "And it came to pass, because the midwives were in awe of God, that God made them *batim* houses!" But the final verse of this episode shows that the male babes were now beyond the help of the midwives or the community and were to be thrown into the River Nile by Pharaoh's own nation. Not just the troops, but former neighbour against former neighbour, once a house united, now a house (as would be commented upon in different circumstances by Luke 11:17) divided against itself.

Reflecting on biblical events, holding the burdens of the present

Other massacres of innocent children come to mind; regrettably there are many current versions of racial campaigns that result in the slaughter of clans, tribes and whole populations. Can we possibly imagine what we would have done as Hebrew or as Egyptian? Let's just concentrate on the spectacular piece of passive resistance of the midwives Shifrah and Puah at the end of the story. Ghandi and Martin Luther King would have been proud! The midwives were builders, helpers and contributors by acting as blockers. Surely their mission would not have been broadcast aloud or mass panic would have set in. No such rumbling from the Hebrews is recorded, so perhaps their instructions were issued in closed court. Although it would have been a difficult public policy to conceal, similar "solutions" were successfully concealed in the twentieth century. If Miriam was one of the midwives, we know that she argued for continued creation of children, despite the 50% risk. Either way, there had to have been collusion between the midwives and their clients, to ensure that they didn't arrive too early in the piece. What the text leaves out allows us to elaborate.

From the Hebrew perspective, Shifrah and Puah were builders and helpers; from the Egyptian perspective they were blockers and saboteurs. To locate ourselves reflectively when we re-enact their efforts in our own lives, we have to now move from the distant experience of the biblical midwives to our lives in which our midwifery is the metaphorical one, but the changes we hope to bring are real. We have to identify an event, an opportunity, a challenge that we were called upon to influence, to change, to staff, to remove, to destroy …

Take a moment to go to one such example, one in which you think you had to take on a necessary but possibly dangerous and potentially explosive task in your community. Were you on a staffing committee, planning a building project, a liturgical change program? Were there multiple, heartfelt but conflicting views about how to make decisions? You wanted to build, but there was need to destroy in the process. You had great conviction and insisted that something beneficial, but not necessarily popular, go ahead. Can you relive the emotions? Can you recall how it felt to thwart others who did not share your position and who wanted the opposite outcome? Can you recall the feeling of achievement when your role yielded a successful 'birth'? The project was completed, you were vindicated and perhaps someone even remembered your part in pushing it through.

Now, it might be the same project or another one, where you felt your role had to be the opposite one. Can you recall feeling with all your heart that the project ought not to be born? Can you recall how intensely you felt about stopping that project? Can you recall who it was that you had to oppose, how hard it was to lose a friend over your stand? Hold that moment … Can you feel the emotions rising, reminding you of the absolute passion you had in mustering your courage? Was it a difficult struggle for the entire community or only between you and one or two others? Were you right? Are you sure? And how do you feel about the people who had to be overruled because they were wrong? Do they still hold it against you? Did they leave? Or have you yourself been on the receiving end of someone else's equal conviction and found yourself sidelined or ousted? Have you felt betrayed because you told something to someone in good faith only to find the confidence not kept and your own position compromised?

The conference session drew into reflective mode. I asked, "Can you feel the intense silence in the room? Can you discern how much attention our feelings are receiving? Are you OK within your own memories or do those episodes from the past cause too much angst, still fresh? Is there something going on in your community right now in which you feel obliged to contribute either to block or to support? How do you feel?" Several minutes of silence elapsed. There was no time for small group break outs or debriefing from skilled facilitators. But emotional work was clearly taking place, not just for the listeners but for myself as well.

If you are a change agent, you have more than your own fair share of weighty baggage to carry around with you. I carry mine and also work hard at being able to turn weighty legacies into insights, which help shape different processes each time there are challenges to resolve. Like everyone in the room, I was saying 'O God, I wish *that* had gone better." The new roof may have been built but a loyal family may have left the congregation as a result of something completely unintended, but which could not be healed. A correct principle may have been enshrined into church rules, but the first consequence would be that someone trusted would have their sense of years of contribution whittled away despite every effort to affirm them. You know, the problem of self-awareness is that it is so painful! When you feel things, they have much more impact than when you don't allow feelings. Our Bible story tells us nothing of the feelings of the two midwives. We have to insert ourselves into their story and by doing so we are alerted at least in some degree to the emotional component of what they did and what we are required to do.

The challenge of integrating the complexity, of needing to do what has to be done but carrying the result of sometimes painful outcomes, is the invitation to use the role models of the midwives to feel courage in the task of getting the right result by being in awe of God and doing the right thing. If you have to both build and block something problematic, how can you do so effectively? Will you begin to frame both sides of the challenge and articulate them so no-one has to carry the secret, so that you smile to yourself about the successful outcome when all is said and done? Having genuinely acted with integrity, if still hurting for yourself and for others who got swept away in a painful process, can you apologise? Can you try for reconciliation? Can you revisit the issues in a confidential way without observers tittle-tattling? And if—having genuinely done all of that, you fail—can you allow yourself to accept that you have fully tried to fix the pain and, while leaving an optimistic door open for future resolution, finally allow what you know about the relationships that have been soured, to slip to the back of consciousness and hold them back from paralysing future good works?

If one of the realities of the world is a niche for every kind of specialty, then we have to embrace parallel understandings and enactments of the holy task of making faith communities that allow for ranges of belief and practice, in your case Christologies and theologies. We have to accept that what we see as right may be right for us, but for others that may not be clear for a while and so our legacy of good, clear thinking about our faiths must yield its offspring in a range of ways. Not all the 'children' will be the same and some will be more challenging than others. We may have been their birth assistants, but the questions we must ask as they grow under our guidance are "Is the generation that *we* birth able to create its own viability? Is it going to be robust enough to take on the changes still ahead, whatever they are?" In other words, will our efforts yield a strong yet flexible generation that can follow on from us?

The clue may be hiding at the end of the Bible passage with which I began. We know that ultimately, after long enslavement and the emergence of Moses as the Jewish Egyptian prince of his generation, the Hebrews will be released after the plagues. These are memorable and significant moments of the story. They loom large in Cecil B de Mille's *Ten Commandments* and provide the blockbuster memories at the end of the Egyptian sojourn. But without the work of the midwives, there could have been no generations of slaves to be liberated from Egypt. The real legacy that would provide for the Hebrew future was slipped into the story quietly and without cinematic fanfare. What does it mean in Exod 1:21 when it says of the midwives, "God made them houses, *batim*"? *Bayit* is the Hebrew word for house, true. It is also the word for a building and the word for the holy Temple whose construction details follow. Do we really believe that Shifrah and Puah received physical houses as their reward, something that would have made them extremely conspicuous in their enslaved setting? Is the reward for doing the right, courageous work of enlivening our own communities, a new house? I am going to propose a different interpretation from the one provided by this translation, an interpretation based upon the context of the entire episode.

Remember how it all began? Joseph was already in service to Potiphar in Egypt when 70 souls went to Goshen during the famine in Canaan. They took their families and their flocks. They settled. They reproduced. They had the legacy of households which were mighty and numerous. Throughout the story and subsequent stories leading to the Exodus the question is about survival, about offspring. The midwives were facilitators of the safe arrival of the offspring of others, despite great risk to themselves. What was their reward? Not, I suggest, a new physical house, but a 'house of generations'. The midwives' very real stake in the continuing households of other families was their blessing and the blessing which accrued to the whole household of Israel, the generations which they helped ensure would be able to follow Jacob.

Their *batim* were not their physical residences but *Beit Yisrael,* the biblical term for the "household of Israel". It is not a real estate term, but a corporate term; a term of identity. What was the reward for the midwives? It was the knowledge that they made the life and death difference to the survival of the whole people and as such merited family households of their own and hence, a share in the nation whose existence depended upon their actions of sabotage and salvation. The legacy of their work was to be able to have generations to follow them. The *bayit*, the house, is the household far beyond that of immediate family members; it comprises collectively the members of the metaphorical extended family.

You, the courageous saboteurs and builders of whatever progressive Christianity is to become, in this room and beyond it, will want to know whether you have been recognised by God, possibly using the same yardstick of performance as that applied to Shifrah and Puah. If you are able to look over your shoulders in a few years and see whether or not you have been gifted with a household of fellow travellers, a networked community, an on-line community of practice, an extensive Facebook or Linked In cohort full of progressive Christians/Christas, then you will have a sense of the result. You will only be successful if your work stands scrutiny by the generation rising behind you, which Marcus Borg assures us is increasingly progressive. If you can see the "extended progressive Christian family house" filling up and becoming mighty, numerous and in awe of God, then you could reasonably feel that you have been blessed in the work of your sacred communities. May that prove to be a blessing for all.

3. Why *Honest to God* blew the roof off the Church and let in the fresh air

Lloyd Geering

Fifty years ago last year (1963), Bishop John Robinson published his little book *Honest to God*.[1] This book sold more quickly and widely than any book of serious theology in the history of the world. I dare to suggest that this record may never be surpassed. Before long its publication had reached a million copies and it was available in 17 languages. It has just been republished in its original form. Thus no theological book was read so widely as this little volume in the whole of the twentieth century. Why was that so?

In some respects it remains a puzzle to this day. It was not because the book was saying anything strikingly new. Those of us engaged in theological teaching at the time found little that was fresh in the book. As we saw it, this book was basically a summarised rehash of the thinking of three theologians whom many of us had been reading and absorbing for some time. We joked that it had taken an illness to force John Robinson to take time off from his busy ecclesiastical schedule to catch up with his reading.

First, he sketched Paul Tillich, who had written two popular and widely read books: *The Shaking of the Foundations*[2] and *The Courage to Be*[3]. The first two volumes of Tillich's massive three-volume *Systematic Theology* were published in the 1950s[4], and Robinson quoted from them. In his search to find a satisfying way of understanding the meaning of 'God', Robinson fastened on Tillich's definition of God as 'the ground of our being'. This showed, as Robinson said, that theology is not about a particular Being called God but about the ultimate questions posed by our very existence, or being.

Secondly, Robinson turned to the impact of Dietrich Bonhoeffer, whose letters from a Nazi prison[5] provided a rich collection of seed thoughts that

---

1   Robinson, *Honest to God.*
2   Tillich, *The Shaking of the Foundations.*
3   Tillich, *The Courage to Be.*
4   Tillich, *Systematic Theology.*
5   Bonhoeffer, *Letters and Papers from Prison.*

many of us were then mulling over. In particular, Robinson was fascinated by Bonhoeffer's new assessment of Jesus as 'the man for others', rather than as a divine figure.

Thirdly, but much less prominent, was the influence of Rudolf Bultmann. His demythologising of the New Testament had become known to scholars outside of Germany only after World War II. Then Robinson added a chapter on "The New Morality", writing with approval of an article by Joseph Fletcher. But Fletcher's book on situation ethics, which was to cause a stir not unlike that of *Honest to God*, was yet to be written, appearing only in 1966[6].

Thus Robinson was pulling together the thoughts of a number of theologians who were then at the leading edge of Christian thought. If he had done this in a simpler and more lucid manner than was present in the originals, that would perhaps explain the sudden and widespread interest. But *Honest to God* is not a particularly easy book for the theologically illiterate to read. Some of us were critical of it at the time just for this reason. To us it seemed a bit of a hotchpotch. Its critics claimed it was woolly and revealed many inconsistencies. Even Robinson himself later said that if he had known it was going to be read so widely he would have written it in a much more accessible style.

So why did it become a runaway bestseller? In small part it was due to a set of chance events surrounding the time of its publication. Not long beforehand, Bishop Robinson had achieved widespread public notoriety over his appearance in a celebrated court case where he publicly defended the publication of the unexpurgated text of *Lady Chatterley's Lover*. Thus the name of Bishop Robinson was already being bandied about in the public arena and this meant that the journalists were on the alert for anything unusual. So the public press chose to announce the arrival of Robinson's little new book with these words on the billboards: "Our image of God must go".

The public impression created from the very beginning was that Robinson was making a break with Christian orthodoxy on the basic issue of the reality of God. Certainly that is made clear in the preface where we read, "Whatever we may accept with the top of our minds, most of us still retain deep down the mental image of 'an old man in the sky'"[7]. Certainly, if we

---

6   Fletcher, *Situation Ethics*.
7   Robinson, *Honest to God*, 13.

keep talking of and praying to, "Our Father in heaven", how can we avoid having this image of God?

Robinson was not denying the reality of God, but calling for "a restating of traditional orthodoxy in modern terms". For such a recasting, he judged that "the most fundamental categories of our theology—of God, of the supernatural and of religion itself—must go into the melting pot". Yet he was not the first to call for such a radical reconstruction, as we shall presently see. So why the stir?

What was new about this book was that it was written by a bishop. Theologians may question and explore, but bishops are expected to be the authoritative guardians of the faith. Moreover it was written in a personal style in which Robinson confessed his own difficulties with orthodox Christian doctrines. He judged them to be expressed in thought-forms and language that had long become obsolete in the world outside of the church. He guessed that his book would surprise some and so he concluded his short preface with these words "What I have tried to say, in a tentative and exploratory way, may seem to be radical, and doubtless to many heretical. The one thing of which I am fairly sure is that, in retrospect it will be seen to have erred in not being nearly radical enough". Those last words have certainly proved to be all too true.

I conclude that it was the personal and public way in which a bishop—already suspected of being a maverick—openly confessed his own doubts that caused this book to ring bells with hundreds of thousands of church-going people. What came over in the book was Robinson's honesty and frankness about his own theological concerns. Many felt relieved that a bishop was experiencing the same problems as they did with the traditional formulations of the faith.

By the same token, the book brought forth a torrent of criticism, much more than even Robinson had expected to be the case. The Anglican journal, *The Church Times*, commented, "It is not every day that a bishop goes on public record as apparently denying almost every Christian doctrine of the church in which he holds office".

What we in theological colleges tended to overlook was the fact that what was already familiar to us was like a sudden blast of fresh air to those who had no inkling of what had been going on within theological faculties during the previous few decades. Theology was normally published in hardbacks and in theological jargon that prevented the layman from having ready access to them. In *Honest to God*, some of this was put in a nutshell and published as a paperback. Some of Robinson's critics even complained that, by publishing it as a simple paperback, Robinson was making available to untheologically trained minds the weighty matters of theology they were not yet ready to understand.

So the book gave rise to widespread debate, and within six months the publisher, David Edwards of the SCM Press, had published a second book, *The Honest to God Debate*.[8] This put together a selection of the thousand letters to Robinson, many extracts from hundreds of reviews, along with articles by David Edwards, David Jenkins, John Macquarrie, and Alasdair MacIntyre. The latter, an Oxford philosopher, concluded that Robinson had become an atheist like himself and believed Robinson's desire to restate the faith in modern terms was "a desperate attempt that cannot succeed". He thought Robinson's book simply reflected the changing face of religion in UK. His concluding words were: "The creed of the English is that there is no God and that it is wise to pray to him from time to time".[9]

Yes, the book did reflect the changing face of religion, and not only in UK but in much of the Christian world. One of the reasons it became such a bestseller is that it appeared just at the right time. When we now turn to look at *Honest to God* in its historical context, we can see its importance as a marker in an ongoing process. In this respect it was the first of several related events that characterised the decade of the 1960s. This was the year in which Martin Luther King made his epoch-changing address, "I have a dream." In 1966, the front cover of *Time* magazine drew the attention of the world to the 'Death of God' theologians: Thomas Altizer, William Hamilton, and Paul van Buren. In 1966, the Jewish 'Death of God' rabbi, Richard Rubenstein, wrote his *After Auschwitz*. Also in 1966, Joseph Fletcher published his *Situation Ethics*[10]. This caused a stir reminiscent of *Honest to God*, and was followed similarly, but in 1968, by a volume documenting the response *The Situation Ethics Debate*[11]. In New Zealand, 1966 was the year in which we had our own widespread theological debate on the resurrection of Jesus, culminating in the notorious 1967 'heresy trial'.

---

8   Edwards, *The Honest to God Debate*.
9   Ibid., 228.
10   Fletcher, *Situation Ethics*.
11   Cox, *The Situation Ethics Debate*.

So the 1960s proved to be a critical turning point for Western Christianity. As one churchman prophetically remarked, "Things will never be the same again". The decline in church attendance began rapidly to accelerate. It was as if *Honest to God* had blown the roof off the church. But though some put the blame on Robinson, and others like him, *Honest to God* was not the cause but only a significant marker in a transition that had started much earlier. Let us now turn to the broader picture of the changing face of religion.

We must go as far back as 1800 or, more specifically, 1799.[12] That was the year in which a rising theological star, Friedrich Schleiermacher, published a book that caused a stir in Germany not unlike that of *Honest to God*. It was called *On Religion: Speeches to its Cultured Despisers*[13]. The latter term referred to the leading lights of the Enlightenment, thinkers such as David Hume, who were subjecting all religious claims to rigorous rational criticism and who were rejecting all appeal to divine revelation.

Schleiermacher's book in its day was much more radical and challenging than *Honest to God*, and yet, instead of being condemned by critics from within the church, Schleiermacher was hailed as the one who salvaged Christianity from its rationalistic, atheistic critics of the Enlightenment. He was a hospital chaplain at the time he burst into print (anonymously at first), but before long he was appointed to a Chair of Theology, first at Halle and soon after to the newly-established University of Berlin, a Chair he held until his death.

He was a very popular teacher and preacher who was so highly admired that nearly the whole of Berlin turned out to honour him at his funeral, when he died at the age of 66. His thinking dominated Protestant thought throughout the nineteenth century, including my own theological teacher, John Dickie. Dickie spoke of him as the most creative Christian thinker since the Reformation. Not surprisingly, Schleiermacher became known as 'The Father of Protestant Liberalism'.

The widespread approval enjoyed by Schleiermacher while he lived tends to disguise the radical change in religious thought that he pioneered. Indeed, he did not himself appreciate or understand just what he was doing, and certainly did not foresee all that his new method would lead to. He was much more of a revolutionary than he intended to be. It was left to others,

12 See my 1991 booklet, *Religious Trailblazers*, ch. 1.
13 Schleiermacher, *On Religion*.

such as John Dickie, to point to what they referred to as his faults and weaknesses. But Dickie was not nearly as critical as Karl Barth and even warned us against Barth and his revival of what was called Neo-orthodoxy. Karl Barth complained, and perhaps justifiably so, that Schleiermacher's new theological method heralded the end of Christian doctrine. He wrote, "The question as to how Schleiermacher did not realise that he was destroying Reformation theology is a mystery which cannot be solved".

Even Schleiermacher retreated somewhat from some of the more surprising statements in his first book when he came to compile his magnum opus—*The Christian Faith*[14]. Yet the German title of that book preserves Schleiermacher's fresh approach in a way that is hidden in its English title. The phrase "The Christian Faith" gives us the impression that the 'Faith' is an objective thing—a 'set of specific beliefs'. And that is how it has long been understood. But it is not what Schleiermacher intended. The German title *Glaubenslehre* does not even mention the word 'Christian' and means literally "The Doctrine of Faith". This title focuses not on God, not on divine revelation and not on beliefs, but on the human experience of faith or trust.

It is in his first two books—*On Religion* and a little known work, *Christmas Eve*—that Schleiermacher (perhaps unintentionally) led theology in a new direction. Only very slowly did that new direction begin to show itself. It was not at all apparent while the momentum of church life carried on as it had in the past. It was still not apparent when I was a theological student in the thirties and forties. That is why the events of the sixties, including *Honest to God*, were felt to be such shock—a virtual theological earthquake—for the very foundations of theology were being shaken.

Schleiermacher, along with Hegel, opened up the way for three seminal thinkers, whose work helped to shape the nineteenth century: Strauss, Feuerbach and Marx. It led Marx to become a militant atheist and expound the communist ideology. It led Feuerbach to understand religion as a human phenomenon, but a most important one, one on which our very humanity depends. Strauss became the pioneer of modern New Testament study and this led to Bultmann and then to Robinson. Tillich became the twentieth century equivalent to Schleiermacher in the nineteenth century, and so to Robinson. In the meantime Karl Barth re-established orthodoxy as Neo-orthodoxy by returning to what obtained before Schleiermacher.

---

14   Schleiermacher, *The Christian Faith*.

But what if one were unaware of those seminal first 50 years of the nineteenth century? My theological education as late as the early 1940s left me in complete ignorance of it, apart from Schleiermacher. And even John Dickie emphasised the faults of Schleiermacher more than his strengths. If even theological students were left in such ignorance, it means that in the early 1960s most people in the pews knew absolutely nothing of the nineteenth century and what it had led to—until *Honest to God* suddenly came as a bombshell. For most church people, there seemed to be only two alternatives: traditional Christianity and unbelief (atheism). Robinson appeared to be in a no-man's land, and moving on the slippery slope towards atheism.

Let me now sketch three ways in which Schleiermacher triggered off the theological changes that led to the bombshell dropped by Robinson. These three features also describe the situation that became more widespread after Robinson and which remains today.

First, Schleiermacher shifted the base on which to engage in the theological enterprise. Traditional theology started from God and the truths that God was believed to have revealed. It was theocentric. (So also was Barth's neo-orthodoxy.) Schleiermacher's new theology started from humankind—from what we experience of the divine. It was anthropocentric. It was basically a shift from the study of divinely revealed truths—dogmatics—to the study of personal religious experience. It was a shift from the objective to the subjective.

The reason why such a radical shift did not seem to make much difference to begin with is that Schleiermacher and his appreciative supporters were so immersed in Christian orthodoxy that it permeated their minds and thinking as well as their hearts. Yet it was already leading Schleiermacher to make statements such as the following from *On Religion*, which even today may surprise:

> Religion answers a deep need in man. It is neither a metaphysic, nor a morality, but above all feeling. ... Dogmas are not, properly speaking, part of religion: it is rather that they are derived from religion. Beliefs in God, and in personal immortality, are not necessarily a part of religion; one can conceive of a religion without God, and it would be pure contemplation of the universe.[15]

---

15   *On Religion*, 93.

As we have just seen, it did not take long for Feuerbach to realise the consequences of what Schleiermacher had done. He studied for a short time under Schleiermacher but lost interest in preparing for the ministry and turned to philosophy and particularly Hegel. But he turned Hegel upside down and then adopted Schleiermacher's anthropocentric basis for philosophy, though he never acknowledged it or seemed to be aware of it. He had probably read Schleiermacher's first book though he never says so. There he would have read:

> The immortality that most men imagine and their longing for it, seems to me irreligious, nay quite opposed to the spirit of piety...the goal and character of the religious life is not the immortality desired and believed in by many ... It is the immortality we can now have in this temporal life ...In the midst of finitude to be one with the infinite and in every moment to be eternal is the immortality of religion.[16]

It is interesting to find that Feuerbach's first publication, and at the age of twenty-four, was *Thoughts on Death and Immortality*[17]. But his seminal work was *The Essence of Christianity*[18]. Here he took Schleiermacher's new anthropocentric base for theology to its logical conclusion. He asserted that theology (the study of God), when properly understood for what it really is, is anthropology (the study of mankind). Theology is the study of the human condition, of our highest human values, of our hopes and our aspirations. As Feuerbach saw it, the supernatural world acclaimed by Christian orthodoxy was largely the projection of mankind's inner world of ideas and values on to a cosmic backdrop.

That is why Schleiermacher, perhaps unintentionally, opened the way to the study of religion as a human phenomenon. There is a direct route from him to Rudolph Otto and his seminal book, *The Idea of the Holy*[19]. Schleiermacher opened the way for the rise of the disciplines of the Psychology of Religion and the Sociology of Religion. It also led to Don Cupitt and the Sea of Faith network, and more recently to progressive Christianity.

Second, Schleiermacher's switch from a divine starting point to a human one took theology out of the hands of the authoritative experts, priests and theologians, and democratised it. Theology became a 'do-it-yourself'

---

16   Ibid., 100–101.
17   Feuerbach, *Thoughts on Death and Immortality*.
18   Feuerbach, *The Essence of Christianity* .
19   Otto, *The Idea of the Holy*.

exercise in which everybody could participate, drawing upon their own inner experience. This is best illustrated by the little known book written by Schleiermacher entitled *Christmas Eve*.[20]

In this, he describes a homely fireside scene at which a gathering of friends—five women and four men—discusses what the celebration of Christmas means to each of them. They were no experts but ordinary people expressing how they thought about their own religious experience. Moreover, at a time when theology and even group discussion was still regarded as a male preserve, we find it is the women who initiate the discussion.

The women interpret the nativity scene in the light of their feelings and experience as mothers. One claims, for example, that she regards Mary as a representation of every mother, who sees her own child as an eternal divine child in whom she looks for the first stirrings of the higher spirit.

When the men subsequently take over the conversation, it moves to a more philosophical and, at times, impersonal level. Leonard, for example, is even said by his friends to be the "thinking, reflective, dialectical, over-intellectual man". He is aware that historical study of the Bible is already introducing uncertainty as to how much is really known about the historical Jesus. He doubts whether the organized church is at all in accordance with what was the intention of Jesus. Ernst counters this scepticism by seeing Christmas as a universal festival of joy. Its continuing significance rests on what Christians have found to be vital in their own Christian experience and does not depend on whether the biblical story of the birth and life of Jesus is historically true.

In contrast to both, Edward—the host—is more speculative and mystical. He notes that in the fourth Gospel there is no mention at all of the birth of Jesus at Bethlehem. Rather it affirms that the Word was made flesh—that Word that was with God and was God. The significance of Christmas for Edward is that "what we celebrate is nothing other than ourselves as whole beings, viewed and known from the perspective of the divine ... What else is humankind than the very spirit of earth, or life's coming to know itself in its eternal being and in its ever changing process of becoming?" (In 1803, and before the idea of evolution had spread, this was surely a most radical thought!)

Joseph, who arrived later in the evening, is a simple, naive and pious Christian who is rather shocked to find the men arguing almost heatedly

---

20 Scheiermacher, *Christmas Eve.*

on such an occasion. He reacts strongly to the coldly rationalist approach of Leonard and tries to restore some cheerful harmony to the evening, leading the party to end with some singing. It was no doubt quite deliberate on Schleiermacher's part to associate harmonious fellowship with the women, and intellectual discord with the men, just as the little story ended, not with statements of belief but with the feelings engendered in a fellowship celebrating their common bonds.

Schleiermacher's little book of 1803 is a fascinating parable of what the theological scene was to become. It uncannily sketches the theological scene in the post-Christian world generally and of the Sea of Faith network in particular. Today there are no more leading theologians to whom we gratefully turn for the authoritative answers to our questions about the meaning of life. Paul Tillich was perhaps the last creative theologian. There have been a few imaginative voices after Tillich, such as John Cobb, John Macquarrie, Gordon Kaufman, and Don Cupitt. In this twenty-first century, academic theology of the traditional style has simply faded into non-existence. Karl Barth was right in declaring that Schleiermacher's new theological method heralded the end of Christian doctrine.

The third way in which Schleiermacher's switch from a divine starting point to a human one led to the modern situation in that it opened the way for dispensing with the word 'God'. Curiously even Schleiermacher himself saw this when he said "Belief in God is not necessarily a part of religion; one can conceive of a religion without God, and it would be pure contemplation of the universe". But to most people then and, for a considerable time thereafter, the idea of 'God' was so axiomatic that it seemed to be indispensable. Even Don Cupitt, as late as 1980, in *Taking Leave of God*, wrote, "God is a myth we have to have"[21]. Yet, only four years later John Macquarrie said in his Gifford Lectures, *In Search of Deity*:

> There was a time in Western society when 'God' was an essential part of the everyday vocabulary. But in the West and among educated people throughout the world, this kind of God-talk has virtually ceased. People once knew, or thought they knew, what they meant when they spoke of God, and they spoke of him often. Now in the course of the day's business we may not mention him at all. The name of God seems to have been retired from our everyday discourse.[22]

21   Cupitt, *Taking Leave of God*.
22   Macquarrie, *In Search of Deity*, 17.

In 1999, Don Cupitt made a study of our everyday discourse and he discovered that, as the word 'God' ceased to be in use, it was replaced by the word 'life'. He found more than 150 life idioms being commonly used today, many of them quite new such as "Get a life!" He concluded that now that theology has been democratised—thanks to Schleiermacher—it is no longer the academic theologians but ordinary people, speaking out of the experience of living, who have been at the leading edge of theology. He called this *The New Religion of Life in Everyday Speech*[23].

Summary

The theistic image of God had to go. It was too small, too human, too personal, and too objective. 'God' remains as a symbol (should we choose to use it)—a symbol that refers to all that transcends us and that also points to the unity of the *universe* we live in.

Honest to God was a significant marker in the process by which Western culture moved from its traditional Christian base to its current non-theistic and post-Christian stance. It started with Schleiermacher but only since the 1960s of the twentieth century did it lead to the increasingly rapid decline of the churches. The nature of this transition is particularly visible in the 'progressive Christian churches' and the Sea of Faith network. Just as the Enlightenment gave us freedom to think, so in the realm of theology we in the West are mostly becoming do-it-yourselfers today.

---

23   Cupitt, *The Religion of Life in Everyday Speech*.

4. Theology from the 'Grass Roots': Signs of new growth since *Honest to God*

Lorraine Parkinson

In this chapter I will consider theological developments in the fifty years since the publication of *Honest to God*. However, as I do so it would not be honest to ignore the truth. The truth is that comprehensive theological questioning was well and truly abroad long before *Honest to God*. It was happening in the nineteenth century, in Melbourne. At that time, the Rev Charles Strong, a former Presbyterian Minister of Scots Church, Collins Street, became the first minister of the liberal, social justice-oriented Australian Church. He taught that Christianity was more endangered by theological obscurantism than by critical historical investigation, natural science or biblical criticism, and that failure to love one's neighbour was more serious than doctrinal doubt. In the end the Australian Church closed because of Strong's outspoken opposition to Australian involvement in World War I. In that context, the optimum time for reform of the church had not yet arrived.

Other thinkers like Strong were also active in that era. One quote from the American Harry Emerson Fosdick will suffice (and remember that this was written close to a hundred years ago):

> There is a widespread, deep-seated, positive desire on the part of many Christians in all the churches to recover for our modern life, for its personal character and its social relationships, the religion of Jesus as distinguished from the accumulated, conventionalized, largely inadequate and sometimes grossly false religion about Jesus.[1]

There is nothing novel about claiming that a new Reformation of the church is both necessary and now underway. In the theological and ecclesiastical ferment that followed the publication of John A. T. Robinson's *Honest to God* in 1963, many voices were heard, urging a re-forming of the church. Clergy and laity alike were leaving the church. 'Death of God' theology

---

1 Fosdick, *Adventurous Religion*, 309.

was gaining ground, somewhat ironically inspired by Dietrich Bonhoeffer's mind-blowing thoughts on living with a God who is absent. But in 1963 the time for a comprehensive re-formation of the church was still not right. There was need to wait for the optimum moment, just as there was in the sixteenth century. As Owen Chadwick commented in the introduction to his *The Reformation:*

> For a century or more Western Europe had sought for reform of the Church "in head and members" and had failed to find it.[2]

The problem was the absence of *kairos*—the right or optimum time. Even Wycliffe's potentially explosive impact on the theological understanding of the masses had come, and gone. The re-formation of the church was in waiting. It was waiting for a time when clergy and laity had reached sufficient understanding of how much was at stake for the church in Europe. That right time duly arrived, along with the right people to stand up and 'seize the day'.

The Protestant Reformation may well have accomplished its theological objectives. Yet in doing so it reinforced the pervasive influence of the state on the life of the church. And even in spite of the wars and social upheavals it spawned, as I have said elsewhere,[3] the Protestant Reformation was a mere blip on the radar, compared with the potential of a new Reformation of Christianity, now underway. This is not about a departure from the church, but about a re-forming of the church. I am certainly with John A. T. Robinson in his later comments concerning *Honest to God*. They were published two years later, in 1965, under the title: *The New Reformation?* Regarding reforming theologians, he wrote:

> I believe in fact that re-formation is a category we must use, and my continued exploration of what a new Reformation might mean is testimony to unavoidable conviction. Until it is finally proved otherwise, Christians must believe that the Church—and they themselves as members of it—can be used rather than discarded.[4]

A Reformation liberates power for change that already exists in an organization or entity. In the case of the church, a new Reformation

---

2   Chadwick, *The Reformation*, 11.

3   In "Teaching the Church Forgot: Jesus' Blueprint for the Best Possible World". Keynote address, Common Dreams 3 Conference, Australian National University, Canberra, 19–22 September 2013.

4   Robinson, *The New Reformation?*, 16.

would free it to take on a new shape, externally and internally. This new shape exists already in the hearts and minds of Christians whose faith is evolving. I and many others are calling the growing new faith of the church, "Evolving Christianity". It is being given life and shape through a 'grass roots theology'—developing among both ordained and lay people. This 'grass roots theology' names change in the church for what it is—a natural manifestation of the need to adapt in order to survive. Not only to survive, but to grow into an intentional community of The Way—as followers of Jesus of Nazareth. Its theological strength comes more from its dynamic questioning of expressions of the sacred than it does from any ironclad answers to that questioning. Its life is built not on the certainty of dogma but on living *in* faith, while asking existential questions *about* faith. Those questions are the basis of an Evolving Christianity for the twenty-first century.

For Robinson, the *kairos* moment for change arrived after he had studied philosophy and systematic theology at Cambridge, and then turned his attention to biblical studies. In 1948 he was appointed chaplain and lecturer in New Testament Studies at Wells Theological College. He began to suspect that theological doctrines might not be as well founded in the New Testament as is often assumed. With that in mind, he decided to place textual studies at the forefront of his thinking. In a book he wrote during that time (called *Jesus and His Coming*), he constructed an elaborate metaphor about the importance of biblical studies for the formulation of theology. This is what he wrote:

> For subterranean rumblings are heard most clearly by those who have their rooms on the ground floor, that is, at the New Testament level of the doctrinal construction. And they are the more noticeable to one who has recently moved downstairs, in the first instance from the floor of the philosophy of religion to that of systematic theology, and then from systematic theology to Biblical studies.[5]

When Robinson wrote *Honest to God*, he leaned heavily on his philosophical skills, in particular relating them to the philosophical approach of Paul Tillich. As some critics have noted, Robinson probably attributed more of his writing about a doctrine of God to Tillich, Bultmann and Bonhoeffer than was at all warranted. He had already written a doctoral dissertation at Cambridge (1945) called, *Thou Who Art*, which in 1988 Alistair Kee argued

---

5   Robinson, *Jesus and his Coming*, 10–11.

was clearly the basis for *Honest to God*.[6] Although it was unpublished at the time of Kee's writing, during the past decade *Thou Who Art* has been published (2006). In the introduction to the dissertation Robinson reiterated his thoughts about the primacy of biblical text over theological doctrine. He wrote: "Theology can extrapolate from but not impose on biblical tradition." *Thou Who Art* is based on Martin Buber's 'I-Thou' philosophy, in which, like Buber, Robinson argues for God as possessing personality. He saw that the New Testament's witness to a God of Love, or God as Love, is only possible if God is in relationship with individual personalities. As he wrote: "Love not only appreciates personality, it bestows it. Life from beginning to end is a responsive existence."[7] One implication of a divine-human relationship based on love is that God can only be in respectful loving relationship with the 'other' by limiting divine omnipotence. That includes granting the freedom of the 'other'. This is often acknowledged as pivotal regarding the problem of evil in a world created by a good God. The freedom of a loving God-human relationship is critical for the development of morally integrated human personality.

Robinson believed that the development of a doctrine of God based on the idea of God as Love, or Love as God, would overcome a widespread and increasing alienation from the belief of the church. The problem as he saw it was not lack of faith, or bad faith, but bad theology. He decided that his reinterpretation of the faith would be based on the Bible. His doctoral dissertation is a sustained critique of theology that was guided by criteria incompatible with the biblical understanding of God. The dissertation represents his concern that traditional belief was inimical to the understanding of the average person.

Several pastoral and evangelical concerns motivated John Robinson to write his *Honest to God* and subsequent books. They were issues that had long disturbed him and which were building up in him to a point when they could no longer be denied. The best way to summarise his misgivings is a short quote from *Honest to God* regarding his time as an ordinand of the Church of England:

> The only way I can put it is to say that over the years a number of things have unaccountably 'rung a bell'. One simply knows that if one is to retain one's integrity one must come to terms with them. And then,

---

6   Kee, *The Roots of Christian Freedom*.

7   Robinson, *Thou Who Art*, 67.

equally, there are certain other things which have not rung a bell, certain
areas of traditional Christian expression—devotional and practical—
which have evidently meant a great deal for most people but which have
simply left one cold.[8]

Robinson was out of step with a tradition that had largely gone unquestioned
for far too long. He was greatly relieved to find other theological students of
similar mind. Regarding the traditions that he was being taught about God
and prayer, he wrote:

> There was nothing about it one could say was wrong. Indeed, it was an
> impressive roundabout: but one was simply not on it—and, what was
> worse, had no particular urge to be.[9]

Robinson did not want to deny God. What he wanted to do was to take
God from the mythological 'up there' and the metaphysical 'out there', and
put God back into the midst of life—where Jesus says God belongs. He was
questioning one set of presuppositions and feeling drawn towards another,
in its place. Many Christians going through the same kind of process can
relate very strongly to that. While Robinson's book clearly did not represent
the beginning of questioning the Christian tradition, it doubtless was the
ground on which many questioners of the 1960s and beyond took their
stand. One such questioner described the way his private thinking was
called out into the public realm by his reading of *Honest to God*:

> I was riveted by this book! I could not put it down. I read it three times
> from cover to cover. ... it was an honest book. It talked about issues I
> had not been willing to talk about or even to think about publicly. ...
> John Robinson touched every issue about which I felt a general dis-ease
> in the church's life, and he showed me why.[10]

So said John Shelby Spong, in *Here I Stand,* published in 2000. Spong's
subsequent publications were largely instrumental in delivering the thought
of John Robinson to the grass roots of the church. Spong saw his role as
explaining more fully the need to put aside fourth century images of God
and Jesus.

These days, evolving Christians have mostly moved on from the point reached
by John Robinson. But on that basis they are now strongly motivated to ask

---

8   *Honest to God*, 19–20.
9   *Ibid.*, 20.
10   Spong, *Here I Stand*, 127.

questions about what might constitute the church's foundation for the future. Among others, those questions address how one speaks of God, of Jesus, of personal spirituality, of pastoral care and of the role of the church in society.

Honest to God communicated Robinson's reinterpretation of Christian doctrine within his pastoral and evangelical situation as Bishop of Woolwich. His book had a predominantly lay readership, untrained in theology. Yet the readers knew it was written for them. He was asking the right questions about the faith. He understood the sincerity of theologians and clergy trying to explain the faith according to "the faith once delivered to the saints." But he also noted that even the best of such restatements were failing to convince the contemporary generation. They were failing to make any sense! The message was not so much being rejected; it was not capable of being understood. What was required was not tinkering around the edges, but taking a more comprehensive approach, if the church was not to have lost out to all but a tiny religious remnant. Robinson went so far as to say that "dogmatic theology is a misrepresentation of the gospel".[11] Yet one of his better known statements is this:

> What I have tried to say, in a tentative and exploratory way, may seem to be radical, and doubtless to many, heretical. The one thing of which I am fairly sure is that, in retrospect, it will be seen to have erred in not being nearly radical enough.[12]

Inexplicably, as Alistair Kee points out, Robinson dismissed his own expertise in doctrine of God theology as evidenced in his doctoral dissertation. He declared himself dependent on following the thoughts of contemporary theologians, in particular Tillich and Bonhoeffer. Yet his dissertation already contained the groundwork that underpins *Honest to God*. In fact it led him to this foundational statement of his position:

> Belief in God is the trust, the well-nigh incredible trust, that to give ourselves to the uttermost in love is not to be confounded but to be 'accepted', that Love is the ground of our being, to which ultimately we 'come home'. If this is true, then theological statements are not a description of 'the highest Being', but an analysis of the depths of personal relationships—or, rather, an analysis of the depths of all experience 'interpreted by love'.[13]

---

11   *Honest to God*, 9.
12   Ibid.,10.
13   Ibid., 49.

This has enormous repercussions for Christology. If God is no longer to be thought of as 'out there', as a being inhabiting another sphere of reality, then the traditional Christological model no longer works. Christ cannot be a supernatural being who 'comes to' this world from 'out there'.

One of the first pastoral concerns to 'ring a bell' with Robinson was his recognition that traditional imagery of God makes God remote from ordinary people and their concerns. The triune God of Trinitarian theology—even if regarded as community—is all the same inherently distant from humanity. This is the God who sends Jesus from heaven to earth and then plucks him back out again. As Robinson notes, some people thought he was an atheist. His writings about the collapse of the metaphysical 'God out there', which was meant to take the place of the mythological 'God up there', looked to many to be the complete undermining of belief in God, particularly of belief in the triune God.

Trinitarian imagery of God entails a necessary view of humanity as warped, or 'fallen', in need of the redeeming Son. Yet the human Jesus clearly had confidence in his followers' ability to carry out his teaching. It is self-evident that he did not believe they were sinners from birth, needing to be baptised into his own salvific death! Evolving or progressive Christianity does not subscribe to the doctrine of Original Sin. Yet removing it also removes the props from under Augustine's fifth century Christological propositions. With the removal of that 'original sin' foundation, the whole 'system' of traditional theology ceases to hold its ground. Robinson put into words, in print, what generations had thought and discussed privately. He was so secure in the foundations of his own faith in a God of love that he found complete freedom to reinterpret theological tradition.

His specific writings on Christology did not appear until 1970. In *The Human Face of God*,[14] Robinson made the point that the gospel depiction of the virgin birth was not intended as literal truth, but as mythology—sacred story. However, within the metaphysical setting of traditional theology, the virgin birth (and so much other biblical myth) became for countless Christians, literal truth. On the resurrection, Robinson quoted Gordon Kaufman, Professor of Divinity at Harvard Divinity School in the 1960s. Kaufman wrote:

---

14   *The Human Face of God.*

> The finite objective historical reality correlative to faith was not in fact the reawakened Jesus of Nazareth but the new community of love and forgiveness, recreated and recognized under the impact of the resurrection appearances.[15]

For years, fuel for a new Reformation has been building in the hearts and minds of faithful followers of Jesus. Along the way, many thoughtful Christians have jumped ship. They still love Jesus, but for them the God of the church is way too small—too distant and too different from the God of Love revealed by Jesus. Along the way, congregations have been shrinking. Along the way, younger generations have decided they have no need of the church and its doctrines about Jesus the Christ. They are the "I'm not religious, but I am spiritual" generation. They are the reason for the development of 'New Age' spirituality, including indigenous and Buddhist spirituality. The church itself is seen by two generations as *passé*—old hat.

For those who remain, there is growing need for a spirituality based on faith, not on belief. Harvey Cox expresses that in his book *The Future of Faith,* when he describes the essential difference between the church's 'Age of Belief' and the 'Age of Faith' that is emerging:

> Belief is more like opinion than the deep-seated confidence of faith. We can believe in something without it making much difference to our life. We place our faith in something only if it is vital to the way we live.[16]

They are the vital issues that Paul Tillich called "ultimate concerns". Cox summarised his position in these words:

> As Christianity moves awkwardly but irreversibly into a new phase in its history, those who are pushing into this frontier often look to the earliest period, the Age of Faith, rather than the intervening one, the Age of Belief, for inspiration and guidance.[17]

So much time and effort has been spent, and is still being spent, cogitating about who is Jesus and what was his relationship with God. Instead, uninterrupted and absolute primacy ought to be given to the serious following of Jesus' teachings about the Kingdom of God on earth. A religion based on metaphysics has become a recipe for social irrelevance. It ensures that traditional Christianity is out of touch with the spiritual and

---

15   Ibid., 131.
16   Cox, *The Future of Faith*, 3.
17   Ibid., 19.

existential needs of twenty-first century people. Messing with metaphysics about Jesus and his place in a triune God is guaranteed to create first of all confusion and then indifference. It distracts from a commitment to follow Jesus' teachings about life and to develop intimate relationship with God who is love. Crucially, it has the potential to place theological absolutes in the way of ethical judgments in areas of pastoral concern.

Kee notes that Robinson's reliance on the philosophy of 'I-Thou' and the derivative 'I-thous', implies a social understanding of God.[18] Because his theology is personalist, it is inherently moral. It stands firmly on the biblical injunction to "love the Lord your God with all your heart, with all your soul, with all your mind and with all your strength … and your neighbour as yourself." All theology based on that commandment becomes moral theology. As Robinson states:

> Assertions about God are in the last analysis assertions about Love—about the ultimate ground and meaning of personal relationships.[19]

Yet the truth is that ethics are often treated as an 'add on' to traditional theology.

Robinson points out that ethical decision-making often relies on change—on new knowledge from the human and social sciences. New ethical positions are therefore much closer to where people actually live. To underpin those new ethical positions, he points to what is constant and unchanging—the love of God. That is infinitely more reliable than laws and codes tied to a particular time and place. God is not the unchanging One; that is the assumption of Greek metaphysics. God is the God of history, found in movement and change, as the Bible asserts. This applies in changing views of marriage, contraception and abortion. The old approach from the viewpoint of doctrine has given way to a loving view of the situation of persons involved. In his 1970 book, *Christian Freedom in a Permissive Society*, Robinson commented on the theological absolutism of the papal encyclical *Humanae Vitae*:

> Few will now bother to ask whether the Pope is infallible. The credibility gap is too great. They are much more concerned with whether the pill is infallible.[20]

---

18   *The Roots of Christian Freedom*, 124.
19   *Honest to God*, 126.
20   Robinson, *Christian Freedom in a Permissive* Society, 115.

John Robinson's stand on war emerged very late in his writing career, but it arises from his continuing understanding of God as expressed in *Honest to God.* In his essay *Where Three Ways Meet,* published posthumously in 1987, he concludes a call to the church to take seriously the Beatitude—"Blessed are the peacemakers, for they shall be called children of God"—by reminding us that anti-war advocacy is a part of the full gospel from Jesus, which the church has to proclaim. He ends by quoting the Spanish Catholic theologian Raimon Pannikar, the so-called 'Apostle of interfaith dialogue': "What we need", Pannikar said, "is not a Vatican III—a Jerusalem II is far more urgent."[21]

This is the recognition to which increasing numbers of Christians have come—the necessity of an intentional return to the teachings of Jesus of Nazareth. In this lies the potential of a Christianity that can unite with all people on the inclusive basis of Love.

What makes evolving Christians different from proponents of 'New Age' spirituality is their determination to preserve the church for the future. They do not want to leave the church; they love its potential for good far too much. They do not want to see it die; they want to see it re-formed in the image of the God of Love taught by Jesus. They see the church's new potential as a gathering of followers of The Way, living out the teachings *of* Jesus, and swept clean of the religion *about* Jesus as the Christ. They see clearly that the church based on traditional doctrine is dying, first of all in the West. They also see it re-formed, as the Church of The Way. These are people who would respond positively to a slogan like 'The Church is dead! Long live the Church!' But unlike the monarch who begins his new reign only after the death of the previous king or queen, people promoting a new Reformation in the church see that the transformation is already taking place. There is widespread agreement that the new Reformation is well and truly underway. It is building from the ground up, undergirded by theology from the 'Grass Roots', from those who respond to Jesus' message about God who is Love. (Or as I prefer to say, about Love who is God).

This is the same message about God and life that caused people in Jesus' time to hear him "gladly!" This is the message that is received, internalised and acted upon whenever the church lives out the teachings of Jesus. It encapsulates the sacred story, guidance for life, and experience of God.

---

21   Robinson, *Where Three Ways Meet*, 122.

Desire for experience *of* the divine is well and truly displacing theories *about* the divine. The yearning for a re-formed church reveals a people who do not want to give up on religion, but can no longer subscribe to what they see as an outmoded, irrelevant definition of their faith.

In the public sphere, Evolving Christianity's re-formed foundation is increasingly being heard, in three parts. First, as a non-Christological narrative concerning the life and death of Jesus of Nazareth. Second, as his system of universal ethics for life. Thirdly, as his revelation of God as Love.

Let me conclude by saying that turning away from traditional doctrine toward a re-claiming of Jesus' teachings is not a step backwards, as some would argue. It is coming full circle. It is the means of uniting the past, the present and the future of the church. T. S. Eliot expressed this insight in a poem that meant a great deal to John Robinson. It is called *Little Gidding*, and this is a short excerpt from its final stanza:

> We shall not cease from exploration
> and the end of all our exploring
> will be to arrive where we started
> and know the place for the first time ...[22]

The basis for evolving Christianity and the foundation of a new Reformation can be traced in many ways to what was given to us fifty years ago by John A. T. Robinson—the encouragement to be 'Honest to God'!

---

22   This poem was written between 1941 and 1942 during the German bombing raids on Britain, and published for the first time in the October 1942 issue of *The New English Weekly*. 'Little Gidding' in *Four Quarters* by T. S. Elliot (London: Faber & Faber, 2001).

5. Reflections from the edge of the flood plain

John W. H. Smith

In Australia today we are witnessing quite significant opposition to Christian orthodoxy, particularly from people who refer to themselves as 'progressive' or 'evolving' Christians. This challenge has come as a direct result of wide scale dissatisfaction with the orthodox answers to genuine questions of faith and to the recent enlightening scholarly information gleaned by a renewed search for the Jesus of history.

In preparation for our book, *Why Weren't We Told? A Handbook on Progressive Christianity,*[1] Rex Hunt and I engaged in many in-depth conversations with colleagues while negotiating the articles, cameos and research data. In these discussions we continually referred to the renewed interest in 'progressive Christianity' and the 'historical Jesus' as a 'movement'. Eventually one colleague remarked that he saw this increasing interest not so much as a movement, but more akin to a 'stream of thinking' that is slowly and inexorably spreading over the religious landscape like a river spreading over a 'flood plain'. A river that is seeking a path of the least resistance as it spreads its life-nourishing influence in a dry and barren environment. This image of a dynamic living force certainly seemed a more apt description of what we were experiencing.

Why has this particular 'stream of thinking', at this particular time, captured the interest of so many people and what will be its influence on the religious landscape of mainstream orthodox Christianity in the future?

The following is an article containing my own personal reflections on the mediating factors of this explosion of interest in the 'historical Jesus' and 'progressive Christianity' in Australia over the last thirty years. The possible impact on the future of the Christian church will also be addressed.

Setting the Scene

The quest for the 'historical Jesus' is not a new phenomenon. Robert (Bob) Funk in 2001 documented thirteen 'milestones' in his historical search, in

---

1   *Why Weren't We Told?*

an article in the *Fourth R.*[2] Funk traces the key influencing factors in the quest for the historical Jesus over two centuries beginning with the 1778 Reimarus' essay *The aims of Jesus and His Disciples*, and concluding with his own work: *The Five Gospels* (1993), and *Honest to Jesus* (1996). As Funk writes, the influence of all these milestones can be truly recognised only in retrospect. Hence, the full impact of what is occurring now will not be fully known for some time to come. However, these milestones form the basic premises of our modern historical research and as such they are the foundational building blocks for further exploration.

It is important to recognise that for a majority of scholars, the search for the historical Jesus is not simply an academic exercise. It is also a personal pursuit to find a sense of wholeness of being. Walter Wink states:

> In my struggle to become human, I find myself returning over and over again to those ancient texts that for me still contain the original impulse of Jesus.[3]

Wink further postulates that the meaning of Jesus for the present age has been the unconscious agenda of the 'Jesus-quest' for the last two hundred years. He argues that, "… the driving Spirit behind the quest was the hope of finding our own humanness in God …"[4]

How then did these scholars begin their search for the 'authentic' Jesus?

We owe a great debt of gratitude to the Jesus Seminar scholars and those scholars from the United Kingdom such as Keith Ward, Richard Swinburne and Karen Armstrong—as well as the early pioneers in Australia, including Lloyd Geering, Dudley Hyde, Charles Birch—for the wealth of information currently at our disposal. More recently, New Zealand and Australian scholars, religious practitioners and theologians—both lay and clergy—are equally making a significant contribution to our understanding of the historical Jesus. The initiative of Rex Hunt in publishing, *Why Weren't We Told? A Handbook on Progressive Christianity*, has placed the contributions of contemporary New Zealand and Australian scholars on the same page as the international scholars, albeit with our own idiosyncrasies. The works of Jenks, Webb, Morwood, Hunt, Leaves, Parkinson, Macnab, Preston, Bodycomb, Tacey, Veitch, Loader, and many others are having a significant

---

2   Funk, "Milestones in the Quest for the Historical Jesus".
3   Wink, "The Myth of the Human Jesus," in Hedrick, *When Faith Meets Reason*, 98.
4   Ibid., 100.

impact, not only on the Australian/New Zealand scene but internationally as well.

How have these contributions influenced our thinking and why has it been so well received albeit by a minority of faith seekers? I contend that there are at least five salient points in the rapid rise of interest in the progressive Christian thought and practice in Australia and New Zealand over the last thirty years.

The Influence of New Testament Scholarship

The first is the influence of recent New Testament scholarship. Who are these scholars and why have they excited our imagination? What is the Jesus Seminar and what has been its contribution? Why has this critical scholarship resonated with so many people?

I begin with a Marcus Borg quotation used by Dominic Crossan in *The Birth of Christianity*.

> The Gospels are literally the voices of their authors. Behind them are the anonymous voices of the community talking about Jesus. And embedded within their voices is the voice of Jesus as well as the deeds of Jesus. ... Constructing an image of Jesus—which is what the quest for the historical Jesus is about—involves two crucial steps. The first step is discerning what is likely to go back to Jesus. The second step is setting this material in the historical context of the first century Jewish homeland.[5]

In the late 1970s and early 1980s there was a re-emergence of interest in the historical Jesus, which Funk refers to as the 'Third Quest'. At this time he and Dominic Crossan, frustrated with the controlling seminary and academic institutions and with the support of about thirty other scholars, established the Jesus Seminar under the umbrella of the Westar Institute. Their aim was to initiate a process for the exchange, debate and research of critical New Testament scholarship regarding the historical Jesus. These scholars based their findings on empirical and factual data. They agreed to meet twice a year to analyse the gospels and to share information so as to build a credible body of knowledge around Jesus of Nazareth. Their methodological rigor led them to accept only that information which would pass the test of their rules of evidence.

---

5   Crossan, *The Birth of Christianity*, 140.

How did they achieve this and what was their method? David Galston reports that they started with the words of Jesus, or as he explains it with a 'voice print'. The question they asked was, "what did Jesus say"? Because they believed that, "The quest for the historical Jesus starts not with a theory of history, but with the more unassuming task of hearing a voice."[6] Therefore, history, they concluded, emerges out of the construct of what is said, and not out of a systemic historical model.

The first task of the Seminar was to make an inventory and classify all the words attributed to Jesus from the first three centuries of the Common Era. Through an examination of the canonical gospels as well as independent sources, including those of Jewish historians, they collected more than 1,500 versions of approximately 500 sayings. In addition to the four canonical gospels the Seminar included all other known non-canonical gospels in their deliberations, such as the find at Nag Hammadi which included a number of 'Sayings Gospels', one of them a Coptic version of the *Gospel of Thomas*,[7] The scholars assumed that for a period of some years stories about Jesus were circulated by word of mouth and it is possible that more than ten years elapsed before anything was written down. It was another ten years before they were collated into the gospel form of Thomas. The members of the Seminar agreed to review each of these 1,500 statements with the aim of determining which of them could be ascribed to Jesus, with a significant degree of probability.

The results of these deliberations are recorded in the 1993 Polebridge Publication *"The Five Gospels: The search for the authentic words of Jesus?"* by Robert Funk, Roy Hoover and Seminar members. Funk and the Jesus Seminar followed up this publication with the *"The Acts of Jesus"* released in 1998.

In the words of Dominic Crossan, I make this qualification:

> this research to achieve its aim of portraying the 1st century Jesus required the removal of sedimented layers to find what Jesus actually said and did, and to do this with scholarly integrity and some methodological validity? This does not in any way conclude that the layers removed are illicit, invalid, useless or detrimental. It would be a mistake to claim that the first layer is authentic as if the other two layers were inauthentic. It is

---

6   Galston, "Postmodernism", 15.
7   Hunt, "The Nag Hammadi Library" in Hunt and Smith, *Why Weren't We Told?*, 50–51.

perhaps best to talk of 'original development' and "compositional layers" [rather] than authentic and inauthentic interpretations. [8]

It is this research and the collective collegiality of the Jesus Seminar scholars that provided the foundational material for the many valuable resource books written in the late twentieth and early twenty-first century.

Why is it that these scholars and writers have had such a profound impact on our understanding of Christianity?

Marcus Borg's book, *Meeting Jesus Again for the First Time*,[9] captured for many the vision that grew from this research. People were indeed exploring the person of Jesus of Nazareth from a different perspective and for many it was a unique and fulfilling experience. But why did it resonate with lay people? Primarily this approach raised for many the unresolved questions that had plagued them for many years.

The historical Jesus was being portrayed more as a revolutionary sage than a divine being. Jesus was presented as pointing to the saving power of God to transform and heal, rather than to claim this ability for himself. This Jesus is egalitarian and inclusive in his table fellowship. He makes forgiveness reciprocal and he advocates that the relationship with God does not require a broker. The research also indicates that Jesus had to be set free from the confines of the creeds and doctrines, in particular the doctrine of atonement. Jesus' death as a blood sacrifice was in reality a later layer of information that had no basis in the findings of the Seminar.[10] The research portrayed a radically different figure of Jesus to the one presented by orthodox Christianity. It in turn challenged our conventional understanding of God as portrayed by traditional Christianity. These scholars paint a portrait of Jesus as an enlightened human being; a teacher of wisdom, which came from his intimacy with God. He was a healer, whose powers came from his relationship with the divine and his understanding and experience of this reality. He displayed a compassion for the human misery he witnessed and the exploitation of the marginalised, which he observed. Further, he was aware that disempowerment was brought about through the abuse of social systems.

---

8   Crossan, *The Historical Jesus*, xxxi.
9   Borg, *Meeting Jesus Again for the First Time*.
10   David Clarke, "Atonement" in Hunt and Smith, *Why Weren't We Told?*, 2–4.

David Galston, the Canadian theologian mentioned earlier, writes that the significant detailed research of the Jesus Seminar, 'embraced the person—the historical Jesus and not a religious theme'.[11] This approach affirms that history emerges out of a construct of what is said and done.

The response to this scholarship did not lie within the context of the material only, but in how the material was presented. These scholars did not use academic language to convey their findings. Theology was not the sole domain of theologians but was being conveyed in a language that welcomed a wider audience. For many these easily readable writings acknowledged and gave credence to the doubts and questions that many lay people had been wrestling with for many years. Some in despair had walked away from traditional Christian faith communities and had become in Spong's terms, the "believers in exile".

Writers such as Spong, Funk, Scott, Borg and Crossan were eagerly embraced because they offered people an understandable way of exploring a credible faith. Their writings encouraged people to meet Jesus again and to understand the context or 'matrix' of the first century life of a Galilean peasant. Crossan and Borg use the wisdom saying attributed to a Native American teacher, "I do not know if this ever occurred but I do believe it to be profoundly true." This made so much sense to those who were searching for relevance and meaning in traditional Bible stories.

These scholars also encouraged people to "re-imagine a world" where God reigns by positioning themselves as eye witnesses to the events recorded in scripture. This was powerful and quite heady stuff for people who for the first time had been introduced to the practical application of New Testament scholarship in a language that made sense to their personal experience and knowledge.

However, all of this information could only have impact if the mood of the audience is sufficiently in sync to resonate with it. On considering this matter I became aware of an interesting parallel between the information being supplied to the general Christian community and the growth in the individual's spiritual development. At a Progressive Christian Network of Victoria (PCNV) meeting in 2013, Chris Page suggested that people exploring their faith journey in the light of New Testament scholarship went through a series of stages. He referred to these stages as *Enchantment,* which

11   Galston, "Postmodernism", 11ff.

is coming to an understanding of the person of Jesus as portrayed by the orthodox Christian faith. The stage of *Disenchantment* kicked in when this depiction of Jesus did not measure up to how they understood the world through their own 'knowledge' and 'experience'. The third stage that of *Re-enchantment* occurs when people discover a new way of relating to the Jesus of history through the detailed knowledge revealed by the New Testament scholars such as the Jesus Seminar. This new understanding allows us to live with *doubt* and *uncertainty*, which may often be the trigger that encourages us to begin *deconstructing* what we have become concerned about and in turn leads us to a delightful *discovery*, as O'Murchu suggests,[12] of ourselves as mature adults capable of a personal relationship with the sacred.

The Formation of Mutually Supportive Discussion Groups

The second salient point in the surge of interest in 'progressive Christianity' has been the establishment of mutually supportive self-discovery groups. These groups arose in response to the need for some honest exploration of questions of faith.

In 2004, Hal Taussig conducted extensive research in North America to test his hypothesis that 'progressive Christianity' was growing at the 'grassroots' level.[13] He discovered that small groups of people wanted to share and support each other with their questions of faith. They were armed with the writings from a wide range of scholars, many of them from the Jesus Seminar. Very often it was those who had felt marginalized by mainstream Christianity who joined the groups. Gay and Lesbian people and others— who were excluded because they dared to challenge the integrity of the doctrines and the creeds associated with formalised religion—were seeking a chance to share questions, frustrations and joys with like-minded, open-hearted people.

In 2010, for similar reasons to those espoused by Taussig, I conducted a much smaller research project.[14] As there is no national register of groups calling themselves "progressive" in Australia and New Zealand, the contacts were made simply by word of mouth through the informal network of colleagues and friends. The results of this research were published as "Living

---

12   O'Murchu, *Adult Faith*.
13   Taussig, *A New Spiritual Home*.
14   In my project, forty 'Requests for Information' were distributed, and twenty-six responses were received.

the Progressive Dream".[15] The conclusions from this study supported those found by Taussig's more extensive research, and perhaps are summed up in the following quotation.

> The principal strength of these groups is that they are vibrant discussion groups, exploring contemporary scholarship in a safe, open and inclusive environment. An atmosphere where nothing is 'taboo', where 'hostility and 'ridicule' is not tolerated and where open and frank ideas are encouraged.[16]

The study programs used the resources of the Jesus Seminar scholars as cited above and supplemented this with information from the new group of writers from Australia and New Zealand, which had only recently begun to emerge. Intentional hospitality was encouraged, often with the opportunity of a shared meal or glass of wine and nibbles.

'Intellectual integrity' was a major theme in many programs. There was a desire among the group participants to share the concerns that arose when enquiring minds and scientific knowledge conflicted with orthodox Christian teaching. Many believed that there was something outside themselves that gave purpose and meaning to life and this could not be confined by the traditional definitions of sacredness. It was not simply a matter of what people didn't believe, but a searching for what they did believe that became the driving force for many groups. In his book, *The Future of Faith,* Harvey Cox postulates three historical stages of faith and concludes that the one we are currently experiencing is the "Age of the Spirit". This stage, Cox claims, is characterised by a search for authenticity in faith and by stripping away the layers of belief that do not stand the test of one's experience and knowledge. You will often hear the statement, "I am not religious but I am spiritual", from people who are turning their backs on organized religion. This stage, Cox also claims, represents a 'protest' against mainstream Christianity, which is based on earlier outmoded stages of faith. He writes that the "Age of the Spirit" is:

> an attempt to voice the awe and wonder before the intricacy of nature that many feel is essential to human life without stuffing them into ready-to-wear ecclesiastical patterns.[17]

---

15   Smith, "Living the Progressive Dream" in Hunt and Smith, *Why Weren't We Told?*, 203–27.

16   Ibid., 225.

17   Cox, *The Future of Faith*, 13–14.

The groups became personal support networks for people when they openly shared their experiences and their desire to seek spiritual wholeness. These men and women became what Bishop Spong refers to as the "believers in exile"[18] or the "church alumni association", although many continued to participate in formal religious communities. For many this meant separating out the community life of the local parish and their particular religious adherence. One colleague related his Sunday morning experience in church, as one of "shuddering with disbelief at the language and the lack of intellectual integrity, but being warmed by the care and love that members of the community showered upon me." Another group leader stated:

> Our group meets before the service each Sunday and walks to church. It travels 100 metres and goes back 150 years.

How the group participants were able to balance and make sense of these conflicting pressures is a testimony to their commitment. In a number of situations the minister/pastor had forbidden them to meet on church premises or advertise their activities on the church notice board. It was interesting to note that the groups that received such overt opposition actually flourished. It was as though the opposition justified their reason for meeting together. Most groups met in homes where participants claimed they had the opportunity to feel less restricted by a 'churchy' atmosphere. This also encouraged people outside a community of faith to participate more openly.

The groups continue to provide an open and relaxed way to explore personal spiritual interests without the restricting overlays of religious straitjackets. Where the group was led by a layperson and not clergy it was bonus for some, because it enabled them to share their concerns and doubts about their faith more comfortably. Each member of a group program had their own personal faith journey and while I was gathering information about these small groups an initiator of one of the largest told me his personal story.

Bill Andrews was about to abandon the church when by chance he heard Bishop Spong delivering an address in Canada in 1996. He speaks of this event as a 'renaissance'. Bill had been questioning the orthodox interpretation of the life of Jesus. He questioned the miracles, the virgin birth, and the resuscitated body at the resurrection. He was seen primarily as a troublemaker and not taken seriously. Bill was just one of many people

---

18   Spong, *Why Christianity Must Change or Die.*

who embarked on an attempt to achieve, what Bob Funk refers to as at least "a modicum of intellectual integrity". Bill employed what the founder of Methodism, John Wesley, referred to as "Reason" and "Experience",[19] and he used these instruments—in conjunction with "Scripture" and "Tradition"—to increase his understanding of the sacred.

The Importance of Learning from Personal Journeys

A third salient point began to emerge when we discovered that the stories shared in small groups were a major influence in people pursuing 'progressive Christianity'. These stories were crying out for a wider audience, hence the publication of our second book together, *New Life: Rediscovering Faith. Stories from Progressive Christians.*[20] It was Bill's story that led Rex Hunt and me to seek personal information from others regarding their spiritual journeys.

We managed to obtain twenty-five quite courageous and gutsy personal stories of the journey with progressive Christianity from lay people in New Zealand and Australia. Many of those we approached were known personally to Rex and myself or were contacts from colleagues. I have quite deliberately used the term "courageous" to describe these stories, because they record personal and at times intimate journeys, which expressed individual doubts and questions that go to the very heart of an understanding of one's self as a 'spiritual' human being.

Each of these stories, while quite unique had corresponding similarities. After much deliberation we determined that there were four major reasons in the twenty-five stories as to why people began to explore progressive Christianity. The first category we described as *Progressive Christianity— An Evolutionary Approach*, because seven respondents came to a gradual dissatisfaction with the teaching of their respective religious communities. This resulted in a decision to seek answers to their questions from other sources, such as the material being produced by the Jesus Seminar scholars, and the emerging scholarship being produced by scholars and practitioners from the Antipodes.

---

19   Wesley had claimed that reason and experience should be employed in interpreting what scripture declares, and if scripture conflicts with experience and reason, we should ask why. See Williams, *John Wesley's Theology Today*.

20   Smith and Hunt, *New Life*.

The second sub-category, *Progressive Christianity—Searching for Self,* are stories of six people exploring the spiritual dimension of their lives in the midst of the challenges and changes of life. They were prepared to embrace change even when it meant discarding the faith of their parents. As one writer claimed she was searching for a faith that encouraged and enabled her to be "more fully human".

The third category, *Progressive Christianity—Seeking Integrity,* was for a set of seven writers who especially valued intellectual integrity in their search for a faith. This did not discount the importance of a free-flowing spirituality in their lives, but equally for them there was the need to be intellectually coherent. Many had explored scientific and managerial approaches along with literary and theological aspects in their search for moral and intellectual coherence.

The final sub-category we titled, *Progressive Christianity—Embracing a Faith in Action.* A group of five writers were imbued with the understanding that their beliefs could only be relevant when they took the action necessary to make them a reality. A belief had practical consequences and most of these writers were committed to social justice and the practical outcomes of a living faith.

For all of our contributors the living out of their faith was an ongoing *process* because progressive Christianity was for them a journey and not a destination. Further, they needed a *community* of friends as they journeyed and as they sought to discern the *authentic Jesus* of history. They admitted openly to the importance of an attitude of *religious pluralism*, that progressive Christianity was not the only way or necessarily the best way, but the way that was right for them at this time. *Intellectual integrity* was another important element for most of the writers and this was a strong motivator to explore and put under the microscope their long held and for many cherished beliefs. The vast majority of our contributors were searching for a way to *embrace life with a passion*, rather than adhere to a religion. The journey for most had brought joy, relief, liberation, excitement and a wonderful sense of freedom, but not without a sense of tension. Finally, a realisation of the sacred in the light of so much that is unknown provided them with a sense of *awe and wonder* in a way that was almost indescribable.

Spreading the Message of the New Scholarship Nationally

The fourth salient factor in the groundswell of interest in progressive Christianity in Australia and New Zealand has been generated through the Common Dreams international conferences and the single speaker events of Common Dreams on the Road. There have been three Common Dreams conferences with attendances ranging from 400 to 900 delegates and three Common Dreams on the Road events that have also attracted significant numbers.

The initiative for the Common Dreams conferences came from Rex Hunt and Jonathon Rea who called a meeting of interested colleagues early in 2006. It was agreed to hold the first event in 2007 and to invite Bishop John Shelby Spong to be the keynote speaker. All conferences have been successful in attracting a wide- ranging audience due to the programming team's ability to attract well-known and challenging speakers. Common Dreams is now a financially viable enterprise and is currently planning a fourth event in 2016.

These events have effectively spread the word of the New Testament scholarship in a quite remarkable way. They have provided people in the Antipodes with the opportunity to hear, first hand, from both international and local scholars valuable information for their journey in progressive Christianity. Perhaps more importantly, they have provided an opportunity for people from all over Australia and New Zealand to meet, establish and maintain friendships, and exchange information. We can justifiably say that through these meetings the contacts continue to grow and people no longer feel as isolated in their questions and concerns. This has been an important instrument in promoting the value of the search for Jesus of Nazareth.

In Australia's major cities the number of specialist religious bookshops has decreased significantly. The rise of interest in New Testament scholarship was readily available through on-line connections, however for many of those journeying, the opportunity to browse through the literature and to receive advice on where to start exploring was crucial. The Common Dreams conferences and Common Dreams on the Road provided a bookstall with the assistance of Mosaic Resources, a publishing and wholesale distribution company formerly based in Melbourne. The bookshop has sold over $100,000 worth of books and DVDs at these events, and has been a major influence in spreading the message of progressive Christianity. It also raised approximately $35,000 profit from its operations.

The Importance of Positive Regard

The fifth important point in the growth of knowledge regarding the historical Jesus has been the *manner* in which the story has been communicated. It is perhaps trite to say that it is not just what is said, but how it is conveyed that is important. The collegiality and warmth of regard for each other is to be commended. In Crossan's terms we are truly in a "companionship of empowerment" where—regardless of one's academic qualifications, experience or professional standing—what is said is regarded and recognised as a contribution of value.

No contribution is dismissed out of hand regardless of who utters it. Rex Hunt, in the middle of 2013, initiated an email discussion world wide among progressive Christians about the nature of God. At one time there were over ninety people involved in the communication, ranging from professors to lay people struggling to make sense of the sacred dimension to their lives. All comments were duly regarded and discussed.

It is not only about respect and grace it is also about a genuine concern for the other's wellbeing. There is a real sense of belonging to a caring worldwide community. Recognizing another viewpoint and adding to or building on that has been commonplace among this community of colleagues, which inspires a real sense of belonging.

The Influence of Progressive theology on the Future Church

In the last thirty years, and particularly in the last ten, we have witnessed a significant growth in the number of people who are searching for a sacred dimension to their existence by pursuing an interest in the 'historical Jesus'. The question that this growth brings to the fore is simply what does it mean for the orthodox Christian church?

The evidence from the research into the group activities recorded in *Why Weren't We Told?* and the personal stories of laypeople recorded in *New Life*, reveal that many are seeking a different way of expressing their spirituality other than through the traditional orthodox religious structures. Many seekers journeying in progressive Christianity are searching for an authentic spirituality that coheres with their life experience, something that they have been unable to find in organized religion.

The majority of those attending conferences who belong to progressive religious groups, wish to stay with a community of faith even though many have suffered rejection by daring to ask fundamental questions. A consistent justification for the desire to remain in a faith community has been that through the interpersonal relationships with others they have been aware of a sacred presence.

If 'progressives' are to remain within the confines of a Christian faith community then the church authorities, particularly the clergy, must be prepared not just to tolerate, but also to embrace and make space for alternative ways of experiencing this sacred presence we call God.

A key element for many of the contributors to our research was the embrace of the human Jesus. It automatically follows that to embrace the 'human' Jesus means a questioning and in many cases a rejection of the 'divine' Jesus who has been afforded equal status with God. To accept fully the human Jesus demotes him from the lofty position he occupies in the creeds.

If the orthodox Christian church wishes to include those calling themselves 'progressive Christians' then it needs to be familiar with the New Testament scholarship surrounding the historical Jesus. This information needs to be available in the theological seminaries as well as the faith communities.

Phillip Hughes, Senior Researcher for the Christian Research Association, has analysed the findings of the Australian Bureau of Census from 2001 to 2011. He detected a steady decline in mainstream Christian Church adherence. However, he also noted that there had been a steady increase in the numbers who refer to themselves as "spiritual". A detailed study of these statistics reveals that religion is no longer culturally or ethnically determined through family ties, gender roles, or class. Religious adherence has become a personal lifestyle option, as people seek to determine their unique spirituality; not through creeds, doctrines or infallible proclamations, but simply on the experience of living life fully. It appears that the way we live is driven more by our own individual understanding of sacredness than an article of faith.

There is still a stated need for communities of faith that provide safe, mutually supportive and caring environments. These future groups may be transitory, coming together to achieve an agreed goal and then disbanding. Their measure of success will be more in their ability to nurture, support and give credence to a quite subjective spirituality rather than to require adherence to a formal statement of faith.

Conclusion

The number seeking an alternative faith to that of traditional orthodoxy is certainly growing. For many it is a reaction to the rigid understanding of Jesus as defined by the orthodox Christian faith. The suggestion that this current resurgence of interest in the quest for the historical Jesus is more a 'stream of thinking'—or something akin to a river slowly, but forcefully spreading across the barren landscape of a flood plain than a 'movement'—has some validity. The concept of a movement is suggestive of an organised and planned activity, whereas the overflowing into a flood plain gives more the impression of an evolving almost uncontrollable living force.

A number of writers such as Robin Meyers[21], Phillip Gulley[22], John Churcher[23] and Dudley Hyde[24] have suggested that the task of the future seekers after enlightenment is to 'rescue', 'liberate' or 'save' Jesus from the structures of the traditional Christian Church. These writers are calling us to recognise the historical Jesus outside the bounds of Christian orthodoxy and to affirm the presence of his Spirit active in the world.

Dostoyevsky in his book, *The Brothers Karamazov*[25] tells the story of the Grand Inquisitor. In this story, Jesus returns to earth at the time of the Spanish Inquisition and the Grand Inquisitor recognises him from his healing acts of compassion. As a result he imprisons Jesus and plans to have him burnt at the stake for crimes against the church. The 'crime' is Jesus' failure to accept the devil's temptation to become the supreme sovereign over the world. However, according to the Inquisitor the church is now rescuing the situation and will take back the free will of the people and eventually rule the world. The Church has usurped Caesar and taken up the sword of imperialism and now Jesus is again standing in its way.

During this monologue Jesus does not speak, and at the end of the Inquisitor's speech Jesus kisses him on his "bloodless, ninety year old lips". The Inquisitor shudders but goes and opens the cell door and instructs

---

21 Meyers, *Saving Jesus from the Church*.
22 Gulley, *If the Church Were Christian*.
23 Churcher, *Setting Jesus Free*.
24 Hyde, *Rescuing Jesus from the Church*.
25 Dostoyevsky, *The Brothers Karamazov*, Book 5.

Jesus to leave and never return. Jesus goes out into the "dark alleyways of the city" where he is now set free. His spirit will continue to roam the world offering compassionate healing while questioning those who claim they act in his name.

The rapid growth in the number of people pursuing progressive Christianity has run parallel with what Funk refers to as the "New Quest"[26] for the historical Jesus. It is difficult to determine which came first. Did our doubts and questions regarding Christian orthodoxy trigger the search or did the search trigger our doubts and questions? Perhaps they have just complimented each other. There is a parallel between Jesus' message of God's kingdom being present in the world and the search for life's meaning through an exploration of the 'sacred other' in the world around us.

Is this the task of progressive Christianity: to recognise and identify in the ordinary things of life, as did Jesus, the sacred spirit of the power we call God? Is it also our task to affirm that the spirit of Jesus is not the sole domain of the church, but has been released into the world emulating a river, which has broken its banks and is spreading life-enriching water across the religious landscape? How we respond to these questions will determine the future of faith for many of us.

---

26   Funk, "Milestones in the Quest for the Historical Jesus".

6. Spiritual vitality and intellectual integrity: Shaping progressive/evolving liturgy

Rex A. E. Hunt

Religion includes definitions and deeds, but first of all it is celebration.[1]

[Liturgy] has lost its living roots in the soil of the world and become a pot-plant in the sanctuary of the Church.[2]

In 2006 Jesus Seminar Fellow and New Testament scholar, Hal Taussig, published *A New Spiritual Home*.[3] He listed five characteristics of progressive Christianity. Two of those characteristics are in part the matrix for this chapter: a spiritual vitality and expressiveness; and an insistence on Christianity with intellectual integrity. This new kind of Christian expression is nourished by a wide-ranging intellectual curiosity and critique.

Likewise, the founder of the Westar Institute, the late Robert Funk, in an editorial in the January/February 2005 issue of *The Fourth R*, issued this radical call to a group of scholars and associated church leaders to throw the old forms out and start over again.

> ... design a new Sunday Morning Experience from the ground up ... new music, new liturgy, new scriptures, new ceremonies, new rites of passage.[4]

Sunday Morning

This brief exploration, an expansion of a workshop at the Common Dreams 3 Conference in Canberra in 2013, is about what happens on the other side of the not-so-welcoming church doors, in that event called worship; 'the religious gathering' or the Sunday morning liturgy. In particular, I want to explore what happens when that gathering is shaped by the following elements:

---

1   Vogt, *Modern Worship*.
2   Robinson, *The New Reformation?*
3   Taussig, *A New Spiritual Home*.
4   Funk, "Editorial".

- a progressive/evolving understanding of the wisdom of the historical Yeshua/Jesus, rather than adopting either the 'apocalyptic' Jesus or the Christ of orthodoxy;
- liturgy is seen as essentially as celebration or festival; and
- a southern hemisphere—or 'the landscape is'—perspective that acknowledges the inverted natural seasons compared to the northern hemisphere where the traditional liturgical calendar was shaped.

Generally speaking, as Dennis Smith and Hal Taussig express it, in our traditional Sunday morning Christian liturgy we have "let our emphasis on preserving traditional forms and expression overrule attempts to give vital expression to the life and faith of contemporary participants".[5]

Certainly the church in Australia has been slow to heed the call by many liturgists, including myself, to adapt its worship and even less prepared to inculturate.[6] As a result the dominant traditional 'liturgical' language sounds foreign. Well, as others have argued and I agree, it *is* foreign because it is *imperial*. What we have ended up with is the language of Caesar Augustus: Almighty Lord, Saviour of the World, Son of God, Emperor. David Galston goes so far as to suggest the gospel writers took the imperial garments of Caesar "and inadvertently, if not intentionally, slipped them over Jesus".[7] Result? Christianity ended up with Jesus Caesar! Which has caused Galston's fellow Canadian, Barrie Wilson, to declare it especially ironic that a movement which "started off as a radical challenge to the *Pax Romana* succeeded in becoming the official religion of the Roman Empire".[8]

Traditional Liturgy

So what does traditional liturgy—so radically influenced by medieval theology—look like? Or, perhaps better, how does it 'flow'? In traditional liturgy, both generally speaking but very specifically during the seasons of Lent and Advent, the movement is from confession to pardon, reflecting a presupposition of human guilt. This is an emphasis that—as Australian

---

5   Smith & Taussig, *Many Tables*, 12.
6   One contemporary Eucharistic Prayer that did make it into *Uniting in Worship 2* of the Uniting Church was written by Anita Monro: "You sculpted the planets and set the stars on fire. You moulded Uluru and shaped the ways of the Murray-Darling. You imagined the echidna into being and set the brolgas dancing. You made the great beasts of the oceans just for the pleasure of them …" (See *Uniting in Worship 2*, 317).
7   Galston, *Embracing the Human Jesus*, 14.
8   Wilson, *How Jesus Became Christian*, 255.

progressive, Francis Macnab, has reminded us—is negative, punitive and ineffective. The claim is that human beings owe God a debt. It's called 'sin'. So at this basic level Christian worship is the "act of paying off one's debt to God", who resides somewhere other than on earth.[9] It can be represented as follows:

Traditional Liturgy (Catholic)

Act	Movement	Liturgical Centre
Introductory Rite	Penitential Act	Guilt
Liturgy of the Word	Reading and Proclaiming	Judgment
Liturgy of the Table	Thanksgiving and Receiving	Forgiveness
Concluding Rite	Blessing and Commissioning	Proclaiming

Traditional Liturgy (Protestant)

Act	Movement	Liturgical Centre
Gathering	Adoration, Confession, Forgiveness	Guilt
Service of Word	Biblical readings, Preaching,	Proclaiming/Unity
Sacrament of Lord's Supper	Bread and Wine	Lord's Death
Sending Forth	Blessing, Dismissal	Service

Such a traditional or orthodox concern emphasises a narrow, single line of tradition, where the Christ is the language of its ceremony. So let me be blunt! In traditional Christian worship one can find little if anything of the gospel of Yeshua/Jesus of history, but plenty of the fictional, non-historical,

---

9   David Galston, "Liturgy in the Key of Q". In private circulation from the Westar Institute (2007), 14–15.

'empty shell' called the Christ of faith. These are sentiments shared, albeit more poetically, by Lebanese poet, philosopher and artist, Kahlil Gibran:

> Once every hundred years, Jesus of Nazareth meets Jesus of the Christians in a garden among the hills of Lebanon. And they talk long; and each time Jesus of Nazareth goes away saying to Jesus of the Christians, 'My friend, I fear we shall never, never agree'.[10]

David Galston is particularly direct:

> Gathering in the name of Jesus and gathering in the name of Christ are two different acts set on different foundations with different suppositions and necessarily different liturgies. One cannot be a Jesus follower and a Christ confessor at the same time, at least not with integrity. It even seems incredible that one should try.[11]

As I have suggested elsewhere,[12] even within liturgies prepared by some progressives, the change seems only minimal in two areas: 'shape' and 'content'. By 'shape' I mean: the liturgical movement still flows from confession to pardon, in spite of the way 'confession' and/or 'assurance/absolution is dressed up. (As Marcus Borg has frequently quipped: 'It's 9 o'clock in the morning and we've already been bad!') By 'content' I mean: the liturgy may proclaim belief beyond literalism, but the traditional language persists in many of the hymns, prayers, and creeds.

Progressive minister Jerry Stinson tells of a conversation he had some time back with controversial American Episcopal Bishop James Pike—who was under threat of a heresy trial. While Pike rejected many of the so-called 'fundamentals' of Christianity, when he conducted worship he would "lead people in one or another of the ancient creeds that included saying he believed in the very concepts he rejected".[13] When questioned further, Pike indicated he felt using a creed in worship was a liturgical act and the words of the liturgy did not necessarily need to be true in accord with his beliefs.

A similar position to that of Pike has been adopted by another Episcopal bishop, John Shelby Spong, who recently argued:

---

10   Gibran, *Sand and Foam*, 77.

11   Galston, "Liturgy in the Key of Q", 13.

12   Hunt, "Foreword" in Smith & Hunt, *New Life,* 21.

13   J. Stinson, "The Encounter of Progressive Christian Theology with the Language of Prayer and Ritual on Sunday Morning". Westar Institute/Literacy & Liturgy Seminar. In private circulation, 2006.

I have no problem in joining in the singing of this [Nicene Creed] ancient love song, but it would not occur to me that saying these words in worship somehow committed me to a literalized belief system, based on a 4th century view of reality.[14]

Stinson disagreed with Pike. "I think the words we use on a Sunday morning need to reflect what it is we believe," he wrote. Language, he claimed, is not an indifferent matter: "a change in speech habits is necessary if we are to change attitudes".[15] Others have stated it similarly: we can't keep what we *know* and what we *believe* separated. On the other hand, some suggest that rational clarity is only one kind of language. Liturgy needs "the rich, deep, not entirely rational forms of expression"[16] shaped by metaphor, the poetic, and parable.

Progressive Sunday Liturgy

So then what might progressive/evolving liturgy with 'spiritual vitality' and 'intellectual integrity' look like? In my own progressive liturgical explorations, for example, I have tried to move away from the traditional 'guilt/sin' base and reshaped the weekly liturgy under the heading *Celebration of Life*—all of life—with six encounter points: Gathering, Centering, Exploring, Affirming, Celebrating, Scattering. Those interested can check out my non-Prayer Book or Book of Common Order liturgies on my web site.[17] However, some general or practical features of the *Celebration* liturgy include the following:

1. The active participation of several people as: presider, co-presider, readers, musicians, singers, open time for 'prayers' in the form of joys and concerns—that is, co-operative participation rather than crowd participation or pseudo-togetherness—where people are given the respect to be actors rather than just reactors.

2. Each liturgy commences from the back of the church, among the congregation, rather than out the front/apse.

3. The use of a gong as part of the liturgy (rather than a bell outside calling people to worship) and the lighting of candles—severally, as Community Candle at the beginning of the liturgy, a Care Candle as part of the Joys and Concerns, and Journey Candles at the end of the

14   Spong, "Question and Answer" www.johnshelbyspong.com (9 January 2014).
15   Stinson, "Encounter", 1.
16   R. Jones, "Metaphor and Sacrament". Westar Institute Literacy & Liturgy Seminar. In private circulation (2007), 115.
17   www.rexaehuntprogressive.com

liturgy given to people who are about to spend some time away from the community.

4. A generous use of colour, especially the southern hemisphere hues.[18]

5. Periods of centering silence and private reflection/meditation.

6. Acknowledgement of the changing seasons—spring, summer, autumn, winter—with appropriate liturgical responses including everyday local symbols.

7. Use both biblical and non-biblical readings that are consistent with the spirit of Jesus.

8. Focus on the presence of G_d/the sacred in ordinary places and the ordinary spaces of our lives, with new names or metaphors for G_d/ the sacred.

9. Singing contemporary songs and hymns shaped by a progressive theology and reflecting our location in the southern hemisphere, rather than by doctrine or church tradition grounded in the northern hemisphere.

10. Lament rather than confession.

11. When the 'Lord's Prayer" is used, draw on contemporary expressions in the spirit of the 'Abba' Prayer.

12. Where possible, I share the Contemporary Exploration/Sermon with some trusted people before it is preached, receiving feedback on what and how it is said/understood.

Other progressive liturgists continue to use the traditional liturgical four movements or 'chassis', but with content, language, and atmosphere based on a 'historical' Jesus or wisdom understanding. One such progressive community in Canada shapes its weekly liturgy this way.[19]

---

18   Australian liturgist Dorothy McRae-McMahon says that when she offers people in liturgical workshops choices of coloured cloths to use as a background for symbols of their life, New Zealanders choose emerald greens, rich dark browns and clear blues. Australians mostly choose grey-greens, reddish browns and muted colours generally (McRae-McMahon, "Liturgy in the Southern Hemisphere", 135.)

19   Galston *Embracing the Human Jesus*, 150.

Historical Jesus Community Liturgy

Act	Movement	Liturgical Centre
Liturgy of Gathering	Peace and Solidarity	Common Humanity
Liturgy of Learning	Content and Discussion	Education
Liturgy of Banquet	Living and Celebrating	Compassion
Liturgy of Parting	Thankfulness and Good Tidings	Honesty

The shaping liturgical movement is from debt to *joy*, sacrifice to *banquet*, and deference to *presence*. The theology is a Christ-less Jesus! The leadership is courageous!

With those general comments in mind, in this next section I now want to get specific by looking at extracts from two liturgical moments: Baptism and the Jesus Banquet—the latter traditionally called Eucharist or Holy Communion—through some contemporary progressive eyes. As well, I shall offer two examples of Words of Committal for a Funeral.

Baptism—Celebrating New Life

Jesus did not practise baptism, at least according to the NT Gospels. Indeed in some quarters it is debatable if Jesus—as a Jew—was ever baptised. William Barclay suggests this in his commentary on *Matthew*:

> No Jew had ever conceived that he, a member of the chosen people, a son of Abraham, assured of God's salvation, could ever need baptism.[20]

More recent scholars, especially those associated with the Jesus Seminar, claim the early Christian communities would have lacked motivation for making up such a story. In all probability Jesus was at one time a follower of John and like many others received baptism at John's hands. However, it still needs to be said that when Jesus' baptism is mentioned it is not as an historical report, but as Christian accounts of an existing practice within the Christian community. Further, that tradition is clearly uneasy with the idea of John the Dipper baptising Jesus. Finally, the baptism practised by John was not a 'Christian' baptism liturgy!

Grounding the sacrament of Baptism in the New Testament is tricky business. There is no consistent or single NT view on Baptism, so that effort to ground our current Baptism practices in the NT should be abandoned. Even when

---

20   Barclay, *Matthew*, 52–53.

we examine the genuine Pauline letters it is not possible to determine the origin of Christian baptism. We can only affirm that Paul "already met with baptism"[21] and continued the practice within his own congregations. So the best we can do is ask: what of baptismal practice *today*?

To enforce the orthodox tradition, as well as cater for conservative elements and churches within the global ecumenical movement,[22] most denominations today demand adherence to the following exclusive action and wording concerning Baptism: "[The Sacrament of] Baptism is administered by pouring water on the head of the candidate"—in the name of the Trinity, and only using the prescribed traditional Formula—Father, Son, and Holy Spirit. No inclusive language within the Formula is allowed otherwise the baptism could be deemed *invalid*! And as if to seal the deal, the 'agreed' Baptism Certificate (in Australia at least) between several of the mainline churches could not be issued in the event that any of these 'essentials' were missing. All of this of course, is literalist nonsense!

But what of some progressive additions in response to Hal Taussig's observation of artistic forms and the use a wide variety of non-Christian rituals and meditation techniques which "interrogates Christian assumptions and traditions in order to reframe, reject, or renew them?"[23] A first step, as suggested by Gretta Vosper, is to change the title: calling it a *Celebration* of Baptism rather than the *Sacrament* of Baptism. Vosper writes:

> Baptism, as a sacrament (an efficacious act intended to engage God's participation in an event) requires particular words and actions in order to validate the effect. As something sacramental, however, that acknowledges and celebrates the pre-existence of the sacred within the child, such prescribed words and actions are no longer necessary.[24]

The second is to change or extend the language and symbols. Here are two *extracts* from progressive Baptism liturgies. The first comes from New Zealand and Australian colleagues, Roger Wiig and Doug McKenzie, in the late 1990s, with some adaptation. The second is from my own pen, but much influenced by others. These are followed by two new or recast Baptism formula examples.

---

21   Marxsen, *Jesus and the Church*, 162.

22   This is often expressed through the Lima Liturgy and the World Council of Churches report, *Baptism, Eucharist and Ministry*.

23   Taussig, "Grassroots Progressive Christianity", 5; and *A New Spiritual Home*, passim.

24   Vosper, *With or Without God*, 338.

Baptism Liturgy 1[25]

> For us in Australia, the driest continent on earth,
> > water is a precious commodity ...
> > > Water is everything.
> > > Water is life.
> > We claim the joy of water
> > and the way it sustains and nourishes us.

All **Let it flow and pour and sprinkle for all people.**
That all may know each day the gift of God in water.

> The biblical stories also talk of the preciousness of water.
> These stories remind us that water
> is a blessing and the source and strength of life.
> Without it humanity and all that has evolved could not survive.
> Our stories also remind us that the way of the Sacred
> is the way of compassion and love.
> God's love, like a shower of rain in drought,
> > awakens the sleeping seed within the soul
> > and lures it to blossom.
> God's love, like a paddling pool,
> > inspires the responsive love of children,
> > > jumping, splashing each other,
> > > shivering with wet delight.
> God's love, like a hot shower after a long day's work,
> > cleanses us, reawakens us.
> God's love, like waves crashing on the shore,
> > breaks in on us and enfolds us,
> > leaving us feeling vital and refreshed.

> *The water is poured into the font*

> So let's give thanks for this love
> that reaches out to us in what we say and do in love for this child
> > whom we are welcoming into our midst .

The generous image and use of water in a dry southern hemisphere land is a feature of this liturgy. To underline the importance of the 'everyday' symbolism of water, parents are sometimes invited to bring water from

---

25 Adapted from Wiig & McKenzie, *Baptismal Liturgy*.

their own family home for use in the liturgy. American Jim Burklo also includes an extended water image in one of his baptism liturgies:

> The chalice holds water that comes from (N's) grandparents' hometown in Germany, and it has been blessed by the pastor of her/his family's church. To it is added water from the Pacific Ocean that defines so much of the landscape that surrounds (N) today. This water represents the far-flung cultural wellsprings that will nourish (N) throughout his/her life [26]

Baptism Liturgy 2[27]

In the touch of this water, the ancient symbol of new life,
I baptise you into the love, service, and joy of God:
[Father, Son, and Holy Spirit...]
Source of Life, Companion, Enlivener.

Water is poured over the head of the child

And I name you (NNN).

Take this name and make it your own.
Live in freedom and fullness
as you travel your journey of life.
For your name is more than a collection of words.
It is something which has meaning
and importance to your parents and to us.
It has been chosen for you from every other name.

Thanksgiving for Birth

We give thanks for the birth of (N),
and for the joy which has come to his/her family.
We anoint you with fragrant oil as a sign
of our blessing to you this day.
May you grow in wisdom and understanding.

(touch head with oil)

May you work for justice in the world.

(touch hands)

May you walk in the ways of peace.

(touch feet)

---

26   Jim Burklo, "Baptism Liturgy".
27   Rex Hunt.

Child of the Earth

Poets are also sensitive to events such as this.

At the beginning of his poem Robert Weston writes:

> *Out of the stars in their flight, out of the dust of eternity,*
> *here have we come,*
> *Stardust and sunlight, mingling*
> *through time and through space...*

Each time we gather in sacred or ordinary places
we are reminded that Aboriginal people
have cared for this land since time immemorial,
loving it as their mother.

Others have also come to this land from many places on earth
and this place has now become home to all.

Respecting the relationship between humankind and
the earth insight of Aboriginal people,
(N), we place your feet in this soil/clay.

If child, held up, then feet 'planted' in the soil

You are a child of the Earth.
You have inherited the responsibility of caring for this earth.
Cherish it for all creation.

May the sun and the stars delight
and touch your heart with fire
and so may you find passion to be creative.

The elements of water, oil, and earth/soil all feature in this liturgy celebrating life. One set of grandparents brought clay from the family home more than five hundred kilometres away. They had built their home on the property from the same clay pit. Now their city-born grandson was being 'earthed' in that clay.

But perhaps more importantly, these liturgies have been shaped by language that is more relationship building than "doctrinal specificity and ecclesial distinctiveness"[28], and with the 'southern hemisphere' liturgical challenge in mind. That is, in light of our Australian experiences of 'nature' and 'season' they seek to overcome the dissonance between metaphor and experience[29].

---

28   Scott Cowdell, "Baptism in Australia: Secularisation, 'civil baptism' and the social miracle" in Burns and Monro, *Christian Worship in Australia*, 156.

29   Dorothy McRae-McMahon makes this helpful point: "... the Churches in the northern

Baptism Liturgy 3

Those courageous enough, or with an understanding from parents or the candidate, could consider using an inclusive formula even though it may not conform to traditional WCC standards. Two examples follow, but keep an eye out for the theological thought police …

> I baptise you in the name of the One the generations call Father;
> and of the Son, the Human One who walked among us;
> and of the Spirit who breathes truth and hope among us still.[30]

> I baptise you in the name of Life who created you,
> Wisdom who knew you first,
> Hope by whom you shall be sustained,
> Delight in whom I pray you to live, and
> Love … may you live every day in its embrace.[31]

So what are some of the things that may be said about Baptism from a progressive perspective? Jesus did not baptise. As noted earlier, if Jesus was baptised by John it was not a Christian baptism. We do not know when Christian baptism was introduced. The necessity of baptism for salvation cannot be justified. With biblical scholar Willi Marxsen, we can also say "a practice was taken over which *as a practice*, had already been well known for a long time"[32] but given a different—perhaps utterly different—understanding[33]. If Vosper's suggestion is to be acted on, baptism would then be understood as a *celebration* of the life of the child/candidate "filled as he or she already is with the spirit of the Divine"[34] within a supportive and nurturing community of faith, rather than anything to do with 'sin'—so-called original or otherwise—or 'getting God'!

---

hemisphere do sometimes tend to assume that they have the authority to determine liturgy for the world, or to refer to the countries in the southern hemisphere as though we have similar cultures amongst us" (McRae-McMahon "Liturgy in the Southern Hemisphere", 129).

30   progressivechristianity.org

31   Vosper, *With or Without God.*

32   Marxsen, *Jesus and the Church*, 163.

33   Various understandings have been attached to Baptism: as an initiation rite, the removal of sin, effect redemption, effect new creation, communication with the divine, etc.

34   Vosper, *With or Without God*, 340. Vosper asks three questions of parents around: (1) baptism as a symbol of the celebration of life of the child, filled already with the spirit of the Divine, (2) as we share life stories and those of people of wisdom and faith, we come to know the Divine more fully, and (3) commit yourself and your children to a journey of the spirit within this community of faith.

The Jesus Banquet—Celebrating Community

Jesus was a storyteller with bread! Listening to the stories and turning to modern biblical scholarship, there is general agreement that meals played an important role in the Jesus tradition. Indeed, Jesus seems so closely associated with meals that some of his critics labeled him a "glutton and drunkard" (Matt 11:19). But, while it can be said he did not *institute* the Eucharist or Lord's Supper, it is more difficult to trace the origins of the Christian supper liturgy. As with the origins of Baptism, the NT evidence relating to the 'Supper of the Lord' is complex and inconsistent.[35]

From all that we now seem to know (and do not know) about biblical culture and early Christianities, we can acknowledge that meals played an important role in communal life. The Jesus followers regularly ate together, even before they began to conduct worship services. They wanted to celebrate the meal *of* Jesus—"even if the meal itself and the original understanding of it had already changed greatly".[36] The *complete* meal tradition they followed—primarily the Greco-Roman banquet—was one they inherited and which brought "a wide variety of both Christian and non-Christian concerns to expression".[37]

Here are *extracts* from two different versions of progressive Banquet/ Communion liturgies. The first comes from David Galston (Canada) and the second, more formal, and slightly edited for the purposes of this article, is from Francis Macnab (Australia).

Eucharistic Liturgy 1[38]

> Welcome to this banqueting table.
> > Enjoy the hospitality.

> All   **All human beings are equal.**
> > **All life forms are to be respected.**

> We give thanks for the gifts of the earth,
> > for its love, and its creativity.

---

35   There are at least four NT traditions relating to the institution of the Lord's Supper: **Paul** (1 Cor 11:23–26—and our earliest witness); **Mark** (Mark 14:22–25) closely followed by **Matthew** (Matt 26:26–29); **Luke** (Luke 22:15–20—with a distinctive textual history that continues to puzzle the experts); and **John** (John 13:1–15—which does not mention any special words or actions involving bread or wine).

36   Marxsen, *Jesus and the Church*, 163.

37   Smith and Taussig, *Many Tables*, 103.

38   Adapted from Galston, *Embracing the Human Jesus*, 249.

All   **The earth and all that is in it**
       gives witness to the spirit of life.

v1   We give thanks for the life of Jesus, our sage,
       and the memory of his loving kindness.

v2   He taught that compassion is the heart of God.
       He practiced equality in the simple act of table fellowship.

v1   When he blessed bread, he used his traditional Jewish prayers, saying:

All   **Blessed is the Holy One of Israel,**
       sovereign of all that is who brings forth
       the bread from the ground.

v2   And when he blessed wine, he said:

All   **Blessed is the Holy One of Israel,**
       sovereign of all that is who brings forth
       grape from the vine.

v1   We share in this act of friendship with millions of people
       around the world and with all faithful people of the past.
       With them and in celebration of our community we say:

All   **Gifts to share and sustaining memory**
       Bring people in hope together.
       The banquet's joy and celebration
       Mark the presence of light.

v1   To gather around this table,
       to break bread freely and to share wine openly,
       is to bring justice to life.

v2   True acts of sharing help us
       to be like the human Jesus, who taught:

All   **Be compassionate as God is compassionate.**

v2   And who said:

All   **Give and there will be gifts given to you.**

v1   May the bread we break speak of love.
       May the wine we pour speak of compassion.
       May our commitment to peace bear witness
              to the heart of this community.

v1   As a community we share bread and wine
       to acknowledge the bond of our common humanity.
              This is bread for our journey and wine for our life .
       May we be a people who unite our words
       with our deeds.

There is no mention of 'body and blood' in these prayers, and no hint of a future heavenly feast. The life and teachings of the historical Jesus are central, rather than any emphasis on a risen Christ.

Eucharistic Liturgy 2[39]

> Such an event as sharing bread and wine
> > was common in the time of Jesus.
> Folk gathered for the sacred moment of the meal
> > when bread was broken
> > and the cup blessed.
> It reminded them of their story,
> > the way they believed their God had led them,
> > the hope that was given to them,
> > and the blessing they received.
> We are told:
> > Jesus took the bread and wine
> > and gave that additional blessing of faith for the future day.
> The church through the generations has embraced this event
> > as a central sacrament of the Faith.
> It was to be the substantial symbol of a life-enhancing presence,
> > giving the courage to bring a different spirit to the world…
> This table sets before us the symbols of life.

All **We give thanks to God for our life and the courage we are given to live it.**

> We are here given this sacrament to enhance and enrich our life.

All **We will receive it with thanksgiving and faith.**

> Come then with your sorrows and your joys,
> > with your searchings and your hopes,
> > with your anxieties and uncertainties,
> > with your strengths and possibilities,
> > with your best gratitude and your full and focused life.
> > Wherever we are, we are surrounded by the Good Presence.

All **May the Good Presence change our way of being in the world.**

> We pause in gratitude for our life and the many gifts of life.

All **Again and again, we want our life and our gratitude to be good and generous.**

> Here in this sacred place, we are lifted into
> > the awesome mystery of life.

All **And we reach out to all that is good.**

---

39   Macnab, *A Fine Wind is Blowing*, 99–102.

Here in this sacred place, we are in
    the Presence of the God of all goodness.

All   **And we pause to be open to that Presence and that goodness.**

Here in this sacred place we give words
    to our inner sense of gratitude and hope.

All   **We pause in gratitude for all that has been given;**
       in hope for all that yet will be.

A couple of general suggestions would seem to follow from all this. First, in the less radical—'soft traditional'—form of words the bread and the wine are recognised as 'the occasion' and not as the 'embodiment' of the historical Jesus. Take. Bless. Break. Give. The fourfold pattern of the meal's *action* is celebrated, rather than embodied in so-called *substances* 'for the forgiveness of sins'. (This is a bit of a favourite within Process Theology circles.)

Secondly, in the more radical—'progressive/evolving'—forms of words, we cease to celebrate the Eucharist and replace it with a Celebration of the Jesus Banquet, so the historical Jesus can come to church! Yet, maybe none of this is very radical at all. While none of the New Testament texts provide a liturgical 'script', there are explicit instructions regarding the celebration of the 'Eucharist' in the *Didache*[40]. It is worth noting that these ancient guidelines for celebrating the supper have no references to a Last Supper tradition, no mention of the death of Jesus, and no words of Jesus interpreting the bread and cup in terms of his own death.

Let me highlight that again. in the *Didache*, the meal is not presented as a continuation of something started by Jesus, nor is it interpreted as a commemoration of Jesus' death. The meal is more about community formation and community solidarity.[41] For the record, the *Didache* is entirely silent about Jesus dying for our sins, much like the early layers of the Q Gospel and the *Gospel of Thomas*, and its focus fits comfortably only in the early stage of the Jesus movement when the faith *of* Jesus, rather than faith *in* Jesus, was still at the centre of things.

So what may be said about the Lord's Supper from a progressive perspective? The Jesus Seminar, in its reflection, concluded:

---

40   According to Aaron Milavec ("The Didache"), this is an early Christian church manual—only discovered in 1873—is independent of any other gospel and may date from the middle of the first century.

41   Smith & Taussig, *Many Tables*, 66.

> The last supper ... was not a historical event. Nevertheless, the Fellows were clear that Jesus often ate meals with his disciples and others and that these meals had symbolic value ... Since Jesus ate frequently with his followers, there must have been a last meal with them.[42]

Liturgical revision and experimentation can be fraught with anxiety. Seemingly superficial issues—such as what kind of 'wine' (fermented or unfermented, if any wine at all)—can block progress on more significant points.[43] On a more positive note, there are exciting lessons to be learned from the experimentation by some Unitarian Universalist congregations in the United States especially their alternate communion liturgies celebrating Spring, End of Summer, Flowers; all "written in a human voice".[44]

Funeral Liturgies—Celebrating a Life

We do not know if Jesus buried any family members, or even if he was given a burial after his own death. Chances are—because he died by crucifixion (the usual death of a political rebel) on orders from the nervous and insecure Roman prefect of Judea, Pontius Pilate—his body would have been left to rot, piled with other corpses nearby, carrion for the birds and dogs.

> This ... was the point of crucifixion. The victim was not properly buried; his or her soul was not laid to rest. This was, to ancient sensibilities, the curse of eternal shame.[45]

Progressives who are called upon to conduct funerals are faced with having to decide what theology and words to use when it comes to the Committal. Recently a group of one hundred international progressives shared some thoughts on the Words of Committal. I share two such examples offered during that Internet exchange:

Words of Committal 1[46]

> So we commend to you our God the one you know as (NN).
> We commit her/his body to be cremated
> > ashes to ashes, dust to dust

---

42   Funk, *The Acts of Jesus*, 141–42.

43   This was an issue that almost single-handedly brought the discussions on church union between the Church of England and the Methodist Churches in Britain to a halt in 1970, because of the inability of the two churches to come to a common mind on acceptable eucharistic elements.

44   Seaburg, *The Communion Book*, 25.

45   Patterson, *Beyond the Passion*, 9.

46   Roger Wiig, "Words of Committal". In private circulation (2013).

in sure and certain hope
> that love never fails,
> that memories will contain the essence of life,
> that thanksgiving opens up new beginnings, and
> that the future contains all creative possibilities.
Into that future we all move knowing that (N)
> and all of us are loved infinitely.

Words of Committal 2

The words used in the traditional service are:
> 'ashes to ashes, dust to dust'.
> But before saying our last farewell,
> I suggest that we put a more hopeful meaning into those words.
If, like (N) we discount physical resurrection as mythology,
> these words have a different slant for her/him.
Backward to the earth from which we are made?
Not so!
Those atoms and molecules which constitute her/his physical frame
> are already moving forward!
Every one of them originated in the burst of heat and light
> which created our galaxy fourteen billion years ago.
They persisted in the bodies both animate and inanimate
> that came into being on planet Earth,
> and they reached their fulfilment
> in the lovely life-form and personality of this
> strong, courageous, self conscious human being
And they won't stop there.
> It will be only a matter of time before some of those same constituents
> which presented (N's) visible presence to us
> will be contributing to global change.
They will once again become a part of our wonderful environment
> and even physically a part of us.
This stupendous fact takes us on to holy ground.
It is holy ground because the process of evolution
> is infused with something big ...
> Purposive Presence?
> A Ground of Being?
> A Collective Consciousness?
> Who knows?
But, Something which is quite capable of looking after her/him.
> (N) is safe and at peace.
We are now saying goodbye to the physical presence
> of someone we have loved deeply.

To have loved someone like her/him was to risk the pain of parting.
But not to have loved is never to have lived.
    And the grief we are experiencing
    is the honouring of our love.
Her/his earthly remains are dear to us because
      they provided the tabernacle in which her/his spirit dwelt,
      and which is now being folded up and put to rest.
It is her/his spirit that we entrust to the love
    and mystery of the Eternal.[47]

Not everyone will find these attempts immediately helpful. Some may even conclude they are part of a so-called continuing problem: the 'demystification' of religion—a concern that has been expressed more than once by Australian, David Tacey.[48] On the other hand, some of the feedback I have received about my own liturgies has suggested that—because they are in 'real' language and employ everyday images—the contents must be taken seriously rather than just glossed over. That takes energy and concentration! Well, maybe. They also take energy, concentration and time to shape. No late Saturday night 'rush' with these liturgies!

But I return to the underlying premise of the Words of Committal: one's honesty and integrity, coupled with the raw emotional needs of the grievers, should have considerable attention in all funeral arrangements. This will ensure that death will be a meaningful experience, leading those who mourn back to living and life.

Liturgical renewal is not just a 'progressive' thing. It is central to traditional expressions of Christianity, as well as many renewal movements across denominational boundaries. Sadly, too many past efforts have been either confined to the examination and interpretation of specific historic liturgical texts, or defined in terms of global 'ecumenical convergence', resulting in a bureaucratisation of the liturgy. Revitalisation *per se* does not seem to have been the primary focus. For the sake of such 'convergence', multiple liturgical practices have been suppressed and we have been left with an over-concern for the orthodox line of tradition that, in most cases, just cannot stand up to any rigorous NT scholarship by 'truth-telling' scholars and clergy.

---

47   Eric Stevenson, "Words of Committal". In private circulation (2013).
48   Tacey, *ReEnchantment*.

When liturgy is circumscribed by the issue of orthodoxy, two things happen. First of all, it loses contact with the life and common experience of the people. It then becomes responsive only to doctrinal concerns and loses that essential interaction between tradition and culture. Secondly, it becomes more and more estranged from the creative minds of contemporary culture. Or, to put it in plain, honest 'Australian' terms: it's dead boring![49]

When we do decide to be brave enough to "throw the old forms out and start over again" by designing "a new Sunday Morning Experience from the ground up", let's keep in mind the spirit of progressive liturgy: spiritual vitality and expressiveness, combined with an insistence on Christianity with intellectual integrity. Who knows, maybe in the process we will also reshape 'church', away from its post-Constantinian 'empire' model into something characterised by four 'historical Jesus' features:

> … some form of shared life (fellowship or community); teaching or study (learning); shared meals (symbolic of relationship and hospitality); and reflection /meditation gathered around the needs of members and the needs of the world (what we used to call prayer), and leading to action programs and commitments to specific ways and tasks directed towards meeting those needs.[50]

Such a radical reshaping—or as David Galston puts it: 'taking the historical Jesus to church'—changes both the contours and the sense of church.

> It changes the reason why people gather as community, and, most significantly, it changes the status of Jesus in the tradition of Christianity[51]

Change is! Religion lives only while we are making it up, while our imaginations—especially our critical imaginations—are firing and we are generating new angles, new narratives and new metaphors "because these things are liberating".[52]

---

49 Bodycomb, *Aware and Attentive*, 3.
50 Gunson, *Learning to Live Without God*, 92.
51 Galston, *Embracing the Human Jesus*, 214.
52 Cupitt, *What is a Story?*, 129.

7. An open Bible: Imagining an inclusive scripture.

Gregory C. Jenks

The Bible is a book with staying power. It is a publisher's dream product and, better still, it is in the public domain. While new critical editions of the ancient Hebrew and Greek texts are protected by copyright, there are no licensing fees to the ancient authors and editors of these influential texts. Better still, there seems to be an insatiable appetite for new editions of the Bible, as Timothy Beal documented in a recent monograph.[1]

Despite predictions by some of the cultured despisers of religion, the 'book of books' seems to have retained its capacity to attract readers, and the number of languages into which it has been translated continues to increase. According to the Wycliffe Bible translation organization, by late 2013 the Bible had been translated into more than 2,800 languages.[2] The influence of the Christian scriptures on global culture has been profound, and in 2011 we celebrated the four hundredth anniversary of the publication of the most influential translation of them all, the *King James Bible*.[3]

At the beginning of 2011 my introduction to the Bible for religious progressives appeared,[4] but the draft of the final chapter was already prepared at the time of the 2010 Common Dreams event in Melbourne. That chapter—"Imagining a future for the Bible"—formed the basis of my keynote address to the Common Dreams gathering. Rather than edit that address for this volume, I want to take the conversation somewhat further than I did in 2010, or indeed in the final chapter of that book. Before starting on that exploration, it may be helpful to summarize the key points from the earlier work.

---

1   Beal, *The Rise and Fall of the Bible.*
2   Of these, 513 have a complete Bible, another 1,294 have the New Testament, and 1,010 others have at least one book of the Bible. See: wycliffe.org.uk/wycliffe/about/vision-whatwedo.html.
3   See www.kingjamesbibletrust.org
4   Jenks, *The Once and Future Bible.*

The core question for that address could be stated quite simply: How can we use the Bible with confidence in our kind of world? The "we" in that sentence refers to religious progressives, and that continues to be the audience in mind as I write once more on the question of how the Bible might have a different kind of future from its recent past. No doubt the proposals I will make in this chapter will not commend themselves to religious traditionalists, whether Catholic or Evangelical or charismatic. It is possible that some of my suggestions will be attractive to people of other religious communities, as well as to atheists and agnostics. However, my intention is to engage in a conversation with other religious progressives, and specifically progressive Christians.

The kind of world we inhabit has become no less complex in the few years since I wrote the earlier essay. We continue to find ourselves drawn by the future and restrained by the past. The immediate present and the imminent future are characterized by the interplay of profound and open-ended changes in the way that we understand the world, and ourselves.

As described in my address at the Common Dreams conference in 2010,[5] these changes include a new cosmology, a new anthropology, a new vision of society, and a new spirituality. Those profound changes are partly impacted by new technologies, and they are all experienced under the shadow of a new apocalypticism that despairs of our survival on this fragile planet and anticipates a tragic end to our aspirations. We have good reasons to despair, but we also have good reasons to be optimistic. One of the questions that fascinates me is how religion feeds into that complex set of realities, and whether the Bible functions to promote justice or oppression.

I followed my brief analysis of these complexities with a very short discussion of the kinds of churches I expect to see in our communities over the next few decades. The only significant change in the scenarios I sketched in 2010 concern the possibility of radical reform within the Roman Catholic church following the election of Pope Francis. Like Mikhail Gorbachev in the Soviet Union, Francis finds himself presiding over an authoritarian system that is in urgent need of reform and renewal. Many—but not all—of his actions and pronouncements during the first six months or so of his pontificate have given hope to progressives within the Catholic tradition and beyond. It remains to be seen how this, the renewal process within the

---

5   Ibid., 190–93.

largest of all Christian denominations will unfold, and what impact this might have on the fortunes of those Evangelical and Pentecostal expressions of Christianity that currently seem to be enjoying the ascendancy.

In the middle section of my 2010 address at Common Dreams, I turned to the question of what kind of a future for the Bible might be imagined in such a world and among these kinds of churches. The issues considered at the time included technology, the canon, biblical authority, participation in Bible reading, the cultural impact of the Scriptures, as well as questions of access, justice, and subversion. In many ways this current essay will focus in more detail on many of these questions, and—in particular—on the question of an open canon as the key to the future of the Bible.

The final section of my previous essay on these topics outlined some ways in which religious progressives might reclaim the Bible.[6] Moving from criticism and deconstruction to reconstruction and affirmation is always a difficult transition, as many a political movement has found when it comes into office. I hope the current essay will contribute to the reclaiming of the Bible by religious progressives, and also offer some new options for the Christian Scriptures to contribute to the well-being of all life on our planet.

Open Table, Open Community

It is traditional to describe Jews and Christians as the 'people of the Book,' but Christians are perhaps better described as the people with an open table. At first glance this runs counter to much Christian practice over the years, during which time access to the Eucharistic altar-table has been controlled and restricted by the religious powers-that-be. Yet that in itself may serve to substantiate the point I am making. It is because of the centrality of the table within our experience of Christian community, that access to Holy Communion—and, on the other hand, the threat of "ex-communication"— has been the hallmark of membership and acceptance.

In recent historical Jesus research there has been a rediscovery of the importance of open table fellowship within the practice of Jesus and his earliest followers. John Dominic Crossan placed great emphasis on this 'open commensality' within the program of Jesus.[7] To some extent the significance of shared meals in the Jesus movement reflects the powerful

---

6   This reclaiming of the Bible for the life of the churches was also the focus of Jenks, *The Once and Future Scriptures*.

7   See Crossan, *The Historical Jesus*, especially 261–64.

symbol of the messianic banquet in ancient Jewish eschatology. One of the great symbols of the good life when God's kingdom arrived was the shared feast.[8] In the mission of Jesus, such open table fellowship seems to have been a prophetic enactment of the real presence of the kingdom of God, as well as a focus for criticism by his opponents.

Crossan has identified several complexes of early Jesus traditions that are related to this theme of egalitarian commensality: 19 *What Goes In*, 76 *Speck and Log*, 80 *Blind Guide*, 84 *On Hindering Others*, 101 *Inside and Outside*, 113 *Eating with Sinners*, 124 *Honors and Salutations*, and 126 *Salting the Salt*.[9] To these I would add items such as 1 *Mission and Message*, with its command that the messengers eat what is set before them by those whose sins have been forgiven and infirmities healed.[10]

It seems clear from Paul's instructions in 1 Corinthians 10 and 11, that the Supper of the Lord was at the very heart of the shared life of the earliest Jesus communities. They were people of the table, and the table was open to anyone wishing to participate in the life of the community. To abuse the egalitarian openness of that table was to desecrate the body of the Lord (1 Cor 11:27) and to show contempt for the church (v. 22).

What we find in the New Testament is a description of early Christian communities as intimate circles, with open boundaries. These were inclusive communities in which traditional barriers and divisions ceased to have significance. The classic text for this is found in Paul's letter to the Galatians.

> There is no longer Jew or Greek,
> there is no longer slave or free,
> there is no longer male and female;
> for all of you are one in Christ Jesus. (Gal 3:28)

In the discussion that follows, I want to claim that inclusive character of the earliest Christian communities as a basis for reimagining the Bible in a more open and inclusive way. An open Bible seems highly appropriate for a religious community whose life centres on an open table.

---

8   See Smith, "The Messianic Banquet".

9   For details of the biblical references along with some discussion of these passages, see the relevant items in the Jesus Database: www.jesusdatabase.org.

10   Other items to consider would include: 3 *Bread and Fish*, 16 *Supper and Eucharist*, and 95 *The Feast*.

Cracks in the Canon

Before considering some proposals for an open Bible, it is necessary to consider the bibles that we already have. The plural form of 'bible' in that last sentence is not a typographical error. While most people of faith and many more people beyond the Christian community think otherwise, the reality is that the concept of a single Bible is an exercise in self-delusion. Most Christian communities are complicit in this deception, as it does not serve their needs for control over their members to acknowledge that we have many bibles.

The collection of biblical documents that most people in the West have in mind when the Bible is mentioned is a quite recent configuration of the Bible from the time of the Protestant Reformation in Europe. This is not the ancient Bible of an undivided church, but simply one variant among others. It combines the books of the NT with a Protestant version of the OT based on the Jewish *Tanakh*, rather than the traditional Christian OT found in the Septuagint and the Latin Vulgate. This Protestant/Evangelical canon preserves the order of the books from the ancient Greek and Latin versions, while excluding the books not found in the Jewish Bible. It does not even reflect the form of the Bible in the famous *King James Bible* of 1611,[11] and we have no reason to presume it to be the 'best' form of the Bible. Yet that is the form of the Bible known to most westerners and taken for granted in most discussions about the Bible. I do not recognize any particular authority for that recent configuration of the Bible over other more ancient arrangements.

There are a number of ways in which the existing diversity of the Christian Bible overturns popular assumptions about the antiquity and canonical integrity of the familiar Western Bibles. One of the challenges is a result of European military and political interventions in the Middle East during the nineteenth and twentieth centuries. As the Ottoman Empire began to

---

11   The original *King James Bible* included the books of the OT Apocrypha. It was only late in the nineteenth century that Evangelical editions of the KJV began to exclude these books, partly to save printing costs and partly due to the Protestant principles of the British and Foreign Bible Society whose charter prevented them from distributing copies of the Bible that included the Apocrypha. This led to the famous events in 1902 when a specially bound copy of the KJV was sent to Lambeth Palace by the British and Foreign Bible Society for use in the coronation of Edward VII. It was returned when Frederick Temple, then the Archbishop of Canterbury, ruled that a 'mutilated' Bible—one lacking the Apocrypha—was unacceptable for the Coronation Oath. See Bruce, *The Canon of Scripture*, 113

crumble, European powers competed for spheres of influence from Egypt and the Gulf to Palestine and Lebanon. Napoleon invaded Egypt and unsuccessfully besieged Acre in northern Palestine. The British created a Protestant bishopric in Jerusalem, and began to encourage Jewish migration in a misguided plan to create a pro-British Jewish community in Palestine.[12]

One of the results of all this European meddling in the Middle East was an increased interest in Oriental antiquities, including ancient manuscripts. Due to its dry climate and the presence of a substantial Christian population in antiquity, Egypt proved to be a rich source for ancient papyrus documents.

One of the most significant finds was *Codex Sinaiticus*, an ancient version of the Bible from St Catherine's monastery at the base of Mt Sinai. This had been identified in 1761 by the Italian naturalist Vitaliano Donati, but in 1844 Constantine Tischendorf, a German biblical scholar, took a large portion of the codex to Europe.[13] This codex is now recognized as one of the most significant books in the world, as the oldest surviving copy of the Christian Bible, and as the only book to have survived from antiquity to the present time. Significantly, its OT included the Apocrypha and its NT included two works no longer counted as part of the Bible: the *Epistle of Barnabas*, and the *Shepherd of Hermes*.

Codex Sinaiticus is now just one of many codices, lectionaries and manuscripts that have been recovered during the past two centuries. Collectively, this rich trove of sacred documents establishes beyond doubt that there was far more diversity in the forms of Scripture accepted among the ancient churches than had been realized.[14] Even more importantly, recent research has questioned the philosophical assumptions of textual criticism, with its quest for the 'original' form of the biblical documents.

---

12   The British government was also responding to pressure from English Evangelicals such as Lord Shaftsbury, who believed that the Jewish people needed to be restored to the Land of Israel as a precondition for the return of Jesus Christ. This Jewish restoration movement within certain Evangelical circles in Britain would eventually contribute to the formation of the Zionist Congress by Theodor Herzl in 1897 and, even more significantly, to the publication of the Balfour Declaration in 1917.

13   There are conflicting accounts of the circumstances under which Tischendorf took possession of this manuscript, and these are outlined on the pages of the joint web site that now makes the document available in its entirety (www.codexsinaiticus.org/en/).

14   Along with other ancient manuscripts, *Codex Sinaiticus* also demonstrated the corruption of the *textus receptus* in Western Europe, a version of the Hebrew and Greek texts that formed the basis of the KJV and other major European Bibles.

In the ancient world there was no such thing as a single original version, since every hand-written copy was an original document. We have come to realize that while there were quality control processes to authenticate copies and validate authorship, what we possess in our diverse set of several thousand biblical manuscripts is evidence for the reception history of the Bible, rather than evidence for the textual history of an individual passage.[15]

The diversity of the Bible extends beyond the variations within the manuscript tradition to differences between our approaches to the text as critical readers. We are now more aware than ever before of the literary dimensions of the biblical text, the intertextual relationships within and beyond the canon, and to the significance of the context of the reader for the meaning of the Bible. Even if, like the Qur'an, the Bible were a tightly controlled sacred text with no variations in the manuscripts, we would have significant differences between alternative readings of the text by religious communities and individuals. As a written text the Bible is always susceptible to the hermeneutical strategies of the reading communities that hold it sacred, even when the contents of the Bible are standardized.

Of course, standardisation of the biblical texts is precisely what we do not have, and especially with the explosion of translations and niche editions in the last few decades. Although most of the consumers of the Bible publishers' output are blissfully unaware of the fact, the familiar configuration of the sacred texts that passes for a Bible in the West—and its missionary outposts in former European colonial territories—is just one of many variants. Alongside the Evangelical/Protestant Bible—and enjoying much greater antiquity in many cases—we must also place the Roman Catholic form of the Bible, with its ancient roots in the Latin Vulgate and the Septuagint versions. Then there is the Greek Bible, effectively unchanged in canonical form and content, since the days when the ink on *Codex Sinaiticus* was still wet. In addition, and without being exhaustive, there is the Armenian Bible, the Coptic Bible, the Ethiopian Bible, the Slavic Bible, and the Syriac Bible. When it comes to the Old Testament, of course, the Jewish Bible, the *Tanakh*, trumps all of these ancient versions.

---

15   See Crane, *Israel's Restoration*. In his study of Ezekiel, Crane demonstrates that the primary value of these textual variants is not their contribution to our knowledge of the original form of the document. Rather, these variations indicate how the biblical text was received and interpreted in different historical communities over time.

The most significant differences between these versions of the Bible are the variations in the books that are included in the canon of the respective religious communities. The most accessible example of this diversity is the *New Oxford Study Bible* edition of the *New Revised Standard Version*,[16] which carefully sets out the differences in the OT canon between different mainstream Christian communities. However, even within the 'core' canonical documents common to all traditions there are variations in content in books such as Daniel, Ezekiel, and Jeremiah. While rarely noted, it also represents a significant change to the biblical text when the twenty-two books of the Jewish Bible—a total that matches the number of letters in the Hebrew alphabet—are re-arranged to form the Christian OT. When this happens more than the numerical (cosmic) significance is lost. For most Christian readers of the Bible, Daniel is a prophetic text, but for Jewish readers Daniel is not one of the Prophets, but among the Writings.

Another crack in the perception of a canonical uniformity is represented by the ancient tradition of readings passages from other sacred texts alongside biblical texts in the daily liturgical practices of clergy and religious. The *Book of Hours*, together with the *Breviary* from which it was developed to provide a devotional aid for pious laity, demonstrates a continuous tradition over more than a thousand years, in which the biblical texts are supplemented by readings, hymns, and prayers from a variety of sources. This tradition continues in the spiritual practices of many contemporary Christians who have access to a variety of print and online resources.[17]

Ecumenical and interfaith scholarship has made available a much wider range of resources than would once have been available within a particular religious tradition. People are reading far more widely than is often realized, but this sometimes becomes evident when the time comes to arrange a funeral or a wedding service. At such times there are often requests for non-biblical spiritual readings to be included in the liturgy due to their significance to the family, to the deceased, or to the couple. In my experience, readings from Kahlil Gibran ('the Prophet') and from Rumi are among the most common of these texts. While they have no formal recognition within

---

16   Coogan, *The New Oxford Annotated Bible*.

17   One popular print collection is *Celtic Daily Prayer*, published by the Northumbria Community. An impressive digital equivalent is provided by the Divine Office app (www. divineoffice.org) that offers a full range of the Liturgy of the Hours.

any Christian communities, these writings serve as sacred texts for many Christians and may be more influential than many parts of the Bible.

The final crack in the façade of canonical uniformity is created by changes in technology. The book itself was once leading-edge technology, and the early Christians were early adopters of the technological innovation involved in the shift from scrolls to the codex. The invention of the printing press by Johannes Gutenberg around 1450 was to unleash another spiritual revolution in the form of the Protestant Reformation as mechanical reproduction of texts made the Bible widely available and at low cost. More recent innovations that impacted on the Bible have included radio, film, and television—not to mention computers, the Internet, and mobile digital devices.[18]

Imagining an Open Bible

We have seen that the Bible is not as singular and uniform a collection of religious texts as is commonly assumed. We have also noted that the traditional and contemporary spiritual practice of a great many Christians represents a *de facto* canon that is rather more open than any of the ancient versions or contemporary denominational canons. It is now time to note some of the ways in which an enlarged and inclusive Bible is already a reality for some expressions of Christianity.

First of all, ecumenical editions of the Bible—such as the *New Oxford Annotated Bible* mentioned earlier—offer a precious opportunity for readers of the Bible to experience directly both the shared texts and the variations around the edges of the canon. By seeking to create an English version of the Bible that will meet the needs of several different expressions of Christianity, such a project celebrates our shared inheritance while acknowledging our historical differences. This is a new kind of Bible. In the past, editions of the Bible have been created to serve—and to control—a particular religious community or—in the case of a project such as the *New International Version*—to serve the needs of a niche market that crosses denominational boundaries.

It is possible to go a step further, and intentionally read versions of the Bible that were not intended for the community to which we happen to belong. A Protestant may choose to read a Roman Catholic version such as the *New Jerusalem Bible*. A Catholic may choose to read the *New International*

---

18   For a brief (and already dated) review of technological changes impacting on our present and future use of the Bible, see Jenks, *The Once and Future Bible*, 195–97.

Version. An Evangelical may opt to consult the Jewish Publication Society edition of the Old Testament,[19] or even the *Jewish Annotated New Testament*.[20] The point of such intentional transgressing of the confessional boundaries around our preferred versions of the Bible is to encounter other ways in which the Bible functions as sacred scripture in different religious communities. The first step towards an open Bible may simply be to acquire a diverse set of Bibles.

Another twist to this exercise may be to read one or more ancient versions of the Bible in a contemporary English edition. Options here would include translations of the Septuagint[21] as well as the biblical texts from the Dead Sea Scrolls,[22] not to mention the additional sectarian writings from Qumran such as the Hymn Scroll.[23] Many of the Jewish writings from the OT Pseudepigrapha offer windows into the early reception history of the Bible as Jews from the Second Temple period reflected in the biblical traditions, paraphrased them, and elaborated on them.[24] The Gnostic scriptures from Nag Hammadi offer something of a parallel from early Christian traditions,[25] as do the writings of the Apostolic Fathers and other early Christian writers. One especially interesting early version of the Bible to read may be the form of the NT known to Marcion.[26]

The ground-breaking volume, *The Five Gospels*,[27] published by the Jesus Seminar in 1993 represented a largely unintentional invitation for individuals and faith communities to enlarge their set of gospels by one. By including the *Gospel of Thomas* in the same volume as the four canonical gospels, the Jesus Seminar offered convenient access to this recently discovered gospel for people who otherwise would not have had such easy access to non-canonical texts. This was followed up by the publication of *The Complete Gospels*[28] and, more recently, the *Authentic Letters of Paul*.[29]

---

19   Jewish Publication Society, *Tanakh*.
20   Levine and Brettler, *The Jewish Annotated New Testament*.
21   Pietersma and Wright, *A New English Translation of the Septuagint*.
22   Abegg, Flint, and Ulrich, *The Dead Sea Scrolls Bible*.
23   Martinez, *The Dead Sea Scrolls Translated*.
24   Charlesworth, *The Old Testament Pseudepigrapha*.
25   Meyer and Robinson, *The Nag Hammadi Scriptures*.
26   BeDuhn, *The First New Testament*.
27   Funk and Hoover, *The Five Gospels*.
28   Miller, *The Complete Gospels*.
29   Dewey, *The Authentic Letters of Paul*.

During the last few decades members of the public have gained unprecedented access to alternative sacred writings that have served as scripture for one or more ancient Christian communities. This is happening outside the control—and despite the protests—of traditional religious authorities. The Bible is being pried open against the wishes of its erstwhile guardians. Meanwhile, the partisan decisions of bishops and councils in antiquity—to proscribe particular persons and ban their writings—fail to dissuade the contemporary spiritual seeker. This interest in reading outside the curriculum provided by the approved lectionaries of the churches is being met by publications such as *An Uncommon Lectionary*[30] and *An (un) Common Book of Hours.*[31]

Not surprisingly, from time to time there are suggestions for a redefinition of the Bible. Once little more than a hypothetical case set as an examination question for theological students, the flood of ancient documents being recovered and made available to the public has given new impetus to proposals for a review of the biblical canon. The most recent example—and perhaps most considered—of such proposals was *A New New Testament*, published by Hal Taussig in 2013.[32] That volume was met with a predictable howl of protest and even mockery,[33] but it has also been nominated for several literary awards. It was in many ways a modest proposal for a reimagination of what the Christian Bible might look like in light of advances in biblical scholarship, ancient textual discoveries, and profound cultural change in our society. This volume was intended to prompt discussion, not close it down—as is so often the case with biblical and theological research.

Resistance, Reception, and Renewal

The processes around the reception of canonical texts within a religious community are always complex and contested. People of faith have argued fiercely over particular documents. Edicts and anathemas have been promulgated. Opponents with fewer votes (or inferior military capacity) have been exiled. Heads have rolled. The flames have been stoked. These days the sanctions are less visceral, but expulsion from one's faith

---

30   Butcher, *An Uncommon Lectionary.*
31   Watkins, *An (Un)Common Book of Hours.*
32   Taussig, *A New New Testament.*
33   See for example the stunned reaction of conservative biblical scholar, Daniel B. Wallace: www.danielbwallace.com/2013/03/17/a-new-new-testament-are-you-serious/

community remains a possibility, together with loss of employment as a pastor or teacher.

We can therefore anticipate resistance to any suggestions for a re-opening of the canonical questions. The cracks are obvious to anyone who wishes to look closely at the canonical arrangements, and the historical basis for the *status quo* is far from convincing. Yet the traditional canonical arrangements have been included in the constitutional and regulatory frameworks that govern the common life of particular religious communities.

The Anglican Church of Australia may serve as an example of these realities.[34] Similar arrangements apply in other traditions, and in some cases the constitutional connection with a particular view of the Bible is even more explicit. The key Anglican documents in this matter are the *Book of Common Prayer* of 1662, the *Ordinal*, the *Articles of Religion*, and the Constitution of the Anglican Church of Australia. Taken together these 'formularies' establish the canonical form of the Anglican Bible and its authority within the life of the church. Significantly, the Anglican Church embraces the ancient form of the OT, including the deuterocanonical texts of the OT Apocrypha. In the case of the NT, the Anglican Church does not even bother to list the books, but simply makes the following general reference: "All the Books of the New Testament, as they are commonly received, we do receive, and account them Canonical" (Article 6).

While any proposal for a change to "the Books of the New Testament, as they are commonly received" will be staunchly resisted by traditionalists of various parties, in principle there is no theological barrier to additional documents being included within the NT. Such a process would require an authentic and demonstrated 'common reception' among the faithful, but that is not beyond imagination. As the faithful vote with their feet and choose to participate in faith communities that regularly read sacred texts beyond the traditional Bible, even the most recalcitrant church leaders are likely to acquiesce.

Indeed, the inclusion of the OT Apocrypha within the Anglican Bible may already offer a model for an open NT. By acknowledging that these books—which were not part of the Jewish *Tanakh*—belong to the Bible, the

---

34   For a discussion of some of these issues as they relate to the Anglican Church of Australia, see "The Anglican crisis over the Bible" in Jenks, *The Once and Future Scriptures*, 19–23.

Articles of Religion open the door for a NT Apocrypha to be included in the Anglican Bible as well. Like the OT Apocrypha, such an additional set of books would be "read for example of life and instruction of manners; but … not [applied] … to establish any doctrine" (Article 6). To paraphrase that in current language, such books would not be read to determine the faith of the church but to shape the lives of the faithful.

Such a limited inclusion of a wider set of texts within the Bible would not reduce theological authority of the imperial canon. The legal requirements of each church would still ensure that "those Canonical books of the Old and New Testament, of whose authority was never any doubt in the Church" continued to serve as denominational benchmarks for belief and practice. Once the first major denomination acted to recognize such an open NT, we may anticipate that other branches of the Christian Church would follow suit—in their own good time, and in ways that reflect their own constitutional processes. Within a few generations we may well have a new consensus around those books that are 'commonly received' by the faithful as sacred scriptures worthy of our critical reception.

Such an 'open Bible' would comprise a Scripture without a last page. In principle, the Bible would never formally be closed. We would forever remain open to the possibility that some additional document might gain such acceptance among the faithful that its place within the Bible becomes uncontroversial. A Christianity that matches the radical inclusiveness of its communal life with an open Bible might better reflect the wisdom and imagination of Jesus of Nazareth. It may also be better placed to act as a missional community serving as midwives at the coming of God's kingdom. Amen. Let it be so!

8. Who do you say that I am? Preaching Jesus today

Nigel Leaves

The iconic question that St Mark attributes to Jesus—'Who do you say that I am?' (Mark 8: 29)—is as relevant today as it was two thousand years ago, especially for those who in some way or another are still 'followers of Jesus'. In this chapter, I will reply to Mark's question with reference to four recent books about Jesus that in my view reflect the agenda for what I shall term 'today's Jesus context'. These texts both encapsulate the current debate about Jesus and provide appropriate source material from which to formulate a tentative answer to how we might preach Jesus today. In particular, I will show how these books bring into sharp relief four important 'Jesus themes' that preachers must deal with whenever they undertake either a personal or a homiletic answer to 'Who do you say that I am?'

The Jesus Context

The first of the four books, Bart Ehrman's *Did Jesus Exist?* (2012), was a response to the recent resurgence of 'mythicist' arguments that Jesus was a literary creation rather than an historical person. This issue, stirred up by scholars such as Tom Harpur, D. M. Murdoch, Robert M. Price, Thomas L. Brodie and Earl Doherty, was fueled by the short-lived and now defunct *Jesus Project* (chaired by R. Joseph Hoffman) and further backed by antagonists such as the *American Humanist Association* and 'the New Atheists', especially Richard Carrier.[1]

Whilst Ehrman declares himself to be theologically 'agnostic' and generally skeptical about much of the historicity of the New Testament—a position

---

1   Ehrman, *Did Jesus Exist?*, 332-334, Harpur, *The Pagan Christ*, Price, *The Christ-Myth Theory*, Doherty, *Jesus Neither God Nor Man*, Murdoch, *The Christ Conspiracy*, and Brodie, *Beyond the Quest for the Historical Jesus*. The *Jesus Project* was initiated by R. Joseph Hoffmann and was conducted by the Secular Centre for Inquiry. However, it disbanded after two years due to internal wranglings between scholars and a major dispute between Hoffmann and Paul Kurtz. Hoffmann still has aspirations to recommence the project under the auspices of *The Jesus Prospect* but so far very little seems to have materialized. Richard Carrier's (continuing) response to Ehrman can be followed at http://freethoughtblogs.com/carrier/archives/category/bart-ehrman.

made clear in a series of excellent books about the transmission and contradictions of the scriptural texts[2]—he surprised many by asserting that 'there certainly was a Jesus of Nazareth who existed in history, was crucified under Pontius Pilate, and about whom we can say a good deal as a historical figure'.[3] This stance not only disappointed the 'mythicists' who thought that they had an ally in debunking the historical authenticity of Jesus, but also riled conservative academics because of his insistence that the real historical Jesus was not the same as the Jesus that they were teaching! Like Albert Schweitzer, Ehrman argues that Jesus was an apocalyptic prophet who thought that God would send the cosmic 'son of man' to establish God's empire here on earth after his crucifixion.[4] In short, Jesus might have been mistaken, but he was definitely an historical person. Ehrman cleverly courted controversy by attacking the mythicists, appearing traditional in his defense of the historicity of Jesus, and at the same time promoting a Jesus completely unacceptable to those who might wish to utilize his arguments. Quite a lesson in how to promote and sell a book!

Secondly, Polebridge Press launched Joseph Bessler's *A Scandalous Jesus* (2013) in which he argues that the three 'Quests for the Historical Jesus', far from being dry academic pursuits, altered the way that people thought about the Christian faith. In his view 'historical Jesus research' should be embraced by Christians because it is a 'space in which new models of faith are glimpsed'—and importantly 'lived both within and beyond the boundaries of tradition'.[5] And because their findings have entered the public discourse, the three Quests have affected both the Churches and the general populace. Who Jesus was now affects *everyone*! Albert Schweitzer's 'Jesus', Rudolph Bultmann's 'Jesus', Ernst Käsemann's 'Jesus', Robert Funk's 'Jesus'—and perhaps the local preacher's 'Jesus'—cry out for a 're-imagining of Faith'.[6] These quests have made Jesus 'scandalous', not only because ecclesiastical authorities did not wish him to be unearthed, but also because the debate about who Jesus might have been is now in the public forum.

The third book, Robin Meyers' *Saving Jesus from the Church* (2009), has been championed by Christian liberals/progressives as an outline of

---

2   Ehrman, *Misquoting Jesus, Jesus Interrupted, Forged.*
3   Ehrman, *Did Jesus Exist?*, 335.
4   Ehrman, *Jesus.*
5   Bessler, *A Scandalous Jesus*, 226.
6   Ibid., ch. 12.

the new Christian path. Assuming the mantle of John Shelby Spong, Meyers is a fresh voice and his book a rhetorical re-enfleshment of *A New Christianity for a New World* (San Francisco: HarperCollins, 2002). He outlines an understanding of the faith that is not ordered 'around the axis of sin and salvation' but rather a 'search for meaning in a world that is often meaningless'.[7] Jesus is more a teacher than a Savior, and instead of arguing about outdated Christian metaphysics and doctrines, Christians must follow his essential teachings. In short, Christianity is more about 'being' than propositional 'beliefs'.[8]

Last, but hardly least, Random Press hit the jackpot with Reza Aslan's latest offering, *Zealot*, which overnight rocketed to the top of the *New York Times* bestseller list. To be sure, one cannot overlook the contribution of Lauren Green, *Fox News* Religion correspondent, who provided extraordinary publicity for the book by announcing her incredulity that a Muslim could write about the 'founder of Christianity'. Nonetheless, Aslan's thesis that Jesus was a nationalist zealot (without a capital 'Z')[9] fiercely opposed to the Roman occupation can claim a degree of validity despite its exaggerated nature.

Relying on John P. Meier's assertion that Jesus was 'a marginal Jewish peasant from the backwoods of Galilee',[10] Aslan presents Jesus as one of many Jewish messianic pretenders of that era whose political message opposing Roman imperial rule unsurprisingly led to his death by crucifixion. It was left to Paul (in opposition to James 'the Just', brother of Jesus) to preach another 'Gospel', one that transformed Jewish nationalist aspirations into a religion for non-Jews and focused on belief in Jesus as the long-awaited Savior of the whole world.[11] With the destruction of the Jerusalem Temple, the final defeat of the Jewish resistance at Masada, and the dispersion of Jewish communities, the Pauline religious outlook gained control and was echoed in the later proclamations of Matthew, Luke, and especially John. The long march from Jesus of Nazareth to Jesus 'begotten not made' and the Christian Creeds had begun.

---

7   Meyers, *Saving Jesus from the Church*, 7.
8   Ibid., ch. 2.
9   The Zealot party arose thirty years after the death of Jesus and was most active in resisting Rome between 69 and 81CE.
10   Aslan, *Zealot*, 219.
11   Ibid., ch. 15.

In many ways Aslan's thesis is a remixing of S. G. F. Brandon's ground-breaking *Jesus and the Zealots: a study of the political factor in primitive Christianity* (1967) and Geza Vermes' portrait of Jesus as a charismatic Jew. In response to Lauren Green it might be pointed out that both Vermes, a Jew who became a Christian who reconverted to Judaism, and Aslan, a Muslim who became a Christian who reconverted to Islam, discovered the same sort of Jewish Jesus. [Go figure!] Moreover, as my colleague Greg Jenks has perceptively observed, the content of Aslan's book can be summed up in its subtitle: 'the life and times of Jesus of Nazareth'. Aslan's concern is to uncover the social and religious milieu of Palestine when Jesus was alive. This is exactly the approach of Brandon and Vermes. The question that needs to be more carefully addressed is whether Jesus advocated the path of revolution or preached a message quite different from the prevailing *Sitz im Leben*? Again, the reception to the book's claims, show a continuing interest in the identity of Jesus.

Four Jesus Themes Arising from these Books

These four books bring into focus the contemporary debate about Jesus. In particular they highlight four themes that I consider vital for preachers to address when they undertake the weekly gig in the pulpit. Karl Barth is widely credited with the remark that the preacher needs to have the Bible in one hand and a newspaper in the other.[12] Today, of course, 'newspaper' is a figure of speech for the many social media that disseminate, dissect, and discuss the latest ideas from books. Unlike her predecessor, the modern preacher has more than a tabloid headline or a controversial editorial with which to engage. People are constantly surfing the web, Facebooking, Tweeting, and e-mailing each other on every topic under the sun, including ideas about Jesus. Unfortunately, many churches seem to operate under the assumption that congregations leave their 'virtual' world behind them; but many people sitting in church pews have smart-phones, iPads, laptops and the like that are 'Google-ready' waiting to check up on the speaker's facts and conclusions.

---

12   There is no record of Barth actually writing this. The alleged comment comes from a *Time* Magazine piece on Barth published on May 31, 1963: "[Barth] recalls that 40 years ago he advised young theologians 'to take your Bible and take your newspaper, and read both. But interpret newspapers from your Bible'". The implication for Barth was that the Bible's authority was greater than the newspaper's. The popular saying lessens the force of Barth's original meaning.

So, what are the four themes?

1. Jesus in the public domain and the challenge of the new atheists
2. The many diverse portraits of Jesus
3. The historical Jesus
4. The impact that preaching the historical Jesus would have on the church today

1. Jesus in the Public Domain and the Challenge of the New Atheists

The popularity of all four books makes it clear that Jesus is being discussed in the public domain, a fact nowhere better revealed than in the recent concern of atheists in trying to prove that Jesus didn't exist. Ehrman wonders why mythicists would spend so much time in this endeavor, and answers that it is part of their agenda to undermine belief in God. If it can be proved that Jesus never existed, then the religious house of cards, which depends on belief in God, will come crashing down. As he says: "their agenda is religious, and they are complicit in religious ideology. They are not doing history: they are doing theology".[13]

The implication, of course, is that because Christians proclaim Jesus to be God, if you can prove he wasn't even a human being, then belief in God will vanish. This is exemplified in Raphael Lataster's book, *There was no Jesus, There was no God*.[14] Obviously, that argument fails on two accounts. First, whether God exists is not dependent on *a priori* belief that Jesus existed, for Jesus and God are not *necessarily* interdependent. Second, the variations in ideas on the relationship between Jesus and God are legion, extending from the full-blown Chalcedonian definition to John Hick's 'metaphor' of God Incarnate to Don Cupitt's 'Jesus the philosopher' and a 'non-realist' god.[15] What people say about Jesus might or *might not* lead them to God.

Moreover, for Ehrman the crucial point is not whether God exists but *what kind of Jesus you preach*. He is convinced that the atheists would do better to accept that Jesus did exist and attack Christianity with the portrait of a 'too historical' Jesus who wrongly believed that God would soon intervene and establish a future theocracy. Challenging Christians on their 'false' interpretations of Jesus would prove a far more effective tactic than

---

13   Ehrman, *Did Jesus Exist?*, 338.
14   Lataster, *There was no Jesus*.
15   Hick, *The Metaphor of God Incarnate; and* Cupitt, *Jesus and Philosophy*.

disputing his historicity. As Schweitzer famously put it: "it is good that the true historical Jesus should overthrow the modern Jesus."[16]

Indeed, John Dominic Crossan in *The Power of Parable* (2012) takes up the atheist challenge by asking: "What difference would it make for the Christian vision—if we found with absolute certainty—that Jesus was never a historical figure?" Would it really matter if Jesus were just another parabolic figure, like the "Good Samaritan" or the "Prodigal son?"[17] Crossan gives the example of Martin Luther King Jr. arguing that there is a substantial difference between the vision provided by an actual person and one invented by the author of a fictional tale:

> But because Dr. King was an actual person who did it—rather than just a character in a parabolic novel who imagined it—his vision could not be so easily dismissed. If it were done, it could be done again—and by others. That, of course, is the challenge of Jesus as an actual, factual, historical figure. If any one human being can do anything in life and death, other human beings can do so likewise.[18]

This leads to the second and perhaps the most fascinating of the Jesus themes that a preacher has to deal with: the many diverse portraits of Jesus—a phenomenon that occurs on two levels that I shall call the 'visible' and the 'invisible'.

2. The Many Diverse Portraits of Jesus

The visible level refers to the obvious fact that Jesus has been appropriated by many different Christian communities in diverse cultural settings from the tropical forests of Papua New Guinea to the shantytowns of Johannesburg and the opulent apartments of Manhattan. He has been championed by some as a socialist 'liberation' revolutionary; and by others as a right wing, gun-toting precursor of Texas Republicans. He has been called 'pacifist', 'feminist', 'Marxist', 'liberal', 'conservative', and dozens of other epithets. His name has been invoked to sanction the handling of deadly snakes or swooning as imagined demons are expelled from their bodies. He has been credited with miraculous healings, rescues from every imaginable calamity, and the spiritual salvation of countless individuals. He has been worshipped in hundreds of different rituals—all the way from the pomp and ceremony

---

16   Schweitzer, *The Quest of the Historical Jesus*, 403.
17   Crossan, *The Power of Parable*, 251.
18   Ibid., 252.

of a Papal Mass in the Vatican to a rock concert at a Campus Crusade in South Dakota and the wringing of a chicken's neck in Jamaica. Many Jesuses inhabit the public domain including the female Jesus, the 'Christa'.[19]

But there remains the invisible Jesus, the one that the preacher knows about but never declaims from the pulpit. She knows from her seminary studies that multiple representations of Jesus appear not only in the pages of the New Testament but also in countless revered manuscripts and codices that were omitted, lost or suppressed when the canonical edition was finalized. And only since 1945, after the discovery of the Nag Hammadi collection of thirteen codices, have biblical scholars conceded that the story of Jesus *might* include more than is contained in the canon of the New Testament. In fact, we now recognize the existence of "a *wild diversity* of the early Christian movement during its earliest centuries," with all parties claiming to "represent the views of Jesus."[20] As Charles Hedrick correctly notes:

> For the first three centuries of the Common Era no generally accepted standards defined the 'right way" to be a follower of Jesus—or even whether a right way could be identified among all the different views of him. Diversity of perspective was the rule. The claim that the 'faith once delivered to the saints' (Jude 3) was the 'true' faith was only one claim for authority among the many competing claims that emerged in the early period.[21]

That competition among Christian groups to claim possession of the 'authentic' voice of Jesus has changed little in two thousand years. In today's world 'Jesus' is variously proclaimed by an estimated thirty-nine thousand Christian denominations.[22] In addition, over the centuries he has been diversely represented in art, literature, film, and even secular propaganda.[23] Two examples will suffice.

---

19   As Elisabeth Schüssler Fiorenza comments in *Jesus and the Politics of Interpretation*, 6: "Jesus is an existentialist religious thinker, a rabbinic teacher, an apocalyptic prophet, a pious Hasid, a revolutionary peasant, a wandering Cynic, a Greco-Roman magician, a healing witch doctor, a nationalist anti-Temple Galilean revolutionary or a wo/man-identified man".
20   Ehrman, *Jesus Interrupted*, 191 (my italics).
21   Hedrick, *When Faith Meets Reason*, xiii.
22   The figure of 39,000 (or sometimes 38,000) denominations is quoted in much Christian literature, though is usually not referenced. My source is the Center for the Study of Global Christianity at Gordon-Conwell Theological Seminary South Hamilton, MA, USA (see www.gordonconwell.com). However, they list extensive data on only **9,000** Christian denominations.
23   For a comprehensive overview of how Jesus has been portrayed in celluloid see Tatum,

The most sinister of such representations is the Aryan Jesus. Susannah Heschel's impressive research shows how from 1939-1945 the 'Institute for the Study and Eradication of Jewish Influence on the German Church' attempted to redefine 'Christianity as a Germanic religion whose founder, Jesus, was no Jew but rather had fought valiantly to destroy Judaism, falling as victim to that struggle'.[24] The institute was funded by the German Christian movement (part of the German Protestant Church) and at its height had a membership of 600,000 pastors, bishops, professors of theology, religion teachers and laity. Their perverted scholarship, that denied the Jewishness of Jesus and falsely promoted his Aryan roots, laid the foundations for anti-Semitism that was a short-step away from countenancing the horrors of the concentration camp. One should note that the German Christian movement was larger than the Confessing Church, which remained a minority opposition group.[25]

At the same time on the other side of the Atlantic, Jesus became a 'rugged', 'strong', 'tanned', 'Western' and 'manly' type in Warner Sallman's populist painting *The Head of Christ* (1924 [originally in charcoal]/1941), copies of which were given to American servicemen as they headed off to fight in the Second World War! Sallman's portrait is considered the most popular artistic representation of Jesus, and closest to the way most 'Western' people, even today, imagine him to have looked!

So which of the many depictions of Jesus is most nearly correct?

This leads us to the third theme for the preacher: Who was the historical Jesus?

3. Who was the Historical Jesus?

Which portrait of Jesus is closest to the historical person who lived all those years ago in Palestine? What are the implications of historical Jesus

---

Jesus at the Movies.
24   Heschel, *The Aryan Jesus*, 1.
25   It should also be remembered that **both** the German Christian movement and the Confessing Church considered that the Jews were responsible for the death of Jesus and thus deserved any historical suffering that came their way. The Confessing Church was more welcoming of Jews who became Christians by baptism, acknowledged that Jesus was born Jewish and considered that the 'Old' Testament was part of the Christian Bible. It must be acknowledged that it is only after the Holocaust that Christian theologians began to fully address their own and the Church's attitude towards anti-Semitism, especially the text: "Let his blood be upon us and on our children" (Matthew 27: 25).

research for Christianity and the preacher? Again, all four books critically engage this research.

I have arrived at the dual conviction that the search for the historical Jesus matters greatly and that we can make a good estimate of who he was. It is of equal importance, I believe, that unless we arrive at a personal assessment of who Jesus was we abandon our own faith quest and become what Friedrich Nietzsche (1844-1900) contemptuously labeled 'followers of the herd'.

Most New Testament scholars accept the proposition that Jesus' central proclamation concerned the kingdom/empire/realm of God.[26] As I observed earlier, since the publication of Albert Schweitzer's *The Quest of the Historical Jesus* (1906), the issue of whether it was to be a *future* or *present* empire has become one of the most hotly disputed issues in New Testament studies. The discussion centers on whether Jesus was **either** an apocalyptic/eschatological prophet who thought that the end of the present world order and the arrival of God's empire would shortly follow his death (Schweitzer's own view); **or** whether he was a wisdom teacher who came to call for the establishment of a new and radically inclusive community. This is not some arcane academic argument, for not only does it go to the heart of who Jesus was and the nature of the God he proclaimed, but also it is crucial in deciding "what sort of religion Christianity is"[27] and therefore what we should proclaim today.

I side with those scholars who argue for a sapiential Jesus, a prophetic teacher who announced that God's empire was to be made real *now* by those who accepted his teaching. It was to be experienced as a present reality by those first disciples and to be similarly practiced by subsequent generations. Jesus' theology was thus not dominated by the expectation of an imminent and cataclysmic intervention by God in history, but rather down-to-earth, everyday advice on how God's empire was to be instituted in this world. His unique teaching method of parables and aphorisms marks Jesus as a social revolutionary who founded a short-lived egalitarian community based upon a 'discipleship of equals' that broke down barriers of race, class, gender and ethnicity.[28]

---

26   'Realm' and 'empire' are now widely used to avoid the sexist overtones of kingdom.

27   Stephen J. Patterson in Miller, *The Apocalyptic Jesus*, 163.

28   Elisabeth Schüssler Fiorenza coined the phrase "discipleship of equals". Dominic Crossan, Gerd Theissen *et al.* view Jesus as a social revolutionary.

The parables, widely hailed as "the distinctive voice of Jesus", depict an alternative society in which "the empire of God brings everyone to the same level". Such a social structure was antithetical to the officially sanctioned empire of Rome. As a popularly proclaimed rabbi he advocated an alternative "counter-world", a "shared egalitarianism of spiritual and material resources" that clearly challenged Roman political, economic, and religious domination. This advocacy of "living in relationships of mutual care" is reflected in the ecclesial utopian community portrayed in Acts 4:32–35.[29] Of course, the mere advocacy of such a spiritual and social program by a Mediterranean peasant would have been viewed as seditious by the Roman authorities, and it could lead to only one outcome: arrest for treason followed by crucifixion.

It was his proclamation of this vision of an alternative and thus subversive empire that brought Jesus to the attention of the Roman authorities. And Pontius Pilate, contrary to the Gospel writers' portrayal of his humane and judicious rule, was in fact a brutal Roman prefect who "unleashed a reign of terror" from 26–36 CE. He had no qualms about ordering the crucifixion of a suspected malefactor on the flimsiest of evidence, and he would surely have dealt in summary fashion with a peasant from Nazareth who proclaimed a rival empire.[30]

Significantly, Jesus' message and program of radical inclusivity was *based on his vision of God*. Charles Hedrick connects his theology, his program, and his death in a single concise paragraph.

> He believed in God and found in his personal faith a sense of authority for his public acts and discourse. He believed God was working through him to reclaim complete control of human affairs. *When fully realized, God's imperial rule would bring about a reversal of human values and overhaul the structures of society.* Quite predictably, therefore, Jesus found his natural place among the poor and irreverent on the margins of society, rather than in its main stream. The "righteous" and the religious authorities were particularly subject to his scathing wit and censure. Likely the reversal of values he announced and its implied challenge to

---

29   I have here summarised the ideas of Bernard Brandon Scott, "The Reappearance of Parables" and John Dominic Crossan, "Jesus as a Mediterranean Jewish peasant" in Hoover, *Profiles of Jesus*, 19–40, 161–68. Scott and Crossan differ slightly in that Scott argues that Jesus primarily presented a vision or "glimpsed alternative", whereas Crossan believes that Jesus offered both an alternative vision **and** a concrete social program.

30   Verhoeven, *Jesus of Nazareth*, 26.

the power structures of human society brought about his death. The fact that he was killed by an official act of the governing authority suggests that his public career was viewed, in some sense, as a serious threat to public welfare.[31]

How, then, shall we personify the God of Jesus?

Stephen Patterson neatly focuses the issue by asking two crucial questions: "What is the character of God that comes to expression in Jesus' words and deeds? What did Jesus believe to be true about God that led him to speak of God's empire in the way that he did?" Clearly, the answers we give to these questions will determine not only the kind of God that we believe in, but also the type of Christianity that we seek to advance and preach today.

First, Patterson argues, Jesus' words and deeds reflected a belief that "God is not remote but directly involved in the lives of ordinary people". God is known in the midst of life, can be addressed intimately, and welcomes *all* into his family. There are no outsiders, no expendables, and no one is unclean. Further, "the experience of God is transformative and leads to new acts of love directed towards others". Thus "God calls persons into relationships of radical love and mutual care".[32]

Second, Jesus' words and deeds manifested an inclusive God who invites us to form communities in which the experience of love and care would be institutionalized where, in the words of a modern hymn "people matter, people count".[33] This is the empire of God. Patterson concludes his disquisition with this insightful observation:

> What people experienced in Jesus was a word of love, acceptance, belonging, and value. Jesus spoke about God in just these terms. So when people heard his words and believed them to be true, their experience became not just that of a remarkable teacher. They experienced his words as the Word of God. This was the beginning of the Christian understanding of who God is. It began with the theology of Jesus himself.[34]

It is from this understanding of Jesus' theology that Christians proclaim their faith.

This, of course, leads us to the fourth theme.

---

31   W. Charles Hedrick, "Jesus of Nazareth" in Hoover, *Profiles of* Jesus, 71 (my italics).
32   Patterson, *The God of Jesus*, 113–18.
33   "Sing we of a modern city" (1968) by Frederik Hermanus Kaan (1929–2009).
34   Patterson, *The God of Jesus*, 118.

4. Preaching the Historical Jesus in the Church Today

Both as a scholar and a Christian minister who values community, I have become aware of an increasing demand by the laity that their clergy be not only up to date in their biblical scholarship, but also able to foster the growth of communities where religious ideas can be discussed openly. The caricature of the layperson who has 'a simple faith' is a distortion that must be expunged. Faith is not 'simple' today, nor was it in the past: it never has been. True faith is a roller-coaster experience that continually questions, doubts and inquires. At the heart of such an exploration lie questions about the Jesus who lived two thousand years ago: "Who was he?" "What did he really teach?" "In what sense was he unique?"

Any Christian who denies being more than a little curious about these issues is either dishonest or unwilling to address one of the most important components of his or her faith. Such an excuse is sometimes encountered amongst candidates for the ministry who, having to undertake a course on Christology as a prerequisite for ordination, encounter a 'crisis of faith' when confronted with various portraits of Jesus, and find that none match their own. As one who teaches such a course I continually ask myself why this awareness has not been absorbed at the church level before these putative seekers are invited to begin their ministerial formation? Why do the churches fail to educate their congregations in basic biblical criticism?

At the root of this conspiracy of silence is fear of the effects of biblical criticism, but any program of theological education, whether in church school, local church or seminary, demands some knowledge of historical criticism. Interestingly, even the evangelical theologian Kenton Sparks in *God's Words in Human Words* (2008) openly admits the compatibility of a reverence for Scripture and biblical criticism. He pleads for his fellow evangelicals and their churches to take seriously the results of historical and textual criticism. He calls for 'believing criticism' in which ministers openly admit that Scripture has historical inaccuracies, false scientific claims, and ethical contradictions.

Such admissions would avoid the cognitive dissonance that biblical scholars of every persuasion experience when "their carefully considered, private scholarly conclusions no longer fit into the old fundamentalist wineskins demanded by their institutions".[35] Beyond this question, much is at stake in

---

35   Sparks, *God's Word in Human Words*, 369.

the evaluation of historical critical research. At the heart of the predicament is the inter-relationship between history, faith, and the Church. Tyron Inbody neatly explains the situation:

> Christology is not simply a historical memory of Jesus; it is the interpretation of his significance and the grounds and nature of his significance for Christian faith and life. There can be no Christology apart from the faith of the believer. Yet the faith of the church is tied intimately to the historical person of the first century. Although Christology is about why and what one recalls about Jesus for the life of faith, that faith is inseparable from the historical figure of Jesus of Nazareth.[36]

In other words, what is taken to be true about Jesus (Christology) is related to what both the individual believer and the Church proclaim about him. Yet what is proclaimed must rest on a credible historical basis, for otherwise Christians and the Church commit intellectual dishonesty that can have disastrous consequences:

> If we can indeed "recover" a message that more accurately represents Jesus as a teacher of wisdom and discipleship as a process of imitation, not conversion .... for example, if one believes that Jesus rejected a politics of purity for a politics of compassion, then anti-gay forces in the church today must be subject to the critique not only of 'liberals' but of the gospel itself.[37]

So, when people ask: "Do you believe in gay rights/equality?" our answer should be religiously motivated: "Yes—because that is what the Gospel of Jesus demands of us, just as it demands that I love the refugee, the outcast, the divorcee, the stranger and even the enemy".

Conclusion

In this chapter I have argued that the four Jesus themes raised by the four books under consideration go the heart of the contemporary fascination with Jesus and also challenge contemporary preachers to offer their congregations a credible Jesus. It is obvious that even people without specific religious beliefs still need 'community'—one need only note the growing number of 'atheist churches' that have sprung up in America and recently here in Australia. Diana Butler Bass makes the apposite observation in *Christianity After Religion* (2012) that historically the Church has emphasized the following hierarchy of 'order': believing first,

---

36   Inbody, *The Many Faces of Christology*, 9–10.
37   Meyers, *Saving Jesus from the Church*, 137.

then behaving and finally belonging. She argues that today amongst those she calls 'spiritual people' a 'great reversal' has reordered those priorities to read: belonging, behaving and believing. After all, belonging is what people need most and recalls how Christianity originated:

> It (Christianity) began with an invitation into friendship, into creating a new community, into forming relationships based on love and service.[38]

Progressive Christians have developed an alternative approach founded upon the revolutionary message of Jesus, whose spiritual and social program was to create communities embodying that vision. Indeed, as Marcus Borg reminds us, the ideal of a loving, inclusive community is at the core of the biblical narrative:

> Community is utterly central in the Hebrew Bible and early Christianity. An individualistic spirituality is quite foreign to the biblical vision of life with God. In its worship and practices, the community celebrates life with God, nourishes and mediates the new way of being, and embodies the egalitarian social vision running through the Bible from exodus through the Jesus movement and evident in early Christianity. Christian life in community is meant to create an alternative world, a counter-world, to the world of normalcy and domination.[39]

The role and mission of the Christian community is to live up to that vision of a transformed world that Jesus came to proclaim. One useful 'progressive' Christian manifesto is that given by Robin Meyers:

> I dedicate this book (chapter) to all the men and women who have chosen the parish ministry as their life's work, and yet who do not wish to be considered harmless artifacts from another age. May all those who labor in the most misunderstood, dangerous and sublime of all professions be encouraged and inspired by the possibility that one's head and one's heart can be equal partners in faith. Lest the church end up as a museum piece whose clergy are affable but laughable cartoons, we must once again dedicate ourselves to this wild calling—one that led us away from more comfortable lives and into the only profession where radical truth-telling is part of the job description. May we fear no **one** and no creed, save our own timidity, and may we encourage and support one another in pursuit of religion that is biblically responsible, intellectually honest, emotionally satisfying, and socially significant.[40]

---

38 Butler Bass, *Christianity after Religion*, 205.
39 Marcus J. Borg in Miller, *The Apocalyptic Jesus*, 156.
40 Meyers, *Saving Jesus from the Church*, dedication page.

9. A progressive Christian understanding of prayer

Glynn Cardy

Prayer is more than thoughts or words directed at or towards a deity. It is more, too, than silent contemplation. It is, rather, a way of embodying a vision that encompasses thoughts, words, and silence, as well as sipping coffee, laughing, being arrested, and making love. Prayer then is a big word, a broad word, which describes how to live out faith. St Paul's admonition to 'pray without ceasing' (1 Thess 5:17) only makes sense if it means to live one's faith.

The vision of many progressive Christians is founded upon behaviours and beliefs that reflect mutuality and compassion, and therefore the valuing of human rights, the importance of empowered communities, as well as the creation of human structures and processes that are just, sustainable, and nurturing. God, in this vision, is both the energy of such change and a reflection of the anticipated mutuality and compassion. This vision is overtly political, and so is God. Prayer, as an embodiment of vision, is likewise political.

Making Fire

Prayer, however, has long been held captive by religious institutions and portrayed as primarily a physically and politically passive discipline. The following parable, which uses 'fire' as a metaphor for spirituality, illustrates and critiques this.

> After many years of labour an inventor discovered the art of making fire. He took his tools to the snow-clad northern regions and initiated a tribe into the art—and the advantages—of making fire. The people became so absorbed in this novelty that it did not occur to them to thank the inventor who one day quietly slipped away. Being one of those rare human beings endowed with greatness, he had no desire to be remembered or revered; all he sought was the satisfaction of knowing that someone had benefited from his discovery.

> The next village he went to was just as eager to learn as the first. But the local priests, jealous of the stranger's hold on the people, had him

assassinated. To allay any suspicion of the crime, they had a portrait of the Great Inventor enthroned upon the main altar of the temple; and a liturgy designed so that his name would be revered and his memory kept alive. The greatest care was taken that not a single rubric of the liturgy was altered or omitted.

The High Priest himself undertook the task of compiling a Life of the Inventor. This became the Holy book in which his loving kindness was offered as an example for all to emulate, his glorious deeds were eulogized, his superhuman nature made an article of faith. The priests saw to it that the Book was handed down to future generations, while they authoritatively interpreted the meaning of his words and the significance of his holy life and death.

Caught up as they were in these religious tasks, the people completely forgot the art of making fire.[1]

Prayer—like fire—can provide light and illumination, as well as warmth, comfort, and nurture. Energy, power, and vitality are also among the charateristics of fire and prayer. It is a rich metaphor. De Mello's parable encourages us to make fire—or make prayer—namely, to embody a vision and live it out.

Yet this parable is also a politically subversive one for it suggests that making prayer is out of the control of religion's priests. One doesn't have to come to church to 'make fire'. One doesn't have to agree with the priest to 'make fire'. One doesn't have to swear allegiance to any creed, canons, or Holy Scripture to 'make fire'. Instead religion's activities—be they worship, study, or service—need to be evaluated in terms of how they help others make the fire of prayer. Is religion fostering openness to—and the advancement of—mutuality and compassion? Or is it supporting a hierarchical structure that is concerned about maintaining its position to the detriment of those outside of religion's power?

The parable also suggests that Christians and the Christian God have no monopoly on spirituality's 'fire'. Keith Ward writes:

The uniqueness one can properly find in Jesus is something like the uniqueness one may find in a great work of art. It provides an insight into the deepest nature of things that nothing else can provide. It relates us to the [experience] of God in a way which is rather different from that

---

1   De Mello, *The Prayer of the Frog*, 7.

found elsewhere ... But it would be crass to hold that it is the only, or obviously the best, work of art in the universe.[2]

A progressive understanding of both faith and prayer recognizes that no religion is the only or the true path. Making fire/prayer is anarchistic. It can happen anywhere, among any people, when there is the right attitude and openness to the sacredness within and beyond them. This way of prayer therefore is potentially, like anarchy, politically disruptive.

Roots of Dissent

In the Book of Genesis, chapter 18, there is a story about the patriarch Abraham challenging the ethics of his God. This God, like many gods, reflects the understanding of power held by the dominant elite. Abraham's God is male, omnipotent, and judgmental. This God tells Abraham of his intention to destroy the wicked city of Sodom.

Abraham though protests. He challenges the nature of his God. He suggests to this deity that to be powerful is to be compassionate, rather than judgmental. Abraham—unlike his ancestor Noah, who quietly sailed away while most of humanity drowned (Gen 7:1ff)—argues with his God. He says, "God, what if there are fifty righteous people in that city, will you still destroy it?"(Gen 18:24).

Abraham is concerned not only about the righteous being destroyed along with the wicked, not only about the fate of the wicked, but about the moral compass of his God. He keeps arguing with God: "What if there are thirty righteous or twenty righteous or ten?" He challenges the dominant image of God as a capricious potentate. He challenges this God be compassionate and let compassion rule divine actions.[3]

What is easy to miss from our twenty-first century perspective is that Abraham literally believed in a God who, at any stage in the argument, could have destroyed him. Yet Abraham does not flinch. He does not let fear quell his courage. He does not let the Sodomites alleged wickedness prevent him from defending them in the face of their impending doom.

This prayer of Abraham's is risky. He continues to ask difficult questions, to doubt and challenge his God's judgment and use of power. He is not prepared to be compliant and submissive. Rather he champions those who

---

2   Ward, *A Vision to Pursue*, 70.
3   This interpretation of Genesis 18 is found in Armstrong, *In The Beginning*, 63.

are well outside of divine favour, and his culture's favour. He champions the needs of the wicked and defenceless and stands with courage before the face of the almighty male deity.

A similar audacious courage is portrayed in the Book of Exodus, chapter one. It is a story of two women, Shiphrah and Puah, midwives, who defied the power of the Egyptian god-like Pharaoh (Exod 1:15–21). They were told to kill male Hebrew babies. Shiphrah and Puah, however, believed in the Hebrew God and refused. The penalty for refusing would have been death. When summoned by Pharaoh, they lied: "The Hebrew women are vigorous and give birth before the midwife comes." Shiphrah and Puah understood their religion's priority, and the priority of their profession: to save life had a higher priority than the dictates of any other god or 'domination system'.[4]

These women's actions were prayers: prayers of deception. They were prayers of vulnerable women that increased their vulnerability by siding with the condemned. These prayers portrayed a belief in a different God than that of Pharaoh.

It was a clash between those with little power—female and foreign midwives—and one with lots of power—the male overlord, Pharaoh. The women's prayers were both political and foolish. For by their actions they were valuing the lives of foreign, slave children at the risk of their own lives. They were revealing their belief not only in compassion but also in mutuality, the belief that slave babies had a right to life just as Egyptian babies did.

In these two examples then, prayer is not just words spoken to a deity. It is a way of living and enacting a political and ideological vision. Prayer is protest. It can be dangerous, resulting in punishment and even death. Those who pray in this manner need to be both courageous and foolish. They are holding up a different vision—one of mutuality and compassion— which requires a different understanding of God.

Beginning a Journey towards a God of Mutuality

When raised in a religious context of an omnipotent male deity who creates and endorses hierarchies, coming to a different understanding of God is both a lengthy and personal journey. On that journey not only do concepts of God change and evolve, but so too does the form and content of prayer.

---

4   The phrase 'domination system' is a favourite of Marcus Borg, for example in *The God We Never Knew*, 132ff.

The first prayer I remember learning began with the words: "Our Father, which art in heaven" (Matt 6:9 KJV). I remember, too, the posture of kneeling with head bowed and palms together. The emphasis, though, was on saying the words.

Not that I understood the words. What was the 'art' in heaven? What was 'heaven' for that matter? I was quickly told that 'heaven' was the location of 'Our Father' who wasn't actually our father. Not that one could locate heaven—though it did seem to be more 'up' than 'out' or 'down'. It was all rather tricky.

Yet as time went on, Sunday by Sunday, I realized that the words didn't matter. It was being together, saying them together, and addressing God that mattered. Not that I had many clues about God. But if God was anywhere, God was in church. And a blend of voices—the well-dressed and the not so well-dressed, the knowledgeable and the beginners—all raised in unison was sure to be heard. Or so was hoped.

When I progressed to Youth Group the personalized version of God was all important. Father God was now Daddy God. It was quite nice as a teenager to have a surrogate all-forgiving dad when you might be having difficulty with the flesh-and-blood one. So prayer was a kind of personal chat, with God having to be a good listener.

But such prayers—and the deity they were addressed to—in time ran out of relevance and stalled. Talking can be therapeutic when one needs therapy, but what happens when one doesn't?

Then in my twenties the whole notion of a Father Almighty God who made the planet, directs its future, and calls its human creatures 'sinners', began to unravel intellectually. I was also conscious this God was being manipulated by ecclesiastical elites who wanted to use religion to solidify their power and keep others compliant.

I sought the guidance of those who integrated their politics and spirituality, and who lived and expounded a vision of mutuality and compassion. In the 1970s the Jesuit priest, Daniel Berrigan, was a great exemplar. Berrigan and his brothers confronted the American war machine of the Father Almighty God and the passive compliance of the churches that sang that Goliath's praise. They broke into a missile silo in Pennsylvania and tried to remake the nose cone into a ploughshare.[5] They poured napalm on draft cards. They disrupted trade in Goliath's temple.

Prayer, as I was slowly learning, was more than words, music, silence, or receiving communion. Prayer was a way of living out a vision of a better world, and a better God. Prayer was critiquing the alliance between the Fathers—the political/military fathers and the religious God fathers. Prayer was political and subversive.

Beyond God the Father[6]

Christianity's Jewish roots warn against the pervasiveness of any image for God, for an image can easily become an idol. The predominant image in Christianity for God is that of a powerful male being. It is so pervasive it has become an idol.

For many Christians the maleness of the God they address in prayer is not an issue. It has been the norm in their upbringing and religious enculturation. They mentally translate 'Father' into 'personal' and 'nurturing'. However a minority of Christians see the elevation of maleness into a deified form as not only restricting God to being 'a being', and a gendered being at that, but also such gendering being part of religion's complicity with the secular holders of power, who like their religious counterparts are predominantly male. It is as if male hierarchies need a male god.

For that minority of Christians, with many progressive Christians among them, no single image can satisfactorily take the place of 'Father God'. Rather the images they use in spoken prayers are multiple, and in their multiplicity critique reliance on any one. So God can be 'ocean', 'friend', 'provocateur', 'mystery', 'wind', 'sister', 'compassion', 'night' and 'between-ness'. No one image nullifies the rest. Images that are meaningful though change, as people's experiences change.

Some Christians have departed from the notion that God is a being. They have found other ways of talking, such as referring to God as 'the Holy', 'the Sacred', or 'the Great Compassion'. This way of speaking and imaging can

---

5   For the prophet text that underlies this action, see Isa 2:4.
6   This is a title of book by Daly, *Beyond God the Father*.

be called nontheism[7]. The definition of God I find most meaningful is the transformative power of mutuality.[8]

Other Christians have departed from any images and instead are spiritually sustained by stillness and its silence. When attending a religious service it is the silence, the music, and the feeling of community that mediates the inexplicable 'sacred', with the words being 'noise' in between.

Communal Prayer that Honours the Mutuality called God

Given such difficulties in articulating what we mean by God, and the variety among even progressive Christians, can we still communally and verbally pray? I think—with imagination—it is still possible. I offer the following communal prayers as examples, with comments after each about the way 'God' is addressed.

Learning The Silence

May we learn the silence of humility
The silence of wisdom
The silence of love
The silence that does not need words
The silence of being
May we learn to silence the noises of demand
To silence our appetites
To silence our needs
To listen instead to the voices of compassion
And the presence of the Spirit within. Amen.

This prayer is not addressed to a deity, but is traditional in the sense of acknowledging 'divinity' (the Spirit) within.

In Times Of Grief

In times of grief and pain
In times of suffering and fracture
In times of uncertainty and the failure of God
May we not sink in despair along with all we believed
But have the faith to learn to float
Knowing, hoping, that in time this too will pass. Amen.

---

7   Nontheism has a variety of meanings depending on who is using it, ranging from disbelief in God as a 'being' to a denial of any relevance of the word or metaphor 'God'.
8   This coincides with Carter Heyward's definition of God as "the power of mutual relation". Heyward, *The Redemption of God*.

Note it's the phrase the 'failure of God' that can provoke new thinking.

Let Us Make Room
Let us make room.
To pray is to make room,
to enlarge our hearts,
to be enlarged by the heart of godness,
so that all the unnoticed, unnotable, and notorious
can come on in.
Let us make room.
And be that room.

Note this prayer uses the word 'godness' rather than 'God'—inviting us to think differently about the word God.

Sharing God
With bread and wine,
We give thanks for one another,
For being together, for difference, for communities.
When we share food, we share God. Amen.

Note that this prayer moves us further into thinking differently about the word 'God' and what it means. Here it's interchangeable with a word like 'love'. And lastly:

Words don't do it any more
God.
Words don't do it anymore.
They can't express what I want to say.
So I remain silent, and wait.
I'm in that space between letters.
A blank space.
Yet today it feels more sacred than the filled spaces.
God.

In this prayer the word 'God' is used like punctuation—brackets around one's spiritual journey.

Sustenance to Live Mutually

To live a life of prayer embodying an alternative vision of mutuality and compassion will give rise to conflict. The Father God, the male church hierarchies, and the male hierarchies of power in society generally, do not tolerate alternate visions that can destabilize their ideological hegemony.

To endure such conflict progressive Christians need to find spiritual sustenance. It is often in learning from the least powerful in society—their humour, courage, and hospitality—that such strength is found.

Children are a great source of inspiration, as depicted in a New Zealand version of the old parable "The Emperor's New Clothes". As you might recall it is a parable criticizing power and pride. The Emperor ['Mayor' in this version] thinks he is wearing clothing that only the very intelligent can see and, unprepared to consider he might not be 'very intelligent', actually appears in a public parade naked. I pick up the rhyme as the parade begins:

> The Mayor tried his best to walk proudly, his bare belly wobbled and jiggled.
> Then, during a lull in the cheering, a wee nipper started to giggle.
> 'Mum,' he chortled out loudly, 'The Mayor is doing a streak!'
> 'Shhh,' said his mortified mother, 'That's quite enough of your cheek!'
> But it seemed that the penny had dropped, everyone started to grin.
> The grins turned to sniggers and chuckles, did all of them see only skin?[9]

The child states the unadorned truth. The child's honesty and courage engenders a politically destabilizing humour that brings down the mighty mayor from his puffed-up throne.

Children often encourage us to play, to use our imaginations, to honestly name—and even change—existing realities. They ask 'Why not?' questions. Questioning, imagination, and play are often tacitly disapproved of by powerful hierarchies. They are seen as childish—read, foolish—activities.

One Bible story about foolishness that is seldom read in churches is that of Balaam's ass (Num 22:21–39). The hapless donkey tries to avoid danger three times, and three times is beaten by Balaam, who believes that he is quite entitled to beat an animal. Then the donkey—via a bit of divine magic—talks back to Balaam, admonishing him. Balaam then gets into an argument with the donkey. Finally, Balaam relents and repents.

The story underlines the wisdom of animals and their ability to often see and feel things humans don't. It also encourages the hearers to treat animals well and live cooperatively with them. It is about mutuality and compassion. Tenderly patting an animal, for example, is a prayer in that it manifests the mutuality known as God.

---

9   Gurney, *The Mayor's Flash New Clothes*.

In both the stories above—about the Mayor and Balaam's Ass—humour and courage are closely linked. In the former it was the courage needed to speak up, even when he might have guessed his mother would disapprove. In the latter it was the courage of the donkey in confronting his abuser. Both courage and humour can upset those who think they are mighty.

Bob Fulghum compares the game *Hide and Seek* with the game *Sardines*. In the former the individual hides until found, and then is a loser. The winner is the one who isn't found. And at the end there is only one winner. *Hide and Seek* is a winners-losers vision of the world.

In *Sardines,* the game begins with only one person hiding. But when that person is found the seeker gets into their hiding place with them, as does the next successful seeker, and the next. In the end they are all discovered, chiefly by the sounds of children piled on top of each other and giggling. This is closer to the alternative vision of mutuality and compassion for both the world and Christianity: being found, being together, and lots of laughter. As Fulghum concludes:

> Medieval theologians even described God, in hide-and-seek terms, calling him *Deus Absconditus.* But me, I think old God is a Sardine player. And will be found the same way everybody gets found in Sardines—by the sound of laughter of those heaped together at the end.[10]

'Being together' is vital in sustaining an alternative vision. Creating and maintaining communities of people who will not only challenge the gods of power and domination but will also look after each other and look after the vulnerable in their midst, is essential. Those who are journeying beyond the metaphors of God so prevalent in church and society, and those who understand the cultural and political challenge that this journey presents, need the encouragement, hospitality, and kindness of one another. It is in being together that humour, courage, and the wisdom of children and animals, can be appreciated and nurtured.

Holy Russian Fools

The folk name for the Russian Orthodox Cathedral in Moscow's Red Square is "St Basil's"—he who was known as a holy fool.[11] The holy fool tradition

---

10   Fulghum, *All I Really Needed to Know*, 54ff.

11   Originally an apprentice shoemaker in Moscow, St Basil adopted an eccentric lifestyle of shoplifting and giving to the poor to shame the miserly and help those in need. He went naked and weighed himself down with chains. He rebuked Ivan the Terrible for not paying

has a number of threads, including not only St Basil, but also mediaeval street artists and those of the *yurodstvo* [folly for Christ's sake] who bravely critiqued the hierarchy throughout Russian history.

The Russian Orthodox hierarchy, however, call the Cathedral *Theotokos* ('God-bearer') after the Virgin Mother, Mary. Today though—much to the dismay of the hierarchy—it is popularly called another name, after another group of fools, the 'Pussy Riot Cathedral'.

In February 2012 three women, all in their twenties, were arrested in a Moscow Cathedral for saying a prayer,[12] and then in August that year two were sentenced to prison. They have recently been released. The prayer they offered was short: "Virgin Mother, redeem us of Putin". Vladimir Putin is the President and the Virgin Mother is the protectress of Russia.

In 2007 Putin made a statement later termed 'nuclear orthodoxy'—namely that Russia's nuclear arsenal would protect her from enemies without, and the Orthodox Church would protect her from enemies within. The political and military chauvinism of Putin would form an alliance with the Father God of the Patriarch.

It is important in understanding this protest to realize that the arrested women were Christians. Both Putin's regime and Patriarch Kirill's church are very hierarchical and male in both their leadership and their imaging of the God. The women, therefore, were not only critiquing this religious-political alliance but were suggesting that God could be imaged differently and outside of such centralized control. They had a political and spiritual vision of mutuality.

One of the convicted protesters wrote:

> In our [prayer] we dared ... to unite the visual imagery of [Christian] culture with that of protest culture, thus suggesting that [Christian] culture belongs not only to the Russian Orthodox Church, the Patriarch and Putin, but that it could also ally itself with ... the spirit of protest in Russia.

The Pussy Riot prayer was challenging religion's compliance with and courting of the political power-holders. Yet the women were not only

---

attention in church, and for his violent behaviour towards the innocent. en.wikipedia.org/wiki/Basil_Fool_for_Christ

12   www.youtube.com/watch?v=grEBLskpDWQ

pitting the God of protest culture against the God of 'nuclear orthodoxy', but a feminist God of mutuality against a male hierarchical one.

The group appealed to the feminism of the Virgin Mary against the anti-feminism of Putin and the Church elite. The words and actions of their prayer held out a vision of mutuality between women and men, between laity and clergy, and between the governed and the governors. The State and the Church harshly over-reacted, even by Russian standards.

At the trial, where the women were convicted of 'hooliganism', they purposefully drew a connection between their own actions and the New Testament where those persecuted for blasphemy—like Jesus (Mark 14:55–59), like Stephen (Acts 7:54–58), and like Paul (Acts 23:1–3)—turned out to be the rightful bearers of truth. There were a few Orthodox priests[13] who bravely supported the women, equating their actions with the holy fool tradition. Fr Vinnikov wrote, "God sent them to the Church as He sent Holy Fools, like St Basil".[14]

Their prayer was more than words. It was action that embodied a vision. It was also an act of solidarity with those oppressed by the domination system. Their prayer, too, was costly. Just like Jesus' prayer, when he disrupted trade in the Jerusalem Temple for disturbing the peace (Matt 21:12–13). And it was seen as foolish.

Holy New Zealand Fools

In New Zealand in 1983, nine Christians were arrested for disturbing the peace of race relations. Their prayerful action embodied a political and spiritual vision.

I, along with a fellow ordinand, Rob Ritchie, was arrested for wearing sackcloth and putting ash on my head. We looked foolish. In the Bible, sackcloth and ashes were used as signs of repentance and a challenge to others to repent also.

The context of this protest was the ongoing struggle for redressing the confiscation of Maori land by successive colonial and post-colonial governments. Each year, on Waitangi Day (February 6), the politicians and military would gather to celebrate the myth that New Zealanders were one people.

---

13 Fr Gleb Yakunin, Fr Pavel Adelgeim, and Fr Vyacheslav Vinnikov.

14 grani.ru/blogs/free/entries/199084.html

Our little team of Christian protesters, meant to—and successfully—challenged that myth. To be two peoples in one land requires mutuality: learning how to speak, listen, and learn from each other, redressing of past wrongs, and having transparent processes for the sharing of decisions and resources. This can be difficult, but ignoring the difficulties does not make for just and sustainable solutions.

At Waitangi in 1983 protesters, numbering in the hundreds, with placards and the like, marched and voiced their displeasure. The government had decided to advertise their power with a large police presence, a number dressed in riot gear. The protesters were firmly kept outside the gates.

The government also decided to have their own church service, with a compliant minister, to celebrate how the Father God had endorsed their exclusionist policies for many generations so that New Zealanders were now—as we had always allegedly been—'one people'. Like with Putin's Russia the government wanted an alliance with God.

The church service was held outdoors, and at the end of each row of seating stood a police officer. Before the service began some friends with brown faces, who were sitting quietly praying in their pew, were escorted out for the crime of being Maori.[15] The context of this service therefore was politically charged, before any protest was evident.

Then with a minute before the service was to commence various clergy and lay leaders, from a range of Christian churches, came forward and began taking the service. It was all very comic. The government's tame minister came rushing out, flapping his arms, and instructing the constabulary.

As for the sackcloth and ashes, that came during the intercessory prayers. Under our clothes, and rather itchy I might add, was the sacking. Around our necks was a little bag of ash, which we ripped and poured over our heads. It was all rather dramatic and foolish in the tradition of *yurodstvo*.

The police, though, were very worried about what was in the ash. A Catholic Irish priest,[16] who was arrested also at the same time—for saying a prayer!—yelled out to one of the flustered cops when we were in the holding pen: "Ah, Davey, me boy [he obviously knew the copper], don't you

15   This is a reference to James K. Baxter's poem, "The Maori Jesus", in Weir, *Collected Poems*, 347.
16   The late Fr. Terry Dibble.

read your Bible anymore? It is sackcloth and ashes. And by the way, how's your mother?"

What followed in the days after were police cells, a trial, lots of media, and lots of talking to church groups. The government never again tried to run a church service there. They did though the next year invite the Maori archbishop to speak, who in one of the better moments of his career, uncompromisingly criticised the government's relationship with Maori.

As for us, the Anglican Bishop of Wellington got the front page headlines: "Anarchy says Bishop".[17] He was referring to the fact that we had broken the government's law.

This political action with sackcloth and ashes was a public religious protest for justice for indigenous people. It was based on a vision of mutuality. It was also a protest against the state using the church to sanctify its policies. It was anarchistic, foolish, and dramatic. It was also a prayer.

Conclusion

There are many ways to understand prayer. For a number of progressive Christians prayer is living into and embodying a vision of mutuality and compassion. The words 'mutuality' and 'compassion' also point to how the word 'God' is best understood. God is like a fire of mutuality and compassion; and to pray is to make fire.

There are examples to be found in the Biblical tradition of people praying this way. Abraham's moral compass led him courageously to confront his capricious male deity. Shiphrah and Puah's belief in the right of Hebrew babies to be allowed to live led them to deceive the all-powerful Pharaoh. All three exhibited understandings of mutuality and compassion that for Abraham had theological consequences and for Shiphrah and Puah had political consequences.

To understand God as a way of compassionate mutuality can lead progressive Christians to change from and discard traditional forms of spoken prayers. New words and ways of praying can emerge, as can new images/metaphors for God. What sustains one's spiritual life may also change. The wisdom of children, animals, and community, and the delight of laughing and being together, has fostered both meaning and courage/faith for me.

Most expressions of Christianity—and most political systems—favour male hierarchies. The predominant deity in these cultures is male. The deity

---

17   *The Evening Post* (Wellington, Friday, 25 February 1983), front page.

is also omnipotent, and usually a supporter of the political status quo. It is as if the ambition of politically powerful men is reflected in a God that some consciously worship, but by which many others are subconsciously influenced.

To live out a vision of mutuality, and hold to a similar understanding of God, can lead some of us to confront politically the status quo. Such confrontation will be seen as foolish. The Pussy Rioters, in the tradition of St Basil, prayed by word and action, trying to liberate God and hold out a dream for a different Russia. Similarly, at Waitangi we tried to address the inequities of the then government's policies and their attempt to have endorsement from the Christian God.

At the Pussy Riot trial the original charge was blasphemy. It was alleged to be blasphemous to ask the Virgin Mary to remove the President. However offending God is difficult to prove in a state's criminal court and so they were convicted of 'hooliganism', or what we might call 'disruption'.

To believe in a power of mutuality and compassion, to name that power as God, and to work politically for the expression of that power in both church and state, will lead to conflict with the God and worshippers of domination and control. It might not be like the conflict seen in the Pussy Riot Cathedral or at Waitangi. It might be less visible. It might involve questioning, noncompliance, or humour. Yet conflict is unfortunately inevitable.

10. Eco-theology: The main game for religious progressives[1]

Noel Preston

On my study wall there hangs a beautiful photograph taken by the crew of Apollo 17 during their space journey to the moon. It shows Earth our home, the blue planet set against the inky blackness of space. Earth appears as a ball-like, single organism. We are a privileged generation to have this image and, associated with it, an understanding of the cosmos in its magnificence. But we are also the generation that is responsible for unprecedented damage to Earth's life systems—a system that has been almost five billion years in the making. In our time, the collision between our human story and the Universe story demands some accounting and reconciliation, as well as a revision of the narratives by which we live.

The Christianity I grew up with didn't have much to say about the themes emphasised in this chapter. In fact my early Methodist formation in Queensland was not only human centred but also rarely discouraged the misuse of natural resources or questioned what was called progress. A 1950s understanding of God had little to do with the natural world; indeed, it was something of a heresy to imagine you were nearer to God in nature than you were in church. At the same time, many of my colleagues regarded the biblical account of creation as literal fact. Things have changed. In the new millennium, religion is greener. In many Christian churches there are initiatives described as 'eco-ministry'. Good stories can be told about individual churches trying to make a difference. However, my suspicion is that, by and large, even the greener churches have not substantially embraced the worldview, the new paradigm and the new theology proposed in this account. In mid-life I awakened from a false consciousness that dulled my sensitivity to the whole planetary community of life. Personally, I now speak from the vantage of a multi-layered identity, no longer content with being simply a Christian or an Australian or even a human being,

---

1   This chapter draws on my presentation to Common Dreams 1. However, it is also informed by several other lectures and publications, including workshop presentations to Common Dreams 3, and my most recent book, *Ethics: With or Without God*.

though I am all that. As a member of the community of Earth's beings, my moral universe of responsibility extends to non-human beings and future generations.

I don't intend to say much about the crisis that now confronts earth's community of life. My assumption is that readers have a broad awareness of the gravity of the situation. In the Judaeo-Christian tradition, the Genesis mandate is that we, *homo sapiens,* are to have dominion over the Earth, *the creation,* albeit as responsible stewards.[2] This mandate now haunts us, in the guise of global warming, the threat to eco-systems and loss of biodiversity, depleting energy sources, a deepening water crisis, international security flashpoints, crimes against humanity, gross inequalities between and within nations, and absolute poverty and destitution facing 1.2 billion of a human population rushing toward 9 billion. The situation is unsustainable. There are many performance indicators that mark this crisis. Collectively, our global consumption of resources is 1.23 of our ecological footprint. That is, we humans are already using one and a quarter planet Earths, 23% more than the ecosystems can sustain. And, for those interested in the global social justice gap, the situation is even more dire. The affluent 20 percent of the world's population controls and uses approximately 80 percent of the Earth's resources. There is a link between the global ecological crisis and the injustice within the human community. One feeds the other: out of greed and ignorance we, the affluent, pollute Earth's fragile ecology while out of necessity and ignorance the desperately poor damage the natural environment just to survive.[3] Meanwhile, a materialistic economic system predicated on endless growth promotes a culture of consumerism that, arguably, limits the vision and insight of the human spirit. So humanity has a double-edged, urgent challenge: to achieve environmental sustainability,

---

2   Debate about the responsibility of Christianity for endorsing human misuse of the planetary resources continues in environmental ethics literature since Professor Lynn White Jnr. of the University of California published in 1967 a paper titled "The Historical Roots of our ecological crisis". For discussion of this see Gill, *The Cambridge Companion,* 221ff.

3   As the title to the challenging book by Brazilian Franciscan Leonardo Boff suggests, *Cry of the Earth.* Also, the feminist eco-theologian, Rosemary Radford Reuther, sees the connection from the perspective of women: "Women must see that there can be no liberation for them and no solution to the ecological crisis within a society whose fundamental model of relationships continues to be one of domination. They must unite the demands of the women's movement with those of the ecological movement to envision a radical reshaping of the basic socioeconomic relations and the underlying values of this society." (Preston, *Understanding Ethics,* 200)

on the one hand, and a fairer and more equitable distribution of resources and life opportunities in the human community, on the other. This double-edged challenge is what is now termed *eco-justice.*

Any theology or spirituality that is not eco-centric (i.e., centred on the Earth and its life forms) is grossly inadequate because it fails to take seriously the reality of life—it rests on a faulty narrative. Furthermore, it does not provide humanity with motivation and nurture to make the journey into the future that will sustain the community of life. At its core, progressive theology or religion must be eco-centric. Eco-theology is not an 'add on' to mainstream theology or religious practice, a mere development of the unchanging, dogmatic centre. This is not a flavour-of-the-month theology or sub-set of systematic theology like some regarded 'political theology' or 'feminist theology' or 'pastoral theology'. This is the main game for progressive Christians, especially because eco-theology supports *eco-spirituality* and an *ethic of eco-justice.*[4] Furthermore, eco-theology not only provides a bridge to solidarity with progressives in other religions but also to solidarity with secular groups who share a similar analysis about eco-justice.

There is a large literature on eco-theology, as the references cited in this chapter indicate. This chapter does not have the scope to canvass critiques of eco-theology. Indeed, it provides little analysis of the way many contemporary Christian theologians adopt an ecological perspective by re-formulating traditional doctrines, like the Trinity, the Resurrection or Eucharistic theology. These omissions, if they are that, are not just the result of the need for brevity but, in my view, there is some futility in undertaking theological word games that are not only obtuse but, in the end, do little to motivate the behaviour and sustaining spirituality of people (of faith and non-faith) who are committed to protecting earth's life community. This harsh word is not meant to overlook the helpful influence of others such as Sallie McFague, Rosemary Radford Reuther, Matthew Fox, Thomas Berry, Leonardo Boff, and Australians Charles Birch, Paul Collins, Norm Habel and Denis Edwards who have been pioneers in charting eco-theology within the Christian tradition. Some of their work draws on Christian mystics of much earlier times: for instance, Francis of Assisi, Meister Eckart and Hildegard of Bingen.

---

4   In *Ethics: With or Without God* I explore these themes in greater detail; *eco-spirituality* in chapter 2 and *eco-justice* in chapter 5. *The Earth Charter* is a comprehensive manifesto of *eco-justice*: www.earthcharter.org.

Science and Theology: converging stories

Contemporary eco-theology rests on two awesome narratives that confront humanity, we who are the *cosmos come to consciousness*[5]. On the one hand there is the story of life on Earth which biology and its companion sciences have unlocked in the past 150 years. According to that story, the community of life on earth has evolved across countless generations. The evidence shows that all life is interconnected, not simply through evolution. In every generation, all life forms ultimately depend on each other. The inter-relatedness of all life is expressed in James Lovelock's Gaia hypothesis that suggests that the Earth is best understood as one organic body, a biosphere in which all species of beings, fauna and flora, contribute to the whole. A consequence of this is that when any species undermines the life of the whole, that species puts itself at risk from Gaia's over-riding will-to-life. There is a pertinent story:[6] "Two planets meet in space. One looks ill and complains of having contracted *homo sapiens*. The other, bursting with health, replies: "Don't worry, my friend. I had the same illness, but it went away entirely of its own accord".

In a sense, this scientific knowledge of the continuity of life, and in particular of the evolution of the human species, demystifies our world, unlocking understandings that collide with superstitions and human fears of the so-called supernatural. And yet, in various ways, as human beings relentlessly try to make sense of their lives, the call of what may be named "spirituality" is profound and ever-present. The quest for what theologian Paul Tillich called "the ground of our being" still inspires many. The Gaia theory is a scientific observation that can be expressed mystically: "all is one and one is all". Religious liturgies might express this poetically: "God is the heart, creation the heartbeat". In his Letter from a Birmingham Jail about fifty years ago Martin Luther King Jr. named the ethical implications of this: "We are caught in an inescapable network of mutuality, tied in a single garment of destiny. Whatever affects one directly, affects all."

The second narrative, the story of God and gods (theology), provides meaning in the face of nature's mystery. This story has been told by our human ancestors in various ways; but the story of origins that, consciously or unconsciously, grounds our sense of who we are, has been called "the

---

5   This evocative phrase was coined by Catholic theologian, Karl Rahner.
6   I heard this story in a presentation by Mikhail Gorbachev at the Earth Dialogues in Brisbane, 2006. *Gaia* is the name of the Greek goddess for Earth.

creation" or, by indigenous cultures, "the dreaming". Centuries ago the scientific observations of Galileo and Copernicus removed the image of a three-tiered universe from informed religious speculation. More recently the scientific story of life's evolution, unlocked by Charles Darwin and others, has directly impacted on the story of God, especially a story which speaks of a separate divine being who, unilaterally, created all that we know as life on Earth. Even though theologians represent a realm of expertise that is not to be confused with that of science, the God story is inevitably impacted by scientific theory, method and discovery. To be credible, the story around which theology is woven, and by which religion binds its adherents, must take into account seriously the other story, the Universe story, and its scientific interpretations about life on Earth.

One of the more eminent of contemporary scientific voices is Edward O. Wilson, Harvard University biologist, who instructively observes:

> People need a sacred narrative ... They will refuse to yield to the despair of animal mortality ... If the sacred narrative cannot be in the form of a religious cosmology, it will be taken from the material history of the universe and the human species ... Material reality discovered by science already possesses more content and grandeur than all religious cosmologies combined ... Such are the conceptions, based on fact, from which new intimations of immortality can be drawn and a new mythos evolved[7].

Wilson's observation is profound. He is not saying simplistically that 'scientific truth' trumps 'religious truth'. Rather his more profound point is shared by many scientific and religious teachers. They warn that scientific (empirically verified) knowledge alone cannot provide the *wisdom* which our species needs to address the challenges of sustaining life on earth and of facing that challenge in ethical ways, directed by compassion and justice. However, the warning is double sided: theologians should be wary of attempting to put new wine in old wineskins!

---

7   See Wilson, *Consilience*, 295.

Nature and God[8]

The Universe story of life's evolution, as understood by students of biology and its cognate disciplines, refutes the idea of a being who is unchangeable and in absolute control of such a dynamic and continuously creative process. At the same time we can say that these processes, both purposeful and chancy, are imbued with an awesome and mysterious force of being and becoming which transcends any particular being.

Charles Birch, the eminent Australian biologist and lay theologian, found congruence between his theology and science, particularly through his scientifically informed understanding of the nature of nature—an understanding that is not properly explained in mechanistic or dualistic terms but rather in organic, holistic and ecological terms. Philosophers A. N. Whitehead and Charles Hartshorne, along with theologians Paul Tillich and John Cobb, are Birch's guides in developing a process theology that understands God as a creative power "not unilaterally responsible for any event". "God and the world are co-creators, for God's creativity works through the spontaneity and self-determination of the creatures." Creation is continuous, being becoming being, and (as the Genesis myth[9] portrayed creation) "it is good". Process thought opens space for the god-question that is consistent with a contemporary scientific worldview.[10] This understanding portrays a God who is experienced as a Presence celebrating the dance of life and suffering with creation's suffering, while empowering creation's evolving struggle, toward justice and compassion.

What we name as God may be more accurately described as 'the mystery in which all life is embedded', and that is awesome. Through the centuries, mystics have spoken in poetic, though personal ways about their god, the one who is nameless, the "I am who I am". In process theology the divine mystery is not to be seen as an all powerful God, the all knowing author of all

---

8   This was the title of a small SCM publication by Charles Birch that impacted on my theology during my training for the Methodist ministry in the mid-1960s. A further explanation: in using the noun, God, I have elected to simply use a capital 'G' though I recognise that some may claim this reference bespeaks theistic notions of God.

9   In fact, a process-thought reading of the Genesis creation stories reveals the co-creation idea. For instance, in Gen 1:11, 12, 24.

10   The quotations in this paragraph are from Birch, *Science and Soul*. For a short essay on Process Theology see Val Webb in Hunt and Smith, *Why Weren't We Told,* 63. Webb is cited by George Stuart, the contemporary hymn writer in a hymn titled "Divine Persuasion". See No. 9 in *Singing a New Song*, 2, 23.

things including suffering and illness, but rather as a compassionate presence with us in life's experiences. The everywhere God in here, in contrast to an elsewhere God out there (theism), is an embodied God, the God within all bodies "in whom we live and move and have our being" (Acts 17:28), as Paul reminded the ancient Athenians. This scientific, philosophical and theological understanding is also consistent with an eco-centric approach. God transforms our relationship to nature because the Earth itself, Gaia, may be understood as 'the body of God' as does theologian Sallie McFague. All life is embodied and connected in that body, though saying that "Earth is the body of God" is not to say "the Earth *is* God!"

My lifelong experience and expression of "god-ness", guided by interpreters scientific and theological, brings me to an explanation that rejects theism's idea of an interventionist God. Technically this explanation is known as pan-en-theism (which means "God in all", so, God in us and all others, in being itself). From this I draw a crucial conclusion for so-called progressives: the main dividing line between progressive and traditional understanding in religions is that between theism and pan-en-theism. Of course this is a particular challenge within the Abrahamic faiths (Judaism, Christianity and Islam). However, it also liberates twenty-first century human beings to engage with other human beings in the quest for a common spirituality and ethical stance that is supportive of the struggle for eco-justice. That said, I am not excluding theists from joining this quest and this cause.[11]

In *The Phenomenon of Man* the Jesuit paleontologist, Teilhard de Chardin, describes how nature's matter and life forms tend toward mutuality, connectedness, interrelatedness and attraction. From this primitive evidence, he intuits signs of love at the heart of creation. According to de Chardin:

> Cosmic energy is love, the affinity of Being with being. It is a universal property of all life and embraces all forms of organized matter. Thus the tendency to unite: the attraction of atom to atom; molecule to molecule; or cell to cell. The forces of love drive the fragments of the universe to seek each other, so that the world may come into being.[12]

To me, godness is that power within the process of life experienced as unconditional love (*agape*) in an intimate and relational and personal way. Alongside the apparent randomness of life, *agape* love points to the

---

11   This 'quest' is the main theme of my newly-released *Ethics: With or Without God.*
12   Quoted by Morwood, *It's Time*, 136–37.

possibility of a redemptive purpose within life, through the evolution of consciousness in human beings.

One key New Testament statement (1 John 4:8) resonates with pan-en-theism: "God is Love … for Love is of God." And further we may say, "Love is God" (although my theology lecturer about 50 years ago warned me against that transposition, allegedly because it robs godness of otherness and transcendence).[13] The God who is Love is in me, like a presence with whom I can relate. Compassion, that expression of love *par excellence*, literally "suffering with", is at the heart of the process. The call is to so believe and so act that *agape* love in its many forms is the centre-point of a life of spirituality. Love is at the heart of what is good religion and good living. "Perfect love," to quote the New Testament again, "casts out fear" (1 John 4 v.18) while fear is at the heart of bad religion and bad living. On the other hand, faith is empowering and liberating when it evokes a sense of belonging to a larger reality that contributes to one's life and receives their contribution to that life.

According to Birch[14], "The presence of the world in God is expressed by George Matheson, afflicted by blindness when he wrote the following hymn.

> O Love that will not let me go
> I rest my weary soul in Thee
> I give Thee back the life I owe
> that in thine ocean depths its flow
> may richer, fuller be.

Birch comments, "the last three lines express the author's feeling that his life has contributed to the ocean of God's life of feeling …".

The Jesus Story and Eco-theology

If we take seriously (as I do), first, the interrelatedness of all life and, secondly, theology as primarily a human search for meaning, then in formulating eco-theology we must be open to many religious traditions. The emergence of hybrid spiritualities—the 'catholic, buddhist, greenie', for instance—makes sense. However, it is necessary to create new or revised approaches from *within* particular traditions. So, in this section I focus

---

13   I note that some people find difficulty in naming "love" as the ultimate virtue, let alone as the essence of God. For instance, a better understanding for some might be "God is Goodness".

14   Birch, *Science and Soul*, 177.

on the core belief of Christianity. There is one key question that seizes my attention as a Christian of the twenty-first century: where does Jesus of Nazareth fit in a process theology? That is surely a question for those who, however long ago or in whatever state of being, committed their lives to being disciples of the Nazarene.

I could rephrase the question adopting Dietrich Bonhoeffer's famous inquiry: "who is Christ for us today?" But no, I actually suspect that 'christology' has become part of the problem. Is Jesus 'the Christ'? And what would that mean in the context of the Universe Story let alone the story of human life on Earth? What is the place of Jesus within an eco-theology claiming to be an authentic development of Christianity and seeking to commune with others who may not be Christian but who share a vision for eco-justice and seek an eco-spirituality that nourishes the quest for that vision?

I am not a gospel scholar trying to uncover the original Jesus but I believe the story of this prophetic, healing and mystical teacher who brought hope to his Galilean contemporaries has much to contribute twenty centuries on. I am influenced by the work of scholars who understand him as a wisdom teacher who empowered the marginalized. His *abba* was a God of love whose chief command was to love all others, while Jesus insisted that God was accessible to everyone. Then he was killed. The priestly guardians of the Jewish religious tradition collaborated with Rome's imperialism that also sensed he was a threat to their 'peace' (*pax romana*). But it didn't end there. His impact lives on. Christian theology began developing Christology, theologising about Jesus as more than a human being.

I am one of those who reject what could be called 'Jesus-olatry' (exalting the man, Jesus, to the status of an extra-terrestrial being). Frankly, such 'idolatry' would cause Jesus himself to turn in his grave! Central to those distortions are theories of atonement that reduce the Jesus story, making him a scapegoat sacrificed to win a theistic God's agreement to forgive sins. So, was he the Christ (elevated to the 'godhead')? Not to most early Jewish Christians it seems. The significant exception was St Paul. By the time the Christian scriptures were completed, the historical Jesus was surrounded with *mythos* which made his 'virgin' birth that of a king, and his death that of a saviour and his resurrection that of a god 'ascending' to heaven promising that he would return sometime. Doctrinal developments progressively constructed by church councils created a religion in which Jesus was divinised to the degree that the Catholic Creeds said little of his life and teachings, but a lot about his status as the only way to heaven, as a member of the Trinity.

I am concerned, not cynical, that Christology has become a hindrance, not simply in its implied claim to superiority over other religions, but also in communicating the Jesus Story to many contemporaries who find creedal Christianity incredible. This is a tragedy, for there is transforming power in the story of Jesus the Nazarene. Christianity gave much to the ancient world as it does today, especially when it is a means for liberating the oppressed and cultivating compassion for all life. That said, without the construction of Christology, it is unlikely that the Jesus story would have survived.

The Christ[15] of faith has become a pre-occupation of some who explore eco-theology from a Christian background. Matthew Fox's *Coming of the Cosmic Christ* is one significant formulation of this re-mythologising. In brief, Fox's thesis is that the historical Jesus introduces us to a Christ who is the underlying reality giving an inherent sacredness to the Cosmos. Fox cites authorities from St Paul to the medieval mystics who talk this way: "in him were created all things in heaven and on earth: everything visible and invisible" (Col 1:16). So, an ecologically (and mystically) informed approach to what is traditionally called 'the incarnation' has been put this way:

> Understood this way, the death of Christ becomes an icon of God's redemptive co-suffering with all sentient life as well as with the victims of social competition. God bears the cost of evolution, the price involved in the hardship of natural selection.[16]

I find it difficult to know how to deal with such assertions. Within the historical framework of Christian doctrine, it might be said that such re-appraisal legitimates a proper, ecological understanding of the Christ myth. Anyway, does an 'eco-Christology' do any harm? But is it necessary? Is it based on an elaborate myth that has to be demythologised as far as certain Christian progressives are concerned for the key message of the Jesus story and its impact for good to be preserved? Central to the Christ myth are theories of atonement that, appallingly, reduce the Jesus story to a Saviour

---

15   To clarify, the title 'Christ' is not Jesus' last name. It is derived from the early Greek word for Messiah.

16   Niels Gregerson, quoted by Edwards, *Ecology at the Heart of Faith*, 59.

who is sacrificed to win a theistic God's agreement to forgive sins. In time, and in the hands of certain Roman prelates and their successors, this power over sin and salvation wedded to the sacraments of Baptism, Confession, and Eucharist became an occasion for abusive power and control.

Eco-theologians like McFague, Reuther, and Fox reject this atonement and redemption paradigm and redefine sin from an ecological perspective. Sin is essentially human action that disrupts the interrelatedness of life, and results in human beings denying their proper place in the process of life's creativity. Eco-theologians also reject the pivotal place given to Original Sin in Christianity. Instead, Fox speaks of Original Blessing and Kevin Treston explains the Genesis story of the Fall, as 'emergence for life' rather than a 'fall from grace'. Another consequence of this ecological approach is to see sin in a collective and systemic way, not simply the misdeeds of individuals.

The Canadian eco-theologian, Bruce Sanguin, has written a very helpful essay about Jesus,[17] which misleadingly is titled "When *Christ* (my italics) is Cosmic". The title is misleading because his essay is not about the maze of Christology. Rather, it declares that following 'Christ' is submission to the "Heart and Mind manifest in Jesus of Nazareth". Sallie McFague is another whose eco-theology is not shackled by an esoteric Christology. Her most recent title[18] interprets the Jesus Story by focussing on the idea of *kenosis*, a New Testament Greek term, meaning "self-emptying" used in Philippians 2. She offers this paradigm to twenty-first century Christians and others as the key to addressing the global eco-justice crisis. Kenotic theology speaks of the self-sacrificial God who is Love, a "counter-cultural love". Practising and nurturing kenotic spirituality and living is the costly gift needed to confront this crisis. This is the kind of love revealed in the Jesus Story, "the man for others", as Bonhoeffer wrote.

There is congruence between the Universe Story and the Jesus Story, notwithstanding the conjuring christologies of some.[19] That said, we can acknowledge that—as a man of his era—Jesus was probably *not* a self-conscious pan-en-theist! One commentator concludes:

---

17   Sanguin in Hunt and Smith, *Why Weren't We Told?*,192–95
18   McFague, *Blessed are the Consumers*, chs 7 and 8.
19   Others say, as part of an evolving cosmos, the Jesus of history is an evolutionary break-through for life on Earth (a mutation and thus incarnate). I will leave that speculation alone.

the experience of God as his *abba* was the source of Jesus' wisdom, his clarity, his confidence, and his radical freedom. Without this it is impossible to understand why and how he did the things he did". [20]

The point about this for eco-theology and eco-spirituality is that, as a mystical prophet, Jesus lived out of a strong sense of unity or 'oneness' with his God giving him a deep awareness of oneness with all, with himself, with other human beings, with all other beings and I suspect, as he spent nights in prayer on the hillsides of Galilee, one with the starry heavens and the cosmos. Here he was at home, here he knew a Presence that nurtured his trust in life and the compassion that was at the centre of his being. Jesus matters twenty centuries after he lived, when life on Earth is under threat, because he showed that human life can be transparent to the creative Love which is God.

Eco-theology in Summary

Lloyd Geering has always been ahead of his time, and still is. In 1999—at the turn of the millennium, when he was well into his eighties—he wrote *The World to Come*, subtitled "from Christian past to global future". He forecasts the end of religion as we knew it and rightly argues that religion's future will be tied to our common global destiny and a global culture that "will rest on a shared view of the universe, a common story of human origins, a shared set of values and goals, and a basic set of behavioural patterns to be practised in common".[21]

Reflecting this, an authentic eco-theology, Christian or otherwise, will be:

1. *pan-en-theistic* rather than theistic, that is, its understanding of God is not of an interventionist theistic God but rather that of a creative loving presence in all being;

2. *eco-centric* and not anthropocentric, that is, it rejects human-centred theology, which subtly endorses our species' destructive dominance of nature through human technology, in favour of a view that takes seriously the intrinsic value of all life;

3. *inclusive* not exclusive, not just in a gender, race or species sense, but also, in recognising that truths to live by may be revealed in varying and multiple ways;

20   Nolan, *Jesus Today*, 71.
21   Geering, *The World to Come*, 158–59.

4. *mystical* rather than literalist, that is, valuing the experience of transcendence, especially that triggered through connectedness in the natural environment;

5. *shaped by an over-riding sense of the goodness of life* rather than its undeniable tragedy, and therefore living with gratitude, because life's purpose is more about celebrating original goodness (rather than original sin);

6. *focussed on orthopraxis* (right conduct) more than orthodoxy (right belief) for it is the life on Earth (we live now) that matters;

7. as a narrative theology *its basic narrative is humanity's common story*, the Universe Story (and especially the story of life on Earth) emphasising the responsible place of human beings within that story. It also recalls the stories and teachings of fellow human beings (such as Jesus of Nazareth) whose lives reveal compassion and self-giving (kenotic) love, inspiring an active commitment to eco-justice.

A life fashioned around eco-theology, nurtured by eco-spirituality and giving oneself to the claims of eco-justice is demanding, requiring discipline, restraint and self-sacrifice—and a strong sense that we truly are co-creators along with the empowering Presence of the "love that will not let us go." The advice of the slogans popularised in the 1970s still hold: *think globally, act locally* and *live simply so others may simply live.* Those who take up the challenge, whatever faith motivates them, are a sign of hope for future generations and a portent of the global cultural shift that is needed, to create fairer and more eco-centric cultures. If that cultural shift is to deepen, it will require a spiritual base along the lines we have examined here. For these reasons I insist that eco-theology and its companions, eco-spirituality and eco-justice, are the main game for religious progressives.

11. Is the religious progressive movement only for white fellas?

Jenny Te Paa Daniel

The progressive religion movement is an astonishing social phenomenon both in its original visioning and in its ongoing evocation of a spirit of profoundly imaginative faith-filled hope. In the international gatherings held over the past seven years, the speakers and participants have together contributed an incredibly rich array of religious perspectives, of practical experience, of spiritual insight and of intellectual challenge.

I consider it cause for huge celebration that in the utterly secularised post-colonial twenty-first century so many consider that thinking, speaking and doing the things of God in order to create and sustain communities of peace and justice is necessarily a good thing to do.

What follows is the updated and, where necessary, corrected text of a paper offered to the 2007 Common Dreams Conference held in Sydney, the first international gathering of those primarily from New Zealand and Australia who identify as 'religious progressives'.

It is good to be meeting in Sydney, even though it is not a city where I feel especially safe. Nor am I necessarily understood as a post-colonial Anglican by my local denominational sisters and brothers. However, it is certainly a city where I feel very safe as a Maori woman. After all, there are something like 30,000 Maori living here, the vast majority of whom are no doubt my tribal relations from the northern part of Aotearoa known as *Te Tai Tokerau*.

These strong and unbreakable *whanau* or family ties provided both incentive and ongoing security for the first generations of Maori who migrated here during the 1960s. They came not only to Sydney but all across Australia in search of better social and economic opportunities. And so it is, that despite all of the passionately articulated traditional sporting and economic rivalries between our respective nations, I do still very sincerely acknowledge Australia as being very much an important offshore island of Aotearoa New Zealand!

Increasingly, however, we are becoming far more than simply geographic neighbours. Facilitated by the historic ease of migratory movement between our lands, a new and complex demographic continues to emerge. New kinship ties formed through the interrelating and subsequent intermarriage between the peoples—indigenous and other—of Aotearoa New Zealand and Australia has given rise to a whole new set of understandings about both cultural and national identity on both sides of the Tasman Sea.

Similarly, this same new demographic has resulted as many of those blessed to live in or to have migrated from what is so uncritically and variously described as Oceania, the South Pacific, or the Pacific Islands, have also migrated to one or other of the big brother nation states of New Zealand or Australia in search of new opportunities for social and economic advancement.

I say 'uncritically' because there is still no consensus among scholars or politicians about the most accurate or helpful descriptor of all those island communities that exist alongside Australia and Aotearoa New Zealand. Together, we are contained within the tidal embrace of the Pacific, the greatest of the world's oceans, with an area exceeding that of all dry land on the planet.

What I do know is that both Australia and New Zealand are richly blessed by the unique presence and very significant contributions made to our respective nation states by indigenous peoples from this broad geographic region that I will hereafter refer to as the 'South Pacific Islands'. Notwithstanding the fraught definitional territory into which I am straying, I can confirm that I am using the term 'indigenous peoples' here to mean, those more likely—according to indigenous oral tradition—to trace their genealogy from original inhabitants and to have lived primarily within specific South Pacific Island communities.

I am referring specifically to twelve island-based population groups mostly Polynesian; with the exception of Melanesian peoples of Papua New Guinea, Vanuatu, New Caledonia and the Solomon Islands. All of these islands comprise communities primarily of indigenous peoples with whom both Australia and Aotearoa New Zealand have established mission, trade, aid, defense, free association or other political agreements. These island nations include (in order of descending population):

Papua New Guinea	(population 7.1 million)
Fiji	(887,000)
Solomon Islands	(597,000)
New Caledonia	(256,000)
Vanuatu	(261,000)
Western Samoa	(186,000)
Tonga	(106,000)
Kiribati	(103,000)
Cook Islands	(15,000)
Tuvalu	(11,000)
Niue	(1,200)
Tokelau	(1,300)

The total population[1] of just these named South Pacific islands alone is approximately 10 million. When you include Australia (approximately 23 million) and Aotearoa New Zealand (approximately 4 million), then there may therefore be some 35–38 million people—if you include Hawaii and Rapanui—living within a sea space of some 165 million square kilometres. According to my consistently lousy maths and my even lousier eco-theology, that still means a lot of ocean space for not so many people!

What I so love about the entire South Pacific, especially throughout Polynesia, is the extraordinary range of ethnic and cultural diversity that exists within the languages, art, dance, cuisine, cultural and religious traditions of the peoples who often live in the most indescribably beautiful environments that characterise the region. What I love even more is the extraordinary beauty and sheer goodness of so many of the people.

South Pacific Island people are—by nature and by the circumstances of their living environment—incredibly tenacious, pragmatic, hospitable, creative and utterly self-sufficient. And then there is their predominantly uncritical faithfulness to so many of the Christian churches that have with varying degrees of success both positively affected and negatively afflicted South Pacific peoples over many many years.

The latest and most damningly influential religious menace in the South Pacific is I believe the smooth talking, flashy, racist, sexist, homophobic, prosperity Gospel adherent, tele-evangelist! Nonetheless, the all-pervasive

---

1   The population figures are very approximate only and they have been updated to reflect 2013 estimates.

165

historically established influence of the Christian churches in virtually all the islands of the South Pacific remains a significant part of their enduring charm.

However, the mission schools and theological colleges established alongside the first churches have not created strong educational legacies. As an indigenous academic leader in theological education, I have long critiqued the well meaning but ultimately appalling legacy of those of our forebears who were responsible for the establishment and implementation of theological education (very broadly speaking) from the colonial time of the fledgling mission schools through to the post colonial contemporary denominational seminaries and theological schools that now proliferate in the region.

This in turn has ensured a dearth of highly qualified theologically educated church leaders with critical thinking skills and thus astute and courageous hearts for Gospel activism. Little wonder then that the churches and their leaders are now increasingly part of the enduring problem in preventing Pacific peoples from developing the necessary critical analysis—let alone the key strategies—that would enable them to understand and to respond more appropriately to the very real social, political and economic problems now so readily apparent throughout the region.

This contribution to the emergent progressives religious movement is inspired by my recent experience as a participant and presenter at two significant international conferences on the role of religious communities in the South Pacific. After all, this gathering in Sydney is also geographically located within the South Pacific region.

Both the earlier conferences highlighted the troubling disconnect between the current social, political and economic realities confronting Pacific Island societies and the conservative and all-powerful grip of so called 'traditional' Christian 'teachings'. These 'teachings' are now so deeply embedded within most South Pacific Island societies that there is at times little critical distinction made between what is defined as cultural tradition and what is—or indeed may be—authentically defined as 'Christian' tradition.

Both conferences pointed to the gains made by New Zealand Maori in secular and theological education as they overcome the colonial legacy. Both wondered about Australia's position on such matters and both pondered on the collaborative possibilities that may yet be developed between us all as sisters and brothers in the region, regardless of who has made the best progress to date.

As previously mentioned, indigenous students preparing for church leadership, indeed for ministry whether as lay or ordained, have historically not benefitted as they ought to have done from the theological educational offerings in our region. The systemic injustices of monolingualism and monoculturalism deeply embedded in all education—including theological education—has militated against Maori and South Pacific Island student success for many, many years.

There is, therefore, an urgent need for a large-scale educationally and religiously redemptive project to be undertaken, and it occurs to me that there are many white fellas (and women!) within the progressive religious movement with the professional status, skills and educational qualifications to assist. But a crucial question is whether predominantly white[2] religious progressives have the troubled heart so necessary for engaging with such a challenging redemptive project. More importantly, do they sufficiently understand the increasingly complex geo-political contextual reality of the region?

Politically dominant white Australian leaders have for many years now moved very firmly to prioritise the nation's regional position as a key ally of United States and British interests. Australia's national 'gaze' therefore is toward the west and not the east, which is where all your best South Pacific neighbours live and love. We also long for God's justice. Is it possible for that gaze to be reoriented? Is this potential shift in horizon a shared desire among those responsible for church leadership, particularly those responsible for theological education?

As a completely unscientific survey over a three-month period (which included two reasonably lengthy stays in Australia) I informally canvassed every Australian person I encountered for an indication of their knowledge of the official relationships the Australian government has with any South Pacific Island nation. It was not a very encouraging exercise for all kinds of reasons, ranging from indifference to ignorance. Sadly, the same was true

---

2   Understanding the term 'white fella' to be commonly understood as the aboriginal descriptor for non-Aboriginal Australians, I use it interchangeably with 'white', to denote primarily those Australians descended from the earliest colonial settlers, including convicts transported from the United Kingdom.

for the majority of *Pakeha* New Zealanders with whom I later undertook to ask the same question. It was a deeply troubling set of responses.

Even more troubling was the fact that while most knew or cared little about their government's relationships with the peoples of the South Pacific, virtually all my informants were more than happy to share delightedly their tourist stories of being individually feted and cosseted by the happy and friendly islanders with whom they interacted whilst on cheap packaged vacation tours.

The global phenomenon of the disinterested, ill-informed imperious tourist is as apparent in our region as in any other part of the world. Blissfully unaware of the rumblings of political discontent throughout the South Pacific Islands region, non-indigenous Australians and New Zealanders regularly join with thousands of other global tourists in securing their annual South Pacific island paradise vacational fix.

It is my contention that as neighbours, and therefore as regional citizens in common, we cannot justify not noticing—let alone not acting to transform—the dark underside of life in the South Pacific neighbourhood. As Christians in common surely we cannot continue to avert our eyes, let alone our hearts for justice, every time there is an armed coup, another devastating tribal battle, more allegations of serious political corruption, the plight of illegal immigrants, shocking evidence of high level drug, arms and people trafficking through the region, and so on it goes.

What do our indifference, our ignorance, indeed our averted eyes and hearts, say about our sense of being as neighbours with one another—let alone about being God's people for peace with justice in this, our part of the global 'vineyard'? The challenge, I believe, is to ask ourselves whether or not we truly share in both the delights and the responsibilities of being in right relationship with each other as Christian sisters and brothers in our region, let alone with those of the other great faiths who also now comprise a sizeable faith based group alongside us?

In other words—and employing the exact same words being used to describe the inaugural international gathering of religious progressives— do we as regionally located sisters and brothers in Christ share a 'common dream' for the South Pacific neighbourhood within which we each yearn to have our life and being characterized by peace and God's justice? To what extent do non-indigenous New Zealand and Australian Christians—

arguably the most privileged, at the very least in economic terms—have a responsibility to assist those in the regional neighbourhood who are clearly less fortunate?

I know there is a significant risk in what I am suggesting. Some people will immediately leap to accusations of overly simplistic analysis, potentially naïve political interference, cultural imposition, neo-colonialism, neo-imperialism, reverse racism, and so on.

I summarily reject any such accusations on the basis that I understand religious progressives to be at heart theologians, not party politicians or neo-capitalists. As public theologians we pride ourselves on having both the capacity and the will to influence the public square, to name the issues of pressing human concern, and to challenge those who hold political power, not only to take notice, but also to act in concert against those things that diminish the quality of life for any of God's people. The message is irrefutably political but there is a significantly different morally interested framework of reference at stake.

Secular politics are driven by singular individualised economic self-interest and the unbridled pursuit and retention of power for its own sake, whereas public theologians are driven by an unapologetic determination to ensure that collective well being is able to be achieved and sustained for all and not just for some. There is a morally bound objective to ensure more equitable participation in decision-making and thus the modest redistribution of power and resources, especially to those most in need.

At this point I want to notice and to name what a number of religious progressives may be wondering. What on earth is a Maori lay woman public theologian doing in Australia speaking on the issues of the South Pacific when there are any number of unspeakably tragic issues going on within her own indigenous community?

I raise this as a caution because ideological challenges such as this are not uncommon. What they indicate however is the extent to which the uninterrogated effects of twenty-first century post-colonial identity politics can so readily entrap us. These are the politics that have encouraged the uncritical formation of social groups around a unifying principle such as tribe, ethnicity, gender or sexuality. Groups are usually formed around the longer-term objective of changing/transforming the situation of oppression or injustice being experienced by those in the group.

Critics of identity politics point to the ways in which undue focus upon 'difference' can unhelpfully preclude collaborative approaches to problem solving. Such is the case in the example given; What is she doing involving herself in matters not involving her own people?

This tendency of first becoming instinctively reactionary and defensive whenever anyone who is not 'of our tribe' dares to notice and to speak out about things of grave concern in the neighbourhood, is becoming quite commonplace. Pushback against the 'outsider' critic thus enables 'insiders' deftly to avoid responsibility for being their sisters' and brothers' keepers. Those pushing back react, not by considering the veracity of the observation, but by discrediting the humanity of the observer!

And so to those who would dare to suggest that problems in the village are for the villagers only to work out, I do beg to differ! Those who articulate this closed border mentality usually have very little to give to the development of flourishing and peace-filled globalised societies.

I will never concede to the oft-made claim that it is not OK for 'outsiders' to initiate neighbourhood discussions over what we observe and what we know to be going on that is not right. The observation of Edmund Burke (1729–1797)—that evil is only able to prosper when good people stand by and do nothing—is instructive. I do truly believe that we are all equally responsible for one another. No one is exempt from acting precipitately in the face of any and all human suffering.

There is also another reason why I am raising the particular issue of collective neighbourhood responsibility and why I am raising it with religious progressives. As an indigenous woman, I am always deeply concerned about the potential loss of what I describe as 'essential shared memory'. This is the project of ensuring the life story narratives, particularly the histories of injustice, are never lost to anyone.

Throughout all the years of my work as a public theologian I have witnessed too many who assert a disturbingly populist understanding of progressive Christianity, let alone religion per se. What I witness is either the complete avoidance of indigenous history and ongoing struggle or worse, the delimiting, discrediting or even the complete erasure of selected aspects particularly of colonial/indigenous history.

I have been further troubled by the political inference articulated by some 'progressives', that 'progress' is in fact from here and now forward. In other words, let whatever was in the past remain there because what matters is moving ahead into 'progressive' imagining and acting, into new ways of being unconstrained by the drudgery, conservatism and injustices of the past.

This attitude effectively dismisses significant religious memories and an entire epistemology of indigenous religious and spiritual wisdom too precious ever to be erased, diminished, overlooked, or forgotten. As an indigenous woman, I know only too well how readily indigenous *taonga* or precious ways of knowing and of being, have so often been unilaterally rendered irrelevant, redundant, of no further use—by those with the power to do so. Therefore, without a prior commitment to a mutually respectful collaborative partnership approach with indigenous peoples, religious progressives will always risk being seen as a movement 'For White Fellas only'.

It does not have to be that way. Progressive religion does not have to be a predominantly 'white' movement, but unless and until indigenous peoples and other people of color are also attracted into belonging on an interdependent basis then the risk of exclusivity remains. What is needed is a collaborative strategy where the unique wisdom, gifts, skills, yearnings, and vision of all peoples might be contributed for the mutual enrichment and for the religiously progressive benefit of all and not just for some.

Indigenous peoples have much to contribute to such a strategy. For example, at the heart of indigeneity, as with Christianity and all other religious movements, is right relationality. Right relationality with the land and right with one another. The things therefore that indigenous peoples are obligated to protect and to promote are those things which are life-giving for relationships between and among all of humanity and those things which are life-giving for relationships between and among all of God's magnificent creation.

As an indigenous woman, I enjoy ancestral links deep within Aotearoa New Zealand as the homeland of my birth, as well as within those islands and those people from whom all Maori are originally descended, Rarotonga, Raiatea, Rapanui and Hawaii. It is this *whakapapa* or genealogical connection to both land and people, that at once compels and obligates me to speak and to act as I do.

At the same time is it not—or ought it not be—obligatory for all who have been historically invited and thus enabled to make the South Pacific region their chosen place of belonging, to speak and to act with a similarly profound, albeit culturally unique commitment to right relationality? After all we are all sisters and brothers in the same geographic vineyard. We are inextricably regionally connected.

It is this collective, shared, mutual or joint regional responsibility as God's people together in the South Pacific, that is at the heart of my *plea for us all* to reconsider our relational responsibilities with and for one another. We need after all to work out our collective salvation together!

There are very serious issues currently affecting Australian Aboriginal communities, New Zealand Maori, and Pacific Island communities. However, a selective geopolitical survey of the South Pacific region will soon reveal the kinds of priority contextual issues with which religious progressives ought also to be intimately acquainted, about which they ought to be inconsolable, and for whose alleviation they ought therefore to be speaking and acting with great urgency.

Starting with Australia's northeastern shores there is *Papua New Guinea* (PNG), a nation where there has been virtually a permanent official government warning in place for international travelers for way too long. PNG where HIV/AIDS is endemic, where sexual violence against women and children is at devastating levels, where infant mortality is at an all time high level and similarly political instability. PNG, where the Christian churches maintain a powerful social and political presence. In the 2000 census 96% of the population identified themselves as belonging to a Christian Church.[3]

The status of women in PNG churches is still relegated to that of being passive recipients of male church leader largesse at best, sexist bullying at worst. PNG, like so many other Pacific Island nations, is where male-dominated cultural tradition is often used as the great silencer of women who dare to challenge, including within the Church. All of these assertions are extremely complex and are deeply nuanced through the subtle interactions of culture, economics, politics, and spirituality. I know that nothing of the ways in which human societies are organized and interact is ever simple. However, what I do know with absolute certainty is that that

---

3   unwomen-asiapacific.org/docs/WhyDoSomeMenUseViolenceAgainstWomen_P4P_ Report.pdf

every woman's life matters to God especially those who are suffering and dying needlessly.[4]

The Solomon Islands. This is a country to which Australia and New Zealand have recently contributed significantly. Sadly, this contribution has been the intervention force RAMSI, desperately needed because of the extreme levels of violence in a nation of just over half a million citizens. Unable to shake off a well earned global reputation for high-level political corruption, the Solomon Islands is nevertheless a country 'blessed' with the substantial presence of Christian churches. Many of the church leaders have been very active in promoting human rights and many also have been unafraid of naming corruption and injustice. In spite of this, suffering among women and children is utterly disproportionate, while sexual and domestic violence is endemic and utterly under-reported. Even in the midst of such publicly visible suffering the theologically indefensible diminished status of women remains seriously under addressed by the churches.[5]

Fiji, pejoratively known as the coup capital of our region, is now a nation where poverty levels have risen to unprecedented levels. Fiji, where prostitution is now a lucrative source of income for too many young women and a guaranteed source of sexual infection. Fiji now presents with disastrous and increasing levels of HIV and AIDS infections. Here in this incredibly beautiful part of the South Pacific paradise, Christian churches, especially Methodists, dominate the landscape. Women in positions of leadership in a small number of mainstream Protestant Christian churches are politely tolerated. Women and children in Fijian society continue to suffer, too often in silence, the inevitable consequences of impoverishment and loss of democratic freedoms under a military-led regime. Some church leaders have valiantly and sincerely mounted strong and comprehensive anti-violence campaigns, but it is the equally potent culturally-laden patriarchally oppressive systems, structures and attitudes that ensure women and children will remain powerless and dependent and thus continuously over-represented in the statistics of suffering.[6]

---

4   www.childfund.org.au/publications/stop-violence-against-women-and-children-papua-new-guinea
5   www.radioaustralia.net.au/pacific/radio/onairhighlights/solomon-islands-worst-country-for- sexual-violence-against-women-world-bank
6   www.unwomen.org/en/news/stories/2013/11/in-fiji-communities-mobilize-groundup-to-end-violence-against-women-and-girls

Western Samoa. From the superficial tourist perspective, this beautiful place appears relatively stable and settled. But from many Samoan men and women, with whom I am privileged to enjoy close professional and personal relationships, come very disturbing stories suggestive of a less than pristine experience for those most vulnerable in any society. Especially shocking are the findings of the 2005 WHO multi-country report on Women's Health and Sexual Violence. This document, deserving of priority consideration by all Christian churches, shows that 60% of Samoan women interviewed reported experience of physical violence by an intimate partner, 10% reported being beaten in pregnancy, an extraordinary 65% of women over the age of 15 years reported physical violence from a non-partner, i.e. parent, sibling, etc, while 55% felt unable to report violence at all. The reasons given by 86% of the Samoan women for non-reporting included considering the violence 'normal' or 'not serious'. In a small island nation literally awash with churches one would think that this unconscionable level of human suffering would incite unstoppable national outrage and subsequent demand for political action.[7]

The Cook Islands that determinedly lays claim to being the jewel of the Pacific is at once a very settled society that proudly upholds what are uncritically described as 'family values'. Churches proliferate all over the Cooks and attendance is impressive, yet a recent shadow report to government indicated the largest proportion of reported crime in the Cook Islands is for domestic violence.[8] Further reports suggest more than 30% of all Cook Island women experience domestic violence on a regular basis. Concurrently there is no substantial evidence of church leaders taking the necessary lead in addressing the sin of violence against the women of the Cook Islands.[9]

This leaves *Tonga*, in its still somewhat divided state—with some clinging to the last vestiges of an oppressively monarchical rulership system, and the vast majority determined to pursue the implementation of strong

---

7   www.unwomen.org/en/news/stories/2013/11/samoan-helpline-saves-lives

8   www.cookislandsnews.com/2013/August/Wed21/features.htm

9   The recently launched Cook Islands Family Health and Safety Study entitled "Te Ata O Te Ngakau" or "Shadows of the Heart" found that one in three Cook Islands Women have experienced violence of some form at the hand of their partner. But only one in five women reported that violence. That means that 80% of cases of domestic violence are going unreported. Ministry of Health, Cook Islands. 2014.

and viable twenty-first century democracy. Even in this staunchly—often matriarchally—structured society you can place a large 'ditto' under the Samoan statistics without any difficulty at all. As Tongan women and girls suffer domestic and sexual violence, the churches offer at best short term reactionary responses or, at worst, continue to condemn those women who 'ask for it' by endeavouring to step outside of culturally or ecclesially prescribed roles.[10]

Statistically speaking, the situation for too many beautiful, talented, loving, articulate, faith-filled women in the South Pacific region is singularly appalling. While I have chosen to focus on sexual and domestic violence,[11] it follows on that education, health, employment and economic well-being are all affected and the end result is either a diminished quality of life, and/or premature death either for women or for the children and grandchildren blessed into their care.[12]

Priority concern for those who are the least in any society is a Gospel imperative shared by all people of faith. Therefore, it seems unfathomable that the household of God itself could ever be indifferent to human suffering, let alone be complicit—even tangentially—in its continuation.

At a recent high level global gathering of religious, political and academic leaders who were considering the issue of Future Proofing the Pacific,[13] I was asked to address the following question: "what role should religious organisations (in the South Pacific) take in supporting traditional values while imparting skills and attitudes that will support 21st century globalisation …".

As a typically progressive question, it neatly failed to ask the prior question, of the historic role played by religious organizations in both indigenous and settler societies in our region. Throughout the South Pacific there is a predominance of oppressive conservative religious views and attitudes readily apparent, and particularly in those politically unstable societies now most at risk. These are the same societies that are over endowed with churches and missions, many of which were either established alongside or by missionaries and/or church leaders with historic links with either

10   mfftonga.files.wordpress.com/2012/12/tonga-vaw-report-final-2012.pdf
11   www.amnesty.org.nz/our-work/stop-violence-against-women/sexual-and-gender-based-violence-pacific
12   www.rrrt.org/projects/violence-against-women.
13   Conference held at Fale Pasefika, University of Auckland on 30 August 2006.

Australia or New Zealand, or with our colonial master forebears. Predictably, rather than coincidentally, these are also the very societies with the most appalling statistical records of violence against women. When women are attitudinally devalued, diminished, dismissed—as so readily happens in the context of conservative theological understandings and practices—then little wonder there is so little opportunity for women to flourish let alone to succeed.

It occurs to me however that religious progressives as a resources rich group spanning both Australia and New Zealand ecclesial interests are perfectly placed to pioneer a timely and very necessary redemptive response.

The challenge, therefore, is how best to transform the churches—structurally and attitudinally—to which we each belong, so that—irrespective of denominational 'differences'—we become the harbingers of the very best of authentically progressive religious teachings and practices? How do we collectively ensure that our worshipping communities become and remain exemplars of God's justice, that our churches become sites of prophetic wisdom, places of compassionate pastoral practice, which teach and practise ethical thinking and action, and so become 'institutions' that are valued when setting the Christ-like moral compass for all the citizens of our incredibly blessed portion of the beloved community?

The first challenge is to create and to ensure full and diverse participation in forums for public dialogue where all might begin the process of identifying and agreeing priorities for action. The next step is that of strategising how best to resource the religious activists or progressives who are inevitably at the forefront of enabling, encouraging, even shaming churches into becoming truly, believably, effectively and dynamically the beloved communities we all so desperately yearn for them to become for our time and in radically changed circumstances.

The question for religious progressives is whether we actually are comprehensively courageous enough to engage in the geo- and socio-political transformative work at the heart of the Gospel imperative? Have we the will—let alone the moral courage—to confront, critique, and to correct those theologically indefensible practices we see all too often in our regional societal contexts, and which are either ignored, minimised or—worse—theologically sanctioned by the established churches?

The question for *Pakeha* or white fella progressives is, of course, do they engage with the broader regional transformative project, or do they simply detach from their local established religious organisations and begin afresh with a completely self-contained, self-interested, and essentially intellectually abstracted spiritual agenda? The difficulty—in fact the impossibility—for indigenous religious progressives of beginning afresh in the South Pacific context, where cultural and religious tradition are so enmeshed as to be rendered incarnate in the people, makes the 'detached' proposition highly unlikely and therefore inappropriate.

The identity and context questions thus arise. Who are religious progressives and out of which particular contexts are they now contributing to the conversations on re-building 'life-giving, life affirming, life sustaining Christian relationality'?

I believe redemptive work of any kind can be and ought to be undertaken in an intentionally collaborative environment between indigenous and non-indigenous peoples. After all is not the theology of relationality something to do with being 'at one' with one another? Is not the spirit of love after all something to do with entering into one another's sufferings and joys? Does not the discourse of theology over—which Christians claim to have something of a literary franchise—contain relatively unambiguous words like common ground, common dreams, communion, compassion, mutuality, reconciliation, grace, and peace?

I know *Pakeha* liberals working with indigenous peoples fear being accused of being racist imperialists who cannot step aside from being dominant. For some it is the fear of being rejected and/or excluded in turn by indigenous people. For others this fear is now vindicated because you have already been 'told where to go' by indigenous activists! Now I do not for a moment want to try and lessen the agony of being told where to go, but I would simply caution you to remember just what our blessed mentor and Saviour did and said when he was told time and again, where to go.

The danger is that by acting with inappropriate impassivity or by fleeing the bully, liberal *Pakeha* have created space for opportunistic ideologues to occupy the high moral ground. Occupy it they have done, with relatively unfettered freedom and they have used it to articulate what at times are absurd and uncontested cultural claims. It often happens in the struggle for autonomy, inclusion, legitimacy or resourcing, that too little attention is paid to the unmasking of the broad and complex range of ideologically based interests always at stake within any political movement seeking for redemptive action and the restorative means to redress injustice.

One good example of this can be seen in the way in which the 'solution' to justified grievance about sustained educational failure among indigenous peoples has been popularly reframed (certainly within secular education) as a 'cultural recovery' project. Re-claim, re-store, re-cover, re-search and re-vise the tradition. Cultural recovery has thus become the largely uncritiqued contemporary populist catch-cry among indigenous educators and supported by white liberals. The problem is, it is being asserted without any effort to critically discern just exactly what is able—let alone needing and or deserving—to be re-claimed, re-stored, let alone interrogating in whose interests the entire project of cultural recovery is ultimately focused.

In the sometimes chaotic arena of race politics, indigenous peoples can also at times become so preoccupied with protecting cultural uniqueness, with upholding uninterrogated 'traditions', and with uncritically maintaining religious conservatism, that herein lies the danger of failing to see beyond the immediate horizon of what is clearly no longer a pristine South Pacific paradise.

That is why forums such as this gathering of religious progressives are of such critical importance. There needs to be the intentional creation of sacred public space where all people may have an opportunity to restate and debate contemporary 'race matters'. The contemporary social, political, economic, religious playing fields are far from level, but neither are the ruptures created by historic injustice unbridgeable.

I believe it to be possible for all people to be bold and defiant in our criticism of any form of xenophobia. We can be honest and candid about the need for civil responsibility and social accountability for all in our respective societies. Further, we can be charitable, compassionate and generous-hearted toward any political and/or theological perspective from which we can gain insight and wisdom to empower not only ourselves, but especially those most vulnerable around and among us.

It is out of this far more democratic milieu that I now predict the emergence of the real religious progressive project. I imagine religious progressives to be cultural 'prophets', whose visionary tendencies are focussed more on the common humanity; on what it means to be able to become and to remain fully, decently, lovingly, justly human in a complex and diverse world.

I imagine religious progressives as cultural 'prophets' being capable of transcending racial and every other single identity or particularity, with all their prescriptive limitations. In their place we celebrate an open-ended cultural spectrum within which the almost endless options of life-giving and life-sustaining cultural expression represented within the breadth of human diversity may be entitled to their own sense of legitimacy and of fulfilment.

The progressive 'cultural 'prophets' would assign the highest priority to exposing the hidden injustices established and maintained by exploitative economic ideologies. They would challenge and expose the myriad factors that threaten the future social, political, spiritual and economic wellbeing of all citizens, but particularly those most vulnerable, such as indigenous minorities, specifically women and girls.

Such cultural 'prophets' would insist that the voices of women—as those equally created precious human beings in the image and likeness of God— ought never be suppressed or silenced, or denied in any public sphere. Neither should women be limited to what is essentially a ritualised, predictable and purely performative role.

If religious progressives are indeed to be a credibly inclusive, proudly diverse movement, then the very best of hearts and minds must always be engaged in the processes of negotiation, protection, compromise and contribution. These are also times of potential enrichment beyond imagining as all peoples are opened to the possibilities that other traditions, cultural perspectives, and religious movements inevitably present.

I believe the future of the world we wish our grandchildren to flourish within depends on our collective will and wisdom to cooperate, to preserve only the very best of who we are. It also needs our spirit of generosity and our humility to be willing to receive the 'best' gifts, freely given, by those who have been equally blessed with gifts quite different to those of our own.

I want to conclude with a personal story. As an experienced grandmother of four indescribably beautiful little *mokopuna* or granddaughters I have always taken very seriously my grandmotherly responsibilities. One of these is to understand the complex and dynamic nature of this globalised world within which I am now responsible in small part for nurturing and sheltering these precious and as yet vulnerable little ones.

I want my *mokopuna* to know deeply and richly that they are children of the God of love and of justice. I will continue always to teach them that it is into a religious and spiritual realm that they have each been baptized. They are equally precious, equally blessed, equally responsible to become fully whom God created them to be. I want them each to know deeply the richness of the cultural heritages they have each been blessed with from their Maori and Fijian parents and all the ancestors before them. Within the socio-political realm of Aotearoa New Zealand and the wider South Pacific context I want them to be free to flourish, to be educated and ultimately to make their contributions as children of many lands and as citizens of the world. I want them to know deeply and respectfully the beauty of religious movements other than Christianity. I want them to know the many ways in which cultural traditions other than their own can also be abundantly life giving, hospitable, compassionate and just.

So it is—that as one with academic leadership responsibility for those preparing for the precious work of mission and ministry—I urge consideration of my call that is essentially made on behalf of all women of the South Pacific for all religious progressives to contribute to the creation of safe and loving pathways within our religious and cultural communities. These will be pathways that enable us to double our efforts to ensure many more women may take their rightful places at every table of decision making and of political influence; pathways that enable women to double their incalculably valuable contributions to the greater good of our fabulously envied South Pacific societies; and finally pathways that exemplify the fullness of the glory of God's infinitely perfect human creation, as men and women together in all things—acting justly, loving mercy and walking humbly with God.

12. Reclaiming Islam

Sherene Hassan

Aristotle said "it is the mark of an educated man to look for precision in each class of things just so far as the nature of the subject admits."[1] Many of us have become so entrenched in our own ideas, so averse to difference, that we struggle to do this. Nothing exemplifies this more than the xenophobic attitudes towards Muslims that are so pervasive in our society.

As someone who has been a community leader for nearly ten years, I have conducted over 1,000 talks on Islam to diverse audiences. I find staggering the level of misunderstanding that exists regarding a religion that dates back 1,400 years. Clearly, there are a number of areas of contention: *sharia*, and the assumption that Islam promotes misogyny and violence.

The intention of this chapter is to debunk some of the myths associated with Islam and explore the issues of *sharia*, Muslim women, and violence.

Sharia

The topic of *sharia* is often met by the wider community with a hysterical response. This is largely due to the abhorrent abuses of human rights carried out in the name of *sharia*, such as rape victims being stoned to death. It must be pointed out, however, that although cases like this have come to represent *sharia* in the west, most Muslims view this as a departure from Islamic teachings based on pre-Islamic practices, patriarchal misinterpretation and sheer ignorance.

The word *sharia* means 'path to water' and in a religious context, 'path to God'. The objectives of *sharia* are generally considered to be the preservation and protection of five things—a person's life, their religion, their family, intellect and their property and wealth. On this basis, not one 'Muslim' country in the world implements a just *sharia* system. The term *sharia* law is a misnomer because *sharia* is not law but a set of principles. Contrary to widespread opinion—and it must be admitted the misguided opinion of some Muslims—*sharia* is not set in stone. It is dynamic and

---

1 *Nicomachean Ethics* 1.1094b, 24.

fluid, and should take into consideration historical and societal context. The principles behind *sharia* remain the same, but the practicalities and applications are wide and varied and adapt according to time and place. They are judged by an individual scholar on a case-by-case basis, as opposed to a one size fits all approach. According to Muslim scholar Abdul-Azim Ahmed, the only people who attempted to crystallise and codify *sharia* were the British Government during the colonial era when they created the 'Anglo-Muhammadan Law' in an attempt to better control what was an otherwise democratic and decentralised system.[2]

Since *sharia* is based on the Qur'an and *Hadith* (sayings of the Prophet Muhammad, pbuh), it is divine and sacred. However, the application of *sharia* where it manifests in Islamic jurisprudence (*fiqh*) is the human attempt to understand the divine will.

According to Islamic law as enunciated by the caliph Umar, Muslims are supposed to uphold the laws of the land in which they reside, regardless of whether they live in a Muslim majority or Muslim minority country. Umar stated, "It is necessary upon a Muslim to listen to and obey the ruler, as long as one is not ordered to carry out a sin".[3] The term 'Islamic state' is not mentioned in the Qur'an and the Prophet Muhammad himself did not try to implement an Islamic state. It is well documented that the Prophet led a pluralistic society. The Prophet did not impose the prohibitions that existed in Islamic legal tradition on minority groups, so Jews, Christians and Pagans were permitted to drink alcohol, maintain their own places of worship and retain their own dress code.

Historically speaking, thirty years after the Prophet Muhammad's death, the Muslim world experienced a clear conceptual split between religious thought and political action.

Islamic empires were multi-religious and multi-cultural, and religious minorities were governed by their own laws. The term "Islam as a religion and state" was coined in the 1920s as a reaction to Western colonisation of the Muslim world.[4] The fact that there are only 80 legal verses in the Qur'an out of a total of 6,200 further supports the notion that the overwhelming emphasis of the text concerns spirituality.

---

2   On Religion; 5 Things about Sharia: www.onreligion.co.uk/5-things-about-shariah/
3   Sahih al-Bukhari, no. 2796 and Sunan Tirmidhi.
4   www.huffingtonpost.com/sumbul-alikaramali/whos-afraid-of-shariah_b_701331.htm

While it is often stated that Islam is incompatible with democracy, democratic concepts such as *shura* (consultation) and *aqd* (contract between the governed and the governing) are inherent in Islam.

Status of Women in Islam

More than ever, Islam has become inextricably linked with misogyny. One of the contributing factors to this are the many cultural practices that violate the teachings of Islam, yet exist in so-called Muslim countries such as female genital mutilation (FGM), honour killings and forced marriages.

A recent UNICEF report has warned that more than 30 million of the world's girls are at risk of genital mutilation over the next decade.[5] This deplorable act is an African tribal practice that predates Islam. Evidence from mummies indicates that it occurred three thousand years ago.[6] In the twenty-first century, there are Muslim, Christian and animist Africans that practice FGM. Both Christian and Muslim leaders in Egypt have publicly denounced the practice of FGM since 1998.[7] In March 2005, Dr Ahmed Talib, Dean of the Faculty of Sharia at Al-Azhar University, stated: "All practices of female circumcision and mutilation are crimes and have no relationship with Islam."[8] A representative of the Grand Mufti of Egypt, quoted in the same news report, urged state authorities to redouble efforts to halt the practice that, he said, "has social, rather than religious, roots."

The debate about honour killings has been brought to the fore once again in the wake of shocking revelations that cases have recently been reported in Canada. In response, over thirty Imams from the US and Canada signed a *fatwa* unequivocally condemning honour killings, domestic violence and misogyny, which was issued by the Islamic Supreme Council of Canada.[9] Here again we are talking about an ancient practice that dates back to 1,200 BCE.

On a similar note, forced marriages are forbidden in Islam. According to Islamic law, a marriage contract is null and void if either of the two parties entering that marriage is coerced into that marriage.[10]

---

5   www.abc.net.au/worldtoday/content/2013/s3808976.htm
6   See Knight, "Curing Cut or Ritual Mutilation?.
7   www.ghanaweb.com/GhanaHomePage/NewsArchive/artikel.php?ID=77396
8   www.egyptindependent.com/news/mufti-s-deputy-reiterates-female-circumcision-prohibited- religion
9   www.cbc.ca/news/canada/toronto/canadian-fatwa-condemns-honour-killings-1.1161892
10   www.muslimahcompass.org/index.php?option=com_content&view=article&id=427 &Itemid=7

One of the fundamental problems we face is that the actions of Muslims are interpreted as a faithful and legitimate representation of their faith. Thus, if a Muslim girl is forced into marriage the assumption is that this is because of Islam, not in spite of it. The underlying assumption is that all Muslims always act in accordance with their faith. Such an assumption results in the idea of an essentialised religiously determined Muslim. This is not only dehumanising and neglects the obvious diversity and complexity in how Islam is lived out in individual Muslim lives (1.2 billion lives in fact), but it also holds Muslims to a standard to which no other faith community is held. For while we are capable of exercising common sense in not assuming that a self professed Catholic or Jew's actions will be motivated and informed by their faith, we nonetheless presume that any action norm or value enacted by a Muslim is a performance of their religion. Herein lies one of the reasons for the gross conflation between cultural or individuals action, on the one hand and the teachings of Islam on the other.

Islamic teachings espouse equality between the sexes. This is evident in the saying of the Prophet Muhammad, "All people are equal like the teeth of a comb. There is no merit of an Arab over a non-Arab, nor of a white over a black nor of a male over a female."[11] Patriarchal misinterpretation, however, has undermined these egalitarian principles and resulted in institutionalised injustices against women in the name of Islam. These distorted, gender biased interpretations of the Qur'an and *Hadith* have been challenged by numerous female and male scholars.[12] Islamic feminism explicates the idea of gender equality as part and parcel of the Qur'anic notion of equality of all human beings and calls for the implementation of gender equality in the state, civil institutions and everyday life. There are countless examples around the world of women claiming their place in Islamic discourse and becoming agents for change.

In Turkey for example, 400 female scholars (*vaizes*) have been appointed by the government to monitor the work done by Imams across the nation.[13] Human rights organisation, *Sisters in Islam* continues to advocate for legal reform and social equality for women and promotes human rights and

---

11   edoc.bibliothek.uni-halle.de/servlets/MCRFileNodeServlet/HALCoRe_derivate_00002150/ Constructing the Notion.pdf

12   Badran, *Feminism in Islam.*

13   www.csmonitor.com/2005/0427/p04s01-woeu.html

civil liberties both in Malaysia and worldwide.[14] In August 2013, Saudi Arabia's cabinet has passed legislation recognizing all forms of abuse, including domestic violence as offences punishable by law,[15] a significant breakthrough for female activists in the region.

It must be pointed out that although many western feminists claim to champion the cause of Muslim women, in reality their actions are counterproductive. All they achieve by lambasting a faith that has enriched the lives of millions is to alienate the very people they purport to liberate. I have encountered many western commentators who perceive Muslim women to be a monolith; victims of a misogynistic religion. They maintain that enlightenment and liberation can only be achieved through the abandonment of Islamic practice and the aping of western culture. To the Muslim ear, western feminist discourse reeks of colonial imperialism as often feminists only defend a woman's right to choose when she chooses to abandon Islamic norms, not when she chooses to adopt them.

Violence in Islam

A number of commentators have failed to contextualise the verses permitting warfare in the Qur'an. When Islam started in Arabia 1,400 years ago, Muslims suffered persecution at the hands of the pagan Arabs who worshipped 360 idols. The Muslims were instructed by the Prophet Muhammad not to retaliate and to patiently persevere.[16] As a result of this divine requirement for absolute pacifism, many Muslims were tortured and killed by the pagan Arabs. After thirteen years of suffering, verses were revealed in the Qur'an permitting the Muslims to fight back against the disbelievers (22:39–40). There are exhortations to peace which in almost every case follow these violent verses; "Thus if they let you be and do not make war on you and offer peace, God does not allow you to harm them." (Qur'an 4:90).

Sanctity of life is paramount in Islam. It is stated in the Qur'an (5:32), "If one kills an innocent person it is as if they have killed the whole of humanity." Injunctions to blanket violence against non-Muslims stem from misreading of the Qur'an and grow out of social and political conflict.

---

14   www.asianews.it/news-en/Sisters-in-Islam,-Muslim-women-against-religious-extremism-1842.html

15   www.huffingtonpost.com/2013/08/29/saudi-arabia-domestic-abuse-ban_n_3836591.html

16   Aly, *People Like Us*, 162.

A Final Thought

Politicians often employ divisive rhetoric and constantly single out the Muslim community. The more this group is problematised and demonised, the more likely Muslims will become insular and less inclined to engage with the wider community. Commentators are often quick to point out the failure of multiculturalism in Europe and lament that Australia is going down the same path, however, the situation in Europe is vastly different to that of Australia. In Germany, for example, it wasn't until the year 2000 that Turks were allowed to take up citizenship.[17] Professor Jytte Klausen from Brandeis University studied Muslims in six European countries.[18] She identified a direct relationship between restrictive citizenship laws and economic, social and political isolation of Muslims hypothesising that the greater the hurdles to citizenship, the worse the plight of Muslims.

The vast majority of Muslims are committed to justice and promoting social cohesion. By judging Muslims by their worst examples and tarnishing them with the same brush we undermine their humanity and demean over a billion people—one in five of those who inhabit our planet. Clearly a more nuanced approach is needed rather than the constant placing of Islam and Muslims in the dock.

---

17   migrationeducation.de/22.1.html?&rid=205&cHash=b4f5e94683cfb892ed8971ba14bf4
eb8

18   www.strategicdialogue.org/PublicPolicyMuslimsWEB.pdf

13. Leaving the hut

Heather Carter

I have been invited to offer a reflection on the significance of progressive Christianity for me as an Australian woman who has combined family and professional responsibilities, while staying connected with the church. My professional roles have all been connected with the law and I served ten years as a Judge of the Family Court of Australia, preceded by twenty years as a barrister at the Melbourne and Perth Bars and a prior period as a solicitor. My family responsibilities have been probably the most important part of my life. I have three children and they, their spouses and their children, are now again all living in Melbourne—which has not always been the case. The grandchildren range in age from seven to twenty three and give a great richness to my life. My personal interests include cooking, travel, fine dining and wine appreciation, along with a long term interest in the West Coast Eagles AFL team (a legacy from several years living in Western Australia); although my real football connection is to Rugby Union. For someone such as me, what is the practical use of all this 'progressive' theological thought? And what is 'progressive Christianity', in any case? Roger Wolsey offers a description that resonates with me.

> Progressive Christianity is an approach to the Christian faith that is influenced by post-liberalism and post-modernism and proclaims: Jesus as Christ, Saviour and Lord: emphasises the Way and teachings of Jesus, not merely his person: emphasises God's immanence, not merely God's transcendence; leans towards Panentheism rather than supernatural theism; emphasises salvation here and now instead of primarily in Heaven later; emphasises being saved for robust, abundant/eternal life over being saved from Hell; emphasises the social/communal aspects of salvation instead of merely the personal; stresses social justice as integral to Christian discipleship; takes the bible seriously but not necessarily literally, embracing a more interpretive metaphorical understanding; emphasises orthopraxy instead of orthodoxy (right actions over right beliefs); embraces reason as well as paradox and mystery - instead of blind allegiance to rigid doctrines and dogmas; does not consider

homosexuality to be sinful; and it does not claim that Christianity is the only valid or viable way to connect to God (is non-exclusive).[1]

I wish I had known about and understood that much earlier. My Mother and Father were rare churchgoers. They were good people and believed in God, but they did not care much for religion. My sisters and I were taught a simple childish prayer to be said before bed. My older sister and I attended Sunday school as we wished. I continued for several years. I now know that this church was not at all progressive, indeed quite the reverse; but I quite enjoyed it. I confess that I also enjoyed wearing my best clothes. I accepted all the stories at face value and became something of a biblical scholar; that is to say, I could recite large slabs of the Bible and was awarded several prizes for this.

However, over time and with increasing depth, the Bible stopped making sense, not that I could even acknowledge that at the time. To question the stories in the Old Testament was bad enough, but according to the "teaching" I had received, to question the New Testament must be heresy. So I simply stopped going to Sunday School and Church. It no longer seemed relevant and indeed was quite uncomfortable. I had not been seeking spiritual challenge, but intellectual integrity intervened. I do not believe I completely lost my faith, but I suspect I lost my religion, and certainly I lost my theology. I had not heard at that stage George Gershwin's "It Ain't Necessarily So" from Porgy and Bess ("... the things that you're liable to read in the Bible ...").

My recovery of any understanding and acceptance of the Bible only commenced after I discovered it was permissible to doubt.[2] I had earlier come to understand that the Old Testament could be read as stories and myths, but my old "training" shrouded the New Testament with an impenetrable barrier. In particular, scientific and rational difficulties with bodily resurrection and the Virgin Birth raised real challenges to traditional interpretations and doctrines. I never could come to grips with substitutionary atonement. However, I learnt—not in a flash of enlightenment but gradually—that the New Testament should be seen through its own context of history, politics and culture. In turn, this led to my understanding and rejection of what I would now call "bad theology". I

---

1   Wolsey, *Kissing Fish*, ch. 2 (no page number in web edition).
2   See Webb, *In Defence of Doubt*.

need to make it clear that I have become a consumer of progressive religious thought, although I am neither clergy nor academic.

Two ministers in particular were instrumental in starting me on the progressive path. Both were ministers at my parish Church, Ewing Memorial Uniting Church in Melbourne. The first was Rev. Greg Crowe, who has now been called to Ewing twice. In between those two periods, Rev. John Smith was our minister for some five years. Both became and remain my friends. I do not know whether they knew it, but they were also my earliest teachers and guides in progressive Christian theology.

Michael Morwood, the author of *Is Jesus God?*, spoke at Ewing several times. He relieved me of the view of God as an "Elsewhere God," an old man—probably robed in something resembling a dressing gown—who lived somewhere "up there" in the sky and who determined whether and how to punish us. I am now certain that God is a God of love. I am certain that God is not an interventionist God, but I am not certain of much more than that. To me, God is a mystery. I cannot "know" or explain God. As Val Webb asked in her book, *Stepping Out With The Sacred*, "is the Divine within us, within nature, within everything, or is everything within the Sacred?"

"Something for the Spirit" has been a place of real grace for me. It grew from a discussion group of some six people in 2005 to become a monthly meeting where often twenty or thirty people attend on a Sunday evening. A smaller group also meets mid-week. The meetings are held in a private home although very occasionally, when a larger venue is required, we will gather at Ewing Memorial Church. This was a deliberate decision to keep the meetings casual, informal and not too "churchy". We have a bite to eat and drink. Our leader is Lorna Henry and it is her home in which we have continued to meet. Ministers of Ewing attend at times and participate. The attendees may come from Ewing or some other church. Some do not attend any church. A topic is organized. It may be a book, a DVD or a talk and discussion around that follows. The discussion is not constrained. There are no right or wrong ideas. It seems to me that it must be something like the home churches of the early days. It is a small and faith supporting community. Through it, we have been able to read and discuss the readings and thoughts of prominent progressives, including John Shelby Spong, Marcus Borg, John Dominic Crossan, Karen Armstrong, Lorraine

Parkinson and others. I have valued these opportunities to question and explore, and I have valued the support of other members of the group as I have done so.

The "Progressive Christian Network of Victoria" (PCNV) has been another important part of my journey into a more progressive understanding of Christianity. PCNV was launched in early 2006. It aims to promote progressive Christian thought and practice; explore the implications of critical biblical scholarship and the emerging proposals of eminent, contemporary theologians, scholars and others; and to explore alternatives to traditional religious beliefs and practises as well as new ways to understand religious faith. PCNV is non denominational and reaches out to other faith traditions. Some nine or ten events each year are usually arranged, sometimes lectures and sometimes panel discussions. There are over three hundred paying members and about one hundred more people are on the Internet list. PCNV has coordinated and promoted speaking tours by eminent local and international progressives. It publishes a regular newsletter. Books and study resources are catered for by its bookstore.

Through PCNV and Common Dreams conferences, I have been able to meet many leading Australian and International progressive thinkers and writers. It is one thing to read the writings of the progressive thinkers. It is even better to see and hear them speak. Connecting with others who are on the same journey and engaging with the leading progressive religion thinkers has been important to me.

At the recent Common Dream 3 conference in Canberra, I was offered a feast of connections! With over five hundred registrations and a speaking roster headed by Marcus Borg, I enjoyed a smorgasbord of progressive religious thought. A cast of twenty-one people delivered twelve keynote addresses and public lectures, fourteen workshops, presentations or panel discussions.[3]

Finding safe places to pursue the questions that matter deeply is so important. In addition to "Something for the Spirit", PCNV seminars and the Common Dreams conferences, I have been privileged to travel with John Dominic Crossan, Marcus Borg, and their wives, when my husband and I journeyed with them as part of a group travelling through Turkey.

---

3   The line up of international and Australian speakers included Bruce Sanguin, David Felten, Val Webb, Lorraine Parkinson, Aviva Kipen, and Margret Mayman.

We visited many of the places where Paul had been, and others where he may have been. Crossan and Borg are world-renowned biblical scholars and authors. Each night during our odyssey we would learn more of the significance of the history and architecture in which we were immersed which enhanced the context in which we viewed Paul (and Jesus). It was one of the most significant and helpful of my steps along the progressive path.

While grateful for all that I have now learned, I remain resentful that much of the thinking and teaching of students of theology, seminarians and the like did not find its way—as often as it should—into the sermons delivered by many of the clergy I experienced. There was—and sometimes still is—a division between what our ministers learnt and what they tell us. I am totally convinced that the decline of attendance at traditional Churches can be traced to the lack of relevance which people not only experienced in what they were told from the pulpit, but which they also commenced to challenge. Many people appear to have left in frustration.

Of particular concern for me is the lack of young people, whether attending Church or participating in progressive religion groups. The "oldies" may have found a different pathway, but I have met only a few people under 35 or 40 who profess to be interested in either traditional or progressive Christianity. It is even worse for the children. Books and study resources for adult progressives are becoming more readily available but there is an enormous difference in the sort of material that is suitable for children, especially young children.[4]

Peter Kennedy was a Roman Catholic priest at St. Mary's in South Brisbane. His priestly faculties were removed by his Archbishop in 2009 for allegedly contravening some parts of Catholic doctrines. Many of his supporters followed him to St Mary's-in-exile, located at the Trades and Labour Council building in South Brisbane. He once spoke at Ewing and to a PCNV workshop. He told this story which I reproduce with his permission:

> It was time for the travellers to move out from the safety of the hut. The hut they were in was familiar and well lit, but they knew that it could no longer serve them. It was time to venture out into dark and unfamiliar terrain, to seek out a new place of life. As they moved away from the hut,

---

4   One organisation which has addressed this is ProgressiveChristianity.org in USA that has recently prepared and issued a number of resources for Children such as books, songs and significantly, a children's curriculum "A Joyful Path".

the light its windows cast on the world outside grew dim, until there was very little to guide them. They had to move along tentatively. The directions they decided on were often mistaken and they had to rely on each other for any progress they made.

Not all shared the same feelings about what they were undertaking. Where one grew frustrated, another continued to trust. Where one took heart from the adventure, another started to turn back to the light of the hut. It was a strange and unprecedented situation for them all. The only ones who knew where they were going were the ones who turned back, for they were turning to light and familiarity. But anyone embracing the future was at a loss. The only knowledge they possessed was the wisdom that accumulated as they explored their way forward.

That to me sums up the progressive movement. I am still very much at the beginning of my path but I am very sure of one thing: I don't want to go back to the hut!

Afterword: What's the next big challenge for Progressive Christianity?

Bruce Sanguin

No, I'm delighted that liberal theologians do their best to do what Pio Nono said shouldn't be done—try to accommodate Christianity to modern science, modern culture, and democratic society. If I were a fundamentalist Christian, I'd be appalled by the wishy-washiness of their version of the Christian faith. But since I am a non-believer who is frightened of the barbarity of many fundamentalist Christians (e.g., their homophobia), I welcome theological liberalism. Maybe liberal theologians will eventually produce a version of Christianity so wishy-washy that nobody will be interested in being a Christian any more. If so, something will have been lost, but probably more will have been gained.

Richard Rorty[1]

Christianity did indeed need to come to terms with the challenges of modernism, if it was to remain credible. Those challenges to traditional Christianity include: the rise of the authority of a scientific, evidence-based approach to reality, a renewed confidence in reason; biblical criticism; a downplaying of the focus on original sin; and the primacy of personal experience over the authority of the church.

Progressive Christianity—a twenty-first century expression of liberal Christianity—is an attempt to "produce a version of Christianity that is [*not*] so wishy-washy that nobody will be interested in being a Christian anymore".

I have been involved with progressive Christianity for virtually all of my twenty-eight years serving as a congregational minister with the United Church of Canada. In the past eight years I have been privileged to travel and give talks to progressive audiences around the world. So, what do I identify is the next big challenge facing this expression of Christianity?

We are at an opportune moment in history to bridge more successfully the ancient divide between mystery and reason, between the invisible, ineffable forces that shape our lives and the visible, measurable ones, between religion

---

1   The transcript of the original interview is no longer available, but Rohr is cited by Ben Myers, "Faith & Theology" blog: www.faith-theology.com/2008/02/richard-rorty-on-liberal-theology.html

and science. This opportunity seems to come up for grappling by humans every 500 years or so. How do we arrive at a place where these distinct domains are not resolved through division, but rather exist in a relationship of polarity and mutuality? Great creativity, the realm of emergence—or what the prophet Isaiah called the "new thing" that G_d is doing—arises as we hold the tension, and refuse to resolve it one side or the other.

Progressive Christianity stands at a crossroads that has surprising similarities to a particular moment of Greek history. Starting in the early sixth century BCE, the two advancing trends of naturalism and rationalism gained a foothold in the Greek psyche. Naturalism located the causes of human affairs, not in the Olympian gods and goddesses, but rather in nature itself. Rationalism looked, not to the ancient Homeric legends and mythology, but to the intellect and to reason for wisdom and moral guidance. Culminating with the Sophists, who applied both of these trends in the service of pragmatic success in the world, the ancient vision of the archaic Greek consciousness—that the archetypal order of the heavens and the affairs of Earth were inextricably and mysteriously woven, together— was rent asunder.

After a twenty-five hundred year hiatus, modernism emerged, intent upon once again ridding the world of superstition and myth. We are living in an era when the soul of humanity, at least in the Western world, has been almost completely seduced by the modern version of naturalism and rationalism— scientific materialism. Personally I find this metaphysical worldview— essentially, that matter pulled itself up by the bootstraps and produced Shakespeare and the great religions—less credible than a spiritual worldview.

In the Greek world, the odd philosopher, such as Pythagoras, felt a profound sense of disenchantment with the creeping naturalism of Greek philosophy. In response he developed a mystery school in which reason and mystery were granted equal status. Unfortunately, the cult of Pythagoras was so highly secretive that we do not know much about his teachings. The brilliant minds and hearts of Socrates and Plato eventually emerged. Platonic idealism, whatever you might think about it, with its archetypal forms or ideas informing human affairs, was in part, an attempt to allow a dimension of transcendence and mystery to re-integrate the wisdom of the ancients, affirmed in the Jesus prayer: As in heaven, so on Earth.

My basic concern with the trajectory of progressive Christianity is that it is defaulting, often unconsciously, to scientific materialism. Like the ancient Greeks, we seem surprisingly willing to let go of our myth and its core metaphors, symbols, and narratives, and reduce the mystery down to values and virtues.

How, then, do we leverage the enormous potential of living in the creative middle space—the polarity provided by the creative tension that exists between mystery and reason, between science and spirituality?

Resolving this polarity in favour of science and reason results in flatland, a life without depth or horizon, reduced to matter and the meaninglessness of a universe that is going nowhere, very fast. On the other hand, resolving this in favour of mystery and spirituality results in an ungrounded, anything goes, woo-woo spirituality. We need to find a way forward that includes, yet transcends, the valid insights of modernity and post-modernity—the dignity of the individual experience, an evidence-based worldview, biblical criticism, that truth is embedded, without exception in context and perspective, and the ethic of inclusivity.

An evolutionary theology and worldview is one way forward. I have been developing such a theology and practice in the context of congregational ministry for the past twenty years. I am continuing this exploration on my on-line teaching site, *Home For Evolving Mystics* (at brucesanguin.com).

This begins with the premise that if Christianity is to be credible it must take evolution seriously, and by seriously I mean re-imagine theology, ecclesiology, liturgy, and spiritual practice in light of the evolutionary story of the universe. This acknowledges the overwhelming consensus of the scientific community, without necessarily ceding the ground to scientific materialism. We are involved with a universe that is evolving and if G_d—whatever we mean by that term—is in any way involved in the world as we know it, then evolution holds one key to divine knowing (*gnosis*).

> Is evolution a theory, a system or a hypothesis? It is much more: it is a general condition to which all theories, all hypotheses, all systems must bow and which they must satisfy henceforth if they are to be thinkable and true.[2]

I start with the premise that the twenty-first century Christian now is the steward of two sacred narratives, the great story of the evolutionary process, and the story of Scripture. We need to develop literacy in both stories if we are to be credible and relevant. Incidentally it is my experience

---

2   Teilhard de Chardin, *The Phenomenon of Man*, 219.

that many liberal Christians are not literate in either story. We have our work cut out for us! I don't mean that we all need to be scientists, but the broad outlines of the story of evolution, the story of 'deep time', is critical. The broad outline is: matter and energy emerge from the 'no of all nothing'; life emerges from matter and energy; consciousness emerges from life; the capacity for transcendent love emerges from consciousness.

Next, I posit that G_d's first big idea, as the originating mystery, is to materialize or incarnate. From the womb of this originating heart and intelligence, emerges a world made in the image of this undivided one. Evolution then is a divine strategy for making a world that can make itself. But G_d is involved in this process as a divine milieu of love, drawing all of creation towards perfection (or completion) non-coercively. Much of creation has already realized its perfection. Bacteria, for example, reached a perfect state and found their niche, providing the foundation for all of life to emerge on our planet. Humans are that dimension of creation that remains imperfect. This imperfection is also our glory. In this state of imperfection, we experience a yearning for more beauty, truth, and goodness. The enactment of that yearning to transcend our current condition is our capacity for creativity. We are creators. This creativity can be harnessed for love or for destruction. One of religion's primary roles is to shape this creativity to reflect the heart and mind of the originating mystery. This is what is meant by "being made in the image of G_d" in an evolutionary worldview. In us, natural selection has become *actual* selection. Our soul's yearning is to realise—that is, make real—the originating heart and mind of G_d. The evolutionary process itself then is imagined to be moving purposively (but not in a predetermined way) toward this heart and mind. As we awaken to this allurement, as our deepest identity and vocation, we discover our unique purpose. As well, we then tap into what Pierre Teilhard de Chardin called a natural "zest", which is the sacred, evolutionary impulse manifest the heart and mind of G_d.

This means, among other things, that Jesus was not the only occasion of incarnation, as believed in traditional Christianity. He is not an interruption of natural processes, but rather the *eruption* of a natural grace—the flowering of 13.8 billion year evolutionary process. The early church's intuition of his uniqueness was expressed in historic doctrines about Jesus being fully human and fully divine. In an evolutionary paradigm, there is no need to dispute this. Rather, we add another dimension to his uniqueness—

196

fully human, fully divine, and fully cosmic. Theologian, Raimon Panikkar, calls Jesus *cosmotheandric*, recognising that in an evolutionary worldview, the natural cosmic dimension provides context for fully human and fully divine.

One implication of this is that the universe, having arrived at the capacity for a Jesus of Nazareth—the full *personalisation* of the evolutionary process—can now do Jesus! Priest and geologian, Thomas Berry, called evolution a series of "irreversible transformations". By this he meant that once a useful structure, system, or process has emerged, it provides a foundation, or a starting place for more complex structures, and in this case, humans, to emerge. This means that the church exists, in the spirit of Jesus himself, to transcend (and not to copy) Jesus. The question is not "what would Jesus do?"—but rather, "what would the evolutionary spirit, that animated Jesus, do in our day and age"? Everything that was projected on to him historically is actually an externalisation of human potential to realise the image of God in the world. This externalisation, which resulted in many of our creeds, doctrines and dogmas, was a necessary evolutionary step. Jesus became an effective screen upon which to project the human being in the process of moving toward completion—spiritual evolution.

What this means is that the future of progressive Christianity revolves around making mystics. Karl Rahner accurately stated: "the Christian of the future will either be a mystic or he will be nothing at all." My working definition of mysticism comes from Evelyn Underhill's classic book, *Practical Mysticism.*

> Mysticism is the art of union with Reality. The mystic is a person who has attained that union in greater or lesser degree; or who aims at and believes in such attainment.[3]

Underhill points out that we know a thing or a person only by uniting with it. All desire for knowledge is motivated by this longing to know. But for the mystic this knowing is not the analytic, rational mode of knowing (although, there is a place for this way of knowing). Rather it is the intuitive or empathic way of knowing that helps us to know a thing or a person in itself, and not as a projection or an image that reflects our own ego. This definition honours the modernist impulse to grant greater authority to personal experience over traditional forms of authority. To the extent that

---

3   Underhill, *Practical Mysticism*, 3.

historic creeds and doctrines grew out of a purely rationalistic or analytic way of knowing, they can be dismissed. But my sense is that much doctrine actually expresses a deeper mystery that grows out of this mystic sense that comes from empathic or intuitive knowing.

Young people especially are looking for inspiration and not more information. Information they can get though Google. They want a direct experience of Spirit. The brilliance of an evolutionary theology is that it is grounded in such immediacy. To experience the evolutionary impulse, from within, as the yearning for more intimacy, intensity, immensity, and intentionality (or creativity) is to experience Spirit's longing to realise the heart and mind in the world. The practice begins with a more nuanced theology of desire. Christianity, including liberal Christianity, continues to have a rather deep-seated suspicion of desire or human yearning. We tend to lump all desire into a form of yearning that arises out of personal and cultural trauma that stains our desires and directs back to the ego or small self. But we can distinguish—and must—distinguish between this small "y" yearning, and the big "Y" Yearning of the soul, for an increase of beauty, truth, and goodness. This, in fact, may be the core spiritual practice of evolutionary spirituality.

To shift into our Yearning is to connect with our Cosmic Self or even our Christic Self. It begins with a mystic identification with this Yearning to Become, for union with Reality. And Reality, as we have noticed, is this evolutionary process of becoming. This is the most effective way to transcend, while including, the ego. An evolutionary worldview integrates our reptilian and mammalian legacies, which ground us in our earliest instincts for survival, sex, sustenance, and status. But these are contextualised by the intellectual orientation, and the intuitive or felt sense, that we are being swept along by a great tide of love, that is active in the evolutionary process itself. We are, in truth and not just romantically, the interior dimension of the evolutionary process awakening to itself. We are the personalised presence of this process. We are not only determined by history, as is characteristic of other forms of life. We are also *determiners*, capable of conscious evolution. As we exercise and enact this power we are filled with what eleventh-century mystic, Hildegard of Bingen, called *veriditas*, the greening energy of the cosmos itself. We not only envision that future that Jesus called the kin(g)dom of G_d. We are empowered from within to take our part in its realisation. We become the greening energy, personalised.

Sufi mystic/poet Rumi captures this power of realisation, in a poem called *The Theatre of Freedom*.

> In my divine studio
> what I have been working on is this:
> Revealing
> A more realistic picture of God,
>
> Tearing down the cruel walls
> That separates you from the tenderness of Fire.
>
> Someone must be withholding
> The crucial lines
> In all those stories you have heard
> of our Friend,
>
> For there is still too much fear
> And pallor upon your cheeks,
>
> And I rarely see you
> In the marvelous Theatre of Freedom …
> Something has happened to your youthful passion,
> That great fuel
> You once had to define yourself
> Against becoming tamed.
>
> And your eyes now often tell me
> That your once vital talent to extract joy
> From the air
> Has fallen into a sleep
>
> I long for the day when you will join me
> In knowing
> The extraordinary humor
> And all the enchanting realities
> Of the infinite performances of God.[4]

---

4   Ladinksy and Owen (eds.), *The Purity of Desire*.

If the church of the twenty-first century is to survive and thrive, we must turn our congregations into divine studios, like the one Rumi describes. We need to be about tearing down the "cruel walls" that separate us from the "tenderness of Fire"—the love of God that Jesus knew as the deepest core of his own being. This is a love that burns away despair, even in the face of the undeniable crises of our age. But I am convinced that because of our uncritical adoption of the indignities of the modern and postmodernist worldviews, and the subsequent loss of the heart of the Christ mystery, we are losing the battle for the soul of the world. Never was there a more immediate and urgent need for a well-informed, passionate expression of the Christian faith.

There is a cartoon of two men sitting at a table looking at a glass of water that is either half-full or half-empty. The thought bubble above one of their heads reads: "Half-empty". The thought bubble above the head of the other reads: "Half full, but it's probably polluted".

It is my experience that we are, as a group, 'apocaholics'—that is, we are addicted to bad news, apocalyptic scenarios. We seem to revel in how bad the world is, as though if we convince enough people about how awful our species is, we will rediscover our purpose. I was guilty of this myself in my first ten years of ministry. In seminary, I was steeped in an analysis of the evils of our social systems. It was actually the main takeaway. I am grateful for the perspective I received. But I preached the social gospel week after week—until the members of the congregation pleaded with me to preach a sermon about beauty and love every once in a while. If we are going to point out how awful the world is (and yes, our planet is in peril) then we had better have some kind of spiritual resourcing available to deal with the bleak realities. But the problem, as I see it, is that while we have rightly relinquished any belief in a G_d that is going to intervene to save us, we do not really have an alternative.

It has been said that without a vision, the people will perish. It is also true that without hope, the people will stay home on Sunday morning. It has been noticed that within an evolutionary worldview, there is a kind of natural optimism. We do not ignore the realities of our planetary challenges. Rather, we set them within the context of deep time. The universe has shown, both cosmologically and biologically, incredible resilience. The life force is not to be minimised. Earth, for example, has survived five previous extinctions. Earth not only survived, mind you, but actually thrived!

Nassim Taleb, Distinguished Professor of Risk Engineering at New York University Polytechnic School of Engineering, and author of *Anti-Fragility*, suggests that we need to trust this built-in feature of the universe in our life. Things actually need to be picked up and thrown around a bit in order to realise their full evolutionary potential.

The evolutionary worldview notices for example that crises function to provoke the new intelligences required to solve the problems presented by challenging life conditions. The crisis, in other words, is often the birth of a new order. Even as we engage the challenging life conditions that threaten us, we can step back and ponder what new intelligences are emerging as a result. This orientation can help us achieve what theologian Ronald Rolheisser calls the condition of the mellow heart—deeply engaged with reality as it is, and yet trusting that the intelligence, heart, and resilience of a 13.8 billion year process that is positively biased *for* life, and not against it/us, is at work.

A friend of mine and former member of a congregation I served, Trevor Malkinson, writes:

> I spent my twenties at university immersed in the postmodern milieu, and I was an angry critic of much of what I saw in the world around me. The cancer, the 'third world' death squads, the clear cuts, the addiction and the wars, the exploitation and the soulless skyscrapers, the superficial desires and rivers of pop. It could all go fuck itself. I was typical of a certain part of the postmodern ethos, in that I shared a certain dark view of the world, a cynicism, a gloomy negativity toward modernity and capitalism and all that it had wrought. That wasn't all I was, but I was definitely this, and it wasn't until I read Dorothy Soelle's statement that something clicked for me—all this outrage was the exact flipside of a deep love for the world, for life, for Earth and its inhabitants.

Soelle writes that "we are all guardians of joy and responsible for making life's beauty visible and audible". The Psalmist's praise of the Creator, and creation's participation in that praise, is not a denial of injustice. It is rather the very source of our felt sense of indignity. If we are not preaching as much about beauty as injustice, if our liturgies are mere platforms for a social justice agenda, rather than domains of creative emergence, if we convey a cynicism about the world and our lives, without any source of grace with which to engage these powers and principalities, we cannot honestly think that we are proclaiming good news in the spirit of Jesus.

As I have stated earlier, evolutionary theology and practices appeal to a younger generation inasmuch as it includes, but transcends, the tradition. It has the power to lift them above the two choices typically on offer to the contemporary university student: either the bleak materialism of rationalism or fundamentalist religion. An evolutionary paradigm gets us unstuck from the reactive phase, vis a vis, conservative expressions of faith. There is simply no need to engage in the debate. At the same time, we present a source of natural grace, the intimate, but non-coercive presence of a hidden wholeness, traditionally identified with G_d. Finally, it provides a spiritual practice that I call evolutionary mysticism, a direct tapping into a sacred, evolutionary impulse, a shift from the contracting tendencies of egoic yearning, into ever-expansive soul yearnings, allured by the promise of a felt primordial love intimately involved in this great adventure of becoming.

About the contributors

Revd Glynn Cardy was for several years the vicar of St Matthew-in-the-City, Auckland, Aotearoa New Zealand. In July 2013 he announced his resignation from St Matthew's to accept a call to become the minister at The Community of St Luke (Presbyterian) in Auckland. Glynn was a Presenter at the CD3 Conference (2013) in Canberra.

The Hon. Heather Carter is a retired Judge of the Family Court of Australia. She practised earlier as solicitor and barrister for some twenty-five years in Melbourne and Perth. She is an active member of the Uniting Church in Australia and the Progressive Christian Network of Victoria.

Revd David Felten is Pastor at Fountains United Methodist Church, Fountain Hills, Arizona. Together with fellow United Methodist pastor, Jeff Procter-Murphy, David created the *Living the Questions* program. David was a Presenter at both CD1 (2007) and CD3 (2013) Conferences.

Revd Professor Sir Lloyd Geering, ONZ, GNZM, CBE is New Zealand's best-known and most controversial commentator on theological issues. He is the author of at least ten books, his latest being *From the Big Bang to God* (Polebridge, 2013), and served as a workshop leader at the CD2 Conference (2010) in Melbourne.

Sherene Hassan is a director of the Islamic Museum of Australia and has served as Vice-President and Secretary of the Islamic Council of Victoria, the peak body for 90,000 Victorian Muslims, since 2007. Formerly a chemistry and physics teacher, she was a presenter at the CD2 Conference (2010) in Melbourne.

Revd Rex A. E. Hunt is a retired minister of the Uniting Church in Australia, and was chair of the Common Dreams Conference for Religious Progressives from 2006 to 2013. He has published five books, and was a presenter at the CD1 Conference (2007) in Sydney, and a Workshop leader at CD3 (2013) Conference in Canberra.

The Revd Dr Gregory C. Jenks is Academic Dean St Francis Theological College in Brisbane and a Senior Lecturer in the School of Theology at Charles Sturt University. His recent books include *The Once and Future*

Bible (Wipf and Stock, 2011), *The Once and Future Scriptures* (Polebridge, 2013) and *Jesus Then and Jesus Now* (Morning Star Publishing, 2014). Greg was a presenter at the CD2 Conference (2010) in Melbourne, and a panelist and workshop leader at CD3 (2013) Conference in Canberra.

Rabbi Aviva Kipen is the first Australian woman ordained to the Rabbinate and now works in a ministry beyond congregational walls, serving Bet Olam Jewish Funerals, and the Union for Progressive Judaism in the region. A member of Australia's delegation to the ASEAN Regional Interfaith Dialogue Phnom Penh Conference, Aviva was appointed to the Australian Health Ethics Committee in 2012. Aviva was a workshop leader and panelist at the CD2 Conference (2010) in Melbourne, and a presenter at CD3 (2013) in Canberra.

The Revd Dr Nigel Leaves is Canon of St. John's Anglican Cathedral in Brisbane, Australia, and an Adjunct Lecturer in Theology at Charles Sturt University. He is author of several books including *The God Problem* and *Religion Under Attack* and has recently edited *God Encounter* (Morning Star Publications, forthcoming). Nigel was a presenter at both CD1 (2007) and CD3 (2013) Conferences.

Revd Dr Lorraine Parkinson is a retired minister of the Uniting Church. Her ministry included city parishes and part-time university chaplaincy. Her extensive involvement in Christian-Jewish relations in the Uniting Church at Synod and National Assembly levels, has included 10 years involvement in the national dialogue between the Uniting Church and the Executive Council of Australian Jewry. Lorraine was a presenter and workshop leader at the CD3 (2013) Conference in Canberra.

Revd Dr Noel Preston, AM is an ethicist, theologian and social commentator. He retired in November 2004 as the founding Director of the UnitingCare Centre for Social Justice. Previously he held senior academic positions at Queensland University of Technology and Griffith University in the fields of Applied and Professional Ethics. Noel was a presenter and workshop leader at the CD1 Conference (2007) in Sydney and a workshop leader at CD3 Conference (2013) in Canberra.

Revd Bruce Sanguin served as minister in the United Church of Canada for 28 years and is internationally renowned as a speaker, a blogger and author. Bruce was a keynote presenter and workshop leader at the CD3 Conference (2013) in Canberra. He has created *Home for Evolving Mystics*, an on-line membership site dedicated to inspiring and re-Sourcing everyday mystics on their evolving soul-path (www.brucesanguin.com)

Revd John W. H. Smith is a retired minster of the Uniting Church in Australia. His ministries included welfare management, chaplaincy and parish ministry. With Rex Hunt John co-edited *Why Weren't We Told? A Handbook on Progressive Christianity* (Polebridge, 2013) and *New Life: Rediscovering Faith. Stories from Progressive Christians* (Morning Star Publishing, 2014). He was a workshop leader at the CD2 Conference (2010) with David Clark, in Melbourne, and again at the CD3 Conference (2013) in Canberra.

Dr Jenny Te Paa Daniel (Te Rarawa) is a public theologian and professional consultant in higher education. Jenny was Ahorangi or Dean of Te Rau Kahikatea at St John's Theological College in Auckland from 1995 until 2013. She has written and researched extensively on gender justice, theological education and race politics. Jenny was a presenter at the CD1 (2007) Conference in Sydney.

Dr Val Webb has taught religious studies and world religions at universities in the United States and Australia and has written ten books, the most recent an expanded edition of her popular book *In Defence of Doubt: An Invitation to Adventure*. Her book *Like Catching Water in a Net: Human attempts to describe the Divine* won the religion category of the 2007 Best Books USA awards. She has been a presenter at all three Common Dreams Conferences, as well as a workshop leader at CD2 (2010) in Melbourne and a panelist at CD3 (2013) in Canberra.

Appendix: Recent literature by Australian and New Zealand Religious Progressives

Barraclough, Ray. *Why? The Challenge of Giving Explanations for Tragic Experiences in Life.* Burleigh Heads: Zeus Publications, 2010.

Birch, L. Charles. *Science and Soul.* Sydney: University of NSW Press, 2008.

Bodycomb, John. *No Fixed Address: Faith as Journey.* Richmond: Spectrum Publications, 2010.

——. *Aware and Attentive: 'Worship' in evolving Christianity.* Richmond: Spectrum Publications, 2012.

Bouma, Gary D. *Australian Soul: Religion and Spirituality in the 21st Century.* New York, NY: Cambridge University Press, 2007.

——. *Being Faithful in Diversity.* Adelaide: ATF Press, 2011.

Geering, Lloyd G. *From the Big Bang to God. Our Awe-Inspiring Journey of Evolution.* Wellington: Steele Roberts/Salem, OR: Polebridge, 2013.

——. *Such is Life! A Close Encounter with Ecclesiastes.* Wellington: Steele Roberts/Salem, OR: Polebridge, 2010.

——. *Coming Back to Earth. From Gods, to God, to Gaia.* Salem, OR: Polebridge, 2009.

Gunson, John. *Learning to Live Without God.* Melbourne. eBook, 2005.

Habel, Norman. *Exploring Ecological Hermeneutics.* (with Peter Trudinger) Minneapolis, MN: Fortress, 2008.

——. *The Birth, Curse and the Greening of Earth: An Ecological Reading of Genesis 1-11.* Sheffield: Phoenix, 2011.

——. *An Inconvenient Text: Is a 'Green Reading' of the Bible possible?* Adelaide: ATF Press, 2011.

——. *Rainbow of Mysteries: Meeting the Sacred in Nature.* Kelowna, CA: CopperHouse, 2012.

Halsey, R. *Voices from the Void.* Singapore: Trafford Publishing, 2012.

Hunt, Rex A. E. (ed. with Gregory C. Jenks) *Wisdom and Imagination: Religious Progressives and the Search for Meaning.* Melbourne: Morning Star Publishing, 2014.

——. (ed. with John Smith) *Why Weren't We Told: A Handbook on Progressive Christianity.* Salem, OR: Polebridge, 2012.

——. (ed. with John Smith) *New Life: Rediscovering Faith. Stories from Progressive Christianity.* Melbourne: Mosaic Press, 2013; Morning Star Publishing, 2014.

——. *Against the Stream: Progressive Christianity between Pulpit and Pew.* Melbourne: Mosaic Press, 2012; Morning Star Publishing, 2014.

——. *Cards, Carols & Claus: Christmas in Popular Culture and Progressive Christianity.* Melbourne: Mosaic Press, 2013; Morning Star Publishing, 2014.

Jenks, Gregory C. *Jesus Then and Jesus Now: Looking for Jesus, Finding Ourselves.* Melbourne: Mosaic Press, 2014; Morning Star Publishing, 2014.

(ed. with Rex Hunt) *Wisdom and Imagination: Religious Progressives and the Search for Meaning.* Melbourne: Morning Star Publications, 2014.

The Once and Future Bible: An Introduction to the Bible for Religious Progressives. Eugene, OR: Wipf & Stock, 2011.

(ed. and contributor) *The Once and Future Scriptures: Exploring the Role of the Bible in the Contemporary Church.* Salem, OR: Polebridge, 2013.

Leaves, Nigel (ed.). *Encountering God: Face to Face with the Divine.* Melbourne: Morning Star Publications, 2014.

——. *Religion Under Attack: Getting Theology Right.* Salem, OR: Polebridge, 2011.

——. *The God Problem: Alternatives to Fundamentalism.* Salem, OR: Polebridge, 2006.

Loader, William. *Sexuality in the New Testament.* London: SPCK, 2010.

——. *The New Testament on Sexuality.* Grand Rapids, MI: Eerdmans, 2012.

——. *Making Sense of Sex: Attitudes towards Sexuality in Early Jewish and Christian Literature.* Grand Rapids, MI: Eerdmans, 2013.

Macnab, Francis. *A Fine Wind is Blowing: Psalms of the Bible in Words that Blow you Away.* Richmond: Spectrum Publications, 2006.

———. *Discover a New Faith: Energy for a Better Life.* Richmond: Spectrum Publications, 2011.

Morwood, Michael. *Praying a New Story.* Richmond: Spectrum Publications, 2003.

———. *Children Praying a New Story: A Resource for Parents, Grandparents and Teachers.* Sunbury: Kelmor Publications, 2009.

———. *It's Time: Challenges to the Doctrine of the Faith.* Sunbury: Kelmor Publications, 2013)

———. *In Memory of Jesus.* USA: CreateSpace Independent Publishing, 2014.

Murray, S. E. *A Place at the Table. New Hymns written between 2009 and 2013.* Carol Stream: Hope Publishing, 2013.

———. *Touch the Earth Lightly. New Hymns written between 2003 and 2008.* Carol Stream: Hope Publishing, 2008.

Ogden, Steven G. *I Met God in Bermuda: Faith in the 21st Century.* Winchester: O Books, 2009.

———. *Love Upside Down: Life, Love and the Subversive Jesus.* Winchester: O Books, 2011.

Parkinson, Lorraine. *The World According to Jesus: His Blueprint for the Best Possible World.* Richmond: Spectrum Publications, 2011.

Preston, Noel. *Beyond the Boundary: A Memoir Exploring Ethics, Politics and Spirituality.* Burleigh Heads: Zeus Publications, 2006.

———. *Understanding Ethics.* 3rd edition. Sydney: Federation Press, 2007.

———. *Ethics With or Without God.* Melbourne: Mosaic Press, 2014; Morning Star Publishing, 2014.

Smith, E. Durham. *Search for Understanding: The Fullness of Life? Wishful Hope or a Real Possibility?* 2nd edition. Melbourne: Mind Publishing, 2011.

Smith, John W. H. *Honest to Go(o)d.* Melbourne: Morning Star Publications, forthcoming.

———. (ed. with Rex Hunt) *Why Weren't We Told: A Handbook on Progressive Christianity.* (Oregon: Polebridge, 2012)

———. (ed. with Rex Hunt) *New Life: Rediscovering Faith. Stories from*

Progressive Christianity. Melbourne: Mosaic Press, 2013; Morning Star Publishing, 2014.

Stuart, George. *Singing a New Song: Traditional Hymn Tunes with New Century Lyrics*. Sydney: CPRT Sydney, 2006.

——. *Singing a New Song: Traditional Hymn Tunes with New Century Lyrics, Vol. 2*. Toronto, NSW: self-published, 2009.

——. *Singing a New Song: Traditional Hymn Tunes with New Century Lyrics, Vol. 3*. Toronto, NSW: self-published, 2011.

——. *Singing a New Song: Traditional Hymn Tunes with New Century Lyrics, Vol. 4*. Toronto, NSW: self-published, 2013.

Webb, Val. *Like Catching Water in a Net: Human Attempts to Describe the Divine*. New York, NY and London: Continuum, 2007.

——. *Stepping out with the Sacred: Human Attempts to Engage the Divine*. New York, NY and London: Continuum, 2010.

——. *In Defence of Doubt: An Invitation to Adventure*. 2nd edition. Melbourne: Mosaic Press, 2012; Morning Star Publishing, 2014.

White, B. A. *You Who Delight Me: Words of Spirit and Faith*. Wellington, NZ: Steele Roberts, 2012.

Bibliography

Abegg, Martin., Peter W. Flint, and Eugene Ulrich. *The Dead Sea Scrolls Bible: The Oldest Known Bible Translated for the First Time into English*. Edinburgh: T & T Clark, 1999.

Aly, Waleed. *People Like Us: How Arrogance is Dividing Islam and the West*. Sydney: Pan Macmillan Australia, 2007.

Armstrong, Karen. *The Case for God: What Religion Really Means*. New York, NY: Random House, 2009.

———. *In The Beginning: A New Reading of the Book of Genesis*. London: HarperCollins, 1998.

Aslan, Reza. *Zealot: The Life and Times of Jesus of Nazareth*. New York, NY: Random House, 2013.

Badger, Colin R. *The Reverend Charles Strong and the Australian Church*. Melbourne: Abacada Press, 1971.

Badran, Margot. *Feminism in Islam: Secular and Religious Convergences*. Oxford: Oneworld Press, 2008.

Barclay, William. *The Gospel According to Matthew*. Scotland: St Andrews Press, 1956.

Bcal, Timothy K. *The Rise and Fall of the Bible: The Unexpected History of an Accidental Book*. Chicago, IL: Houghton Mifflin Harcourt, 2011.

BeDuhn, Jason D. *The First New Testament: Marcion's Scriptural Canon*. Salem, OR: Polebridge, 2013.

Berry, Thomas. *The Great Work: Our Way into the Future*. New York, NY: Bell Tower, 1999.

Bessler, Joseph A. *A Scandalous Jesus: How Three Historic Quests Changed Theology for the Better*. Salem, OR: Polebridge, 2013.

Birch, L. Charles. *Nature and God*. London: SCM, 1965.

—— *On Purpose*. Sydney: University of New South Wales Press, 1990.

—— *Science and Soul*. Sydney: University of New South Wales Press, 2008.

—— and Cobb, John B. *The Liberation of Life*. Cambridge: Cambridge University Press, 1981.

Bodycomb, John. *Aware and Attentive. Worship in Evolving Christianity*. Richmond: Spectrum, 2012.

Boff, Leonardo. *Cry of the Earth, Cry of the Poor*. Maryknoll, NY: Orbis Books, 1997.

Bonhoeffer, Dietrich. *Letters and Papers from Prison*. London: SCM, 1953.

Borg, Marcus J. *The God We Never Knew: Beyond Dogmatic Religion to a More Authentic Contemporary Faith*. New York, NY: HarperCollins, 1997.

——. *The Heart of Christianity: Rediscovering a Life of Faith*. New York, NY: HarperCollins, 2003.

——. *Meeting Jesus Again for the First Time: The Historical Jesus and the Heart of Contemporary Faith*. New York, NY: HarperOne, 1995.

Bouma, Gary D. *Being Faithful in Diversity*. Adelaide: ATF Press, 2011.

Brodie, Thomas L. *Beyond the Quest for the Historical Jesus: Memoir of a Discovery*. Sheffield: Sheffield Phoenix Press, 2012.

Bruce, F. F. *The Canon of Scripture*. Downers Grove, IL: IVF Academic, 1988.

Burklo, Jim. Baptism Liturgy. *http://tcpc blogs com/musings/2012/12/jim-burklos*-book-of-common-prayer.html

Butcher, John Beverley. *An Uncommon Lectionary*. Santa Rosa, CA: Polebridge, 2002.

Butler Bass, Diana. *Christianity After Religion: The End of Church and the Birth of a New Spiritual Awakening*. San Francisco, CA: HarperCollins, 2012.

Capra, Fritjof. *The Hidden Connections: A Science for Sustainable Living*. New York, NY: Harper Collins, 2002.

Chadwick, Owen. *The Reformation*. The Penguin History of the Church, 3. Harmondsworth, UK: Pelican Books, 1964.

Charlesworth, James H. (ed.). *The Old Testament Pseudepigrapha*. 2 vols. New York, NY: Doubleday, 1983.

Churcher, John. *Setting Jesus Free*. Ropley, UK: O Books, 2009.

Clayton, Philip (ed.). *All That Is: A Naturalistic Faith for the Twenty-First Century*. Minneapolis, MN, Fortress, 2007.

Coogan, Michael D., Marc Z. Brettler, Carol A. Newsom, and Pheme Perkins. *The New Oxford Annotated Bible: New Revised Standard Version*. New York, NY: Oxford University Press, 2011.

Cowdell, Scott. "Baptism in Australia: Secularisation, 'civil baptism' and the social miracle" in Stephen Burns and Anita Monro (eds.). *Christian Worship in Australia. Inculturating the Liturgical Tradition*. Strathfield: St Pauls, 2009.

Cox, Harvey. *The Future of Faith*. New York, NY: HarperOne, 2009.

Cox, Harvey (ed.). *The Situation Ethics Debate*. Philadelphia, PA: Westminster Press, 1968.

Crane, Ashley S. *Israel's Restoration: A Textual-Comparative Exploration of Ezekiel 36–39*. Supplements to Vetus Testamentum. Leiden: Brill, 2008.

Crossan, John Dominic. *The Birth of Christianity: Discovering What Happened in the Years Immediately After the Execution of Jesus*. New York, NY: HarperCollins 1999.

———. *The Historical Jesus: The Life of a Mediterranean Jewish Peasant*. San Francisco, CA: HarperSanFrancisco, 1991.

———. *Jesus: A Revolutionary Biography*. San Francisco, CA: HarperSanFrancisco, 1994.

———. *The Power of Parable: How Fiction by Jesus Became Fiction About Jesus*. New York, NY: HarperCollins, 2012.

Cupitt, Don. *Jesus and Philosophy*. London: SCM Press, 2012.

———. *Taking Leave of God*. London: SCM Press, 1980.

———. *The Religion of Life in EverydaySpeech*. London: SCM Press, 1999.

———. *What is a Story?* London: SCM, 1991.

Daly, Mary. *Beyond God the Father*. Boston, MA: Beacon Press, 1974.

De Mello, Anthony. *The Prayer of the Frog*. India: Gujarat Sahitya Prakash Anand, 1987.

Deane-Drummond, Celia. *Christ and Evolution: Wonder and Wisdom.* Minneapolis, MN: Augsburg Fortress, 2009.

Dewey, Arthur J., Roy W. Hoover, Lane C. McGaughey, and Daryl D. Schmidt. *The Authentic Letters of Paul: A New Reading of Paul's Rhetoric and Meaning.* Salem, OR: Polebridge, 2010.

Doherty, Earl J. *Jesus Neither God Nor Man: The Case for a Mythical Jesus.* 2nd. ed. Ottawa: Age of Reason Publications, 2009.

Dostoyevsky, Fyodor. *The Brothers Karamazov.* (1880) London: Penguin Books, 2003.

Edwards, David (ed.). *The Honest to God Debate.* London: SCM Press, 1963.

Edwards, Denis. *Ecology at the Heart of Faith.* Maryknoll, NY: Orbis Books, 2006.

Ehrman, Bart D. *Did Jesus Exist? The Historical Argument for Jesus of Nazareth.* San Francisco, CA: HarperOne, 2012.

——. *Forged: Writing in the Name of God.* San Francisco, CA: HarperCollins, 2012.

——. *Jesus, Apocalyptic Prophet of the New Millennium.* Oxford: Oxford University Press, 2001.

——. *Jesus Interrupted: Revealing the Hidden Contradictions in the Bible.* San Francisco, CA: HarperCollins, 2010.

——. *Misquoting Jesus: The Story Behind Who Changed the Bible and Why.* San Francisco, CA: HarperCollins, 2009.

Feuerbach, Ludwig. *Thoughts on Death and Immortality.* Berkeley, CA: University of California Press, 1980.

——. *The Essence of Christianity.* New York, NY: Harper Torchbook, 1957.

Fletcher, Joseph. *Situation Ethics.* London: SCM Press, 1966.

Fosdick, Harry Emerson. *Adventurous Religion and Other Essays.* London: SCM, 1927.

Fox, Matthew. *The Coming of the Cosmic Christ.* New York, NY: Collins Dove, 1988.

Fulghum, Robert. *All I Really Needed to Know I Learned in Kindergarten.* New York, NY: Ivy Books, 1986.

Funk, Robert W. "Editorial." *The Fourth R* 18 (2005): 1, 2, 20.

———. *Honest to Jesus: Jesus for a New Millennium*. San Francisco, CA: HarperSanFrancisco, 1996.

———. "Milestones in the Quest for the Historical Jesus" *The Fourth R* vol. 14, no. 4 (2001): 9–11,14–18.

———, Roy W. Hoover, and The Jesus Seminar. *The Five Gospels: What Did Jesus Really Say? The Search for the Authentic Words of Jesus*. New York, NY: Macmillan, 1993.

—— and the Jesus Seminar. *The Acts of Jesus: What Did Jesus Really Do?* San Francisco, CA: HarperSanFrancisco 1998.

Galston, David. *Embracing the Human Jesus. A Wisdom Path for Contemporary Christianity*. Salem, OR: Polebridge, 2012.

———. "Liturgy in the Key of Q". In private circulation from the Westar Institute, 2007.

———. "Postmodernism, The Historical Jesus and the Church" *The Fourth R* vol. 18, no. 5 (2005): 11,14–18.

———. *Quest Learning Centre for Religious Literacy*. www.questcentre.ca

Geering, Lloyd. *The World to Come: From Christian Past to Global Future*. Santa Rosa, CA: Polebridge, 1999.

Gibran, Kahlil. *Sand and Foam*. New York: NY: Alfred A. Knopf, 1926)

Gulley, Philip. *If the Church Were Christian: Rediscovering the Values of Jesus*. New York, NY HarperOne, 2010.

Gunson, John. *Learning to Live Without God*. Melbourne: eBook, 2005. In private circulation.

Gurney, Chris. *The Mayor's Flash New Clothes*. Auckland: Scholastic New Zealand, 2010.

Habel, Norman. *Rainbow of Mysteries*. Kelowna, BC: Wood Lake Publishing, 2012.

Harpur, Thomas W. *The Pagan Christ: Recovering the Lost Light*. Toronto: Thomas Allen, 2004.

Hedrick, Charles W. *When Faith Meets Reason: Religion Scholars Reflect on their Spiritual Journeys*. Santa Rosa, CA: Polebridge, 2008.

Heschel, Sussanah. *The Aryan Jesus: Christian Theologians and the Bible in Nazi Germany*. Princeton, NJ: Princeton University Press, 2010.

Heyward, Carter. *The Redemption of God: A Theology of Mutual Relation*. Washington, DC: University Press of America, 1982.

Hick, John. *The Metaphor of God Incarnate*. London: SCM Press, 1993.

Hoover, Roy W. (ed.). *Profiles of Jesus*. Santa Rosa, CA: Polebridge, 2002.

Hunt, Rex A. E. *Against the Stream: Progressive Christianity Between Pulpit and Pew*. Melbourne: Mosaic Press, 2012; Morning Star Publishing, 2014.

——. "Foreword: Where is Progressive Christianity At? Four Exploratory Cameos ..." in J. W. H. Smith and R. A. E. Hunt (eds.). *New Life: Rediscovering Faith. Stories from Progressive Christians*. Melbourne: Mosaic, 2013; Morning Star Publishing, 2014.

——. and John W. H. Smith (eds.). *Why Weren't We Told?* Salem, OR: Polebridge, 2013.

Hyde, Dudley. *Rescuing Jesus from the Church*. Bayview, NSW: Minkara, 1994.

Inbody, Tyron. *The Many Faces of Christology*. Nashville, TN: Abingdon Press, 2002.

Jenks, Gregory C. *The Once and Future Bible: An Introduction to the Bible for Religious Progressives*. Eugene, OR: Wipf & Stock, 2011.

—— (ed.). *The Once and Future Scriptures: Exploring the Role of the Bible in the Contemporary Church*. Salem, OR: Polebridge, 2013.

Jewish Publication Society. *Tanakh: The Holy Scriptures. The New JPS Translation According to the Traditional Hebrew Text*. Philadelphia, PA: Jewish Publication Society, 1985.

Jones, R. "Metaphor and Sacrament". Westar Institute Literacy & Liturgy Seminar. In private circulation, 2007

Kee, Alistair. *The Roots of Christian Freedom: The Theology of John A.T. Robinson*. London: SPCK, 1988.

Keen, Sam. *Apology for Wonder*. New York, NY: Harper and Row Publishers, 1969.

King, Ursula. *Spirit of Fire: The Life and Vision of Teilhard de Chardin*.

Maryknoll, NY: Orbis, 1996.

Kinsley, David. *Ecology and Religion: Ecological Spirituality in Cross-Cultural Perspective.* Englewood Cliffs, NJ: Prentice-Hall, 1995.

Knight, Mary. "Curing Cut or Ritual Mutilation? Some Remarks on the Practice of Female and Male Circumcision in Graeco-Roman Egypt." *Isis* vol. 92, no. 2 (2001): 317–38.

Knitter, Paul. *Without Buddha I Could not be a Christian.* Oxford: One World, 2009.

Ladinksy, Daniel and Nancy Owen (eds.). *The Purity of Desire: 100 Poems of Rumi.* New York, NY: Penguin Books, 2012.

Lataster, Raphael. *There was no Jesus, There was no God.* North Charleston, SC: Create Space Independent Publishing, 2013.

Levine, Amy-Jill, and Marc Zvi Brettler. *The Jewish Annotated New Testament.* New York, NY: Oxford University Press, 2011.

Loehr, Davidson. "Salvation by character: How UU's can find the religious center" in *Journal of Liberal Religion 1*, 2, 1-14, 2000.

Lovelock, James. *Gaia: A New Look at Life on Earth.* Oxford: Oxford University Press, 1979.

Macquarrie, John. *In Search of Deity.* London: SCM Press, 1984.

McFague, Sallie. *The Body of God: An Ecological Theology.* London: SCM, 1993.

———. *Blessed are the Consumers: Climate Change and the Practice of Restraint.* Minneapolis, MN: Augsburg, 2013.

McRae-McMahon, Dorothy. "Liturgy in the southern hemisphere: The Australian context" in S. Burns and A Monro (eds.). *Christian Worship in Australia. Inculturating the Liturgical Tradition.* Strathfield: St Pauls, 2009.

Macnab, Francis. *A Fine Wind is Blowing: Psalms of the Bible in Words that Blow you Away.* Melbourne: Spectrum, 2006.

Martinez, Florentino Garcia. *The Dead Sea Scrolls Translated: The Qumran Texts in English.* Leiden: E. J. Brill, 1994.

Marxsen, W. *Jesus and the Church. The Beginnings of Christianity.*

Philadelphia PA: Trinity Press International, 1992.

Meyer, Marvin W., and James M. Robinson. *The Nag Hammadi Scriptures: The Revised and Updated Translation of Sacred Gnostic Texts.* New York, NY: HarperCollins, 2009.

Meyers, Robin R. *Saving Jesus from the Church: How to Stop Worshipping Christ and Start Following Jesus.* San Francisco, CA: HarperCollins, 2009.

Milavec, Aaron. "The Didache: A window on gentile Christianity before the written gospels" in *The Fourth R* 18 (2005): 3, 7–11, 15–16.

Miller, Robert J. (ed.). *The Apocalyptic Jesus: A Debate.* Santa Rosa, CA: Polebridge, 2001.

—— (ed.). *The Complete Gospels.* 4th ed. Santa Rosa, CA: Polebridge, 2010.

Morwood, Michael. *Is Jesus God? Finding our Faith.* New York, NY: Crossroads, 2001.

——. *It's Time: Challenges to the Doctrine of the Faith.* Melbourne: Kelmor Publications, 2013.

Murdoch, Dorothy. M. ("Acharya S"). *The Christ Conspiracy: The Greatest Story Ever Sold.* Kempton, IL: Adventures Unlimited Press, 1999.

Nolan, Albert. *Jesus Today: A Spirituality of Radical Freedom.* Maryknoll, NY: Orbis Books, 2007.

Northcott, Michael. "Ecology and Christian Ethics", in R. Gill (ed), *The Cambridge Companion to Christian Ethics.* 2nd. ed. Cambridge: Cambridge University Press, 2012.

Northumbria Community. *Celtic Daily Prayer. Inspirational Prayers and Readings from the Northumbria Community.* London: Collins, 2005.

O'Donohue, John. *Anam Cara: Spiritual Wisdom from the Celtic World.* London: Bantam Press, 1997.

O'Murchu, Diarmuid. *Adult Faith: Growing in Wisdom and Understanding.* Maryknoll, NY: Orbis Books 2010.

——. *Quantum Theology.* New York, NY: Crossroad, 1997.

Otto, Rudolf. *The Idea of the Holy.* Oxford: Oxford University Press, 1923.

Patterson, Stephen J. *Beyond the Passion. Rethinking the Death and Life of Jesus*. Minneapolis MN: Fortress, 2004.

——. *The God of Jesus: The Historical Jesus and the Search for Meaning*. Harrisburg, PA: Trinity Press, 1998.

Pietersma, Albert, and Benjamin G. Wright. *A New English Translation of the Septuagint: And the Other Greek Translations Traditionally Included under That Title*. New York, NY: Oxford University Press, 2007.

Preston, Noel. "Exploring Eco-Justice: Reframing Ethics and Spirituality in an Era of Globalization." The 2002 Felix Arnott Lecture. Brisbane: St Francis College, 2002.

——. *Beyond the Boundary: A Memoir Exploring Ethics, Politics and Spirituality*. Gold Coast: Zeus Publications, 2006.

——. "Ethics *sans frontiers*: The Vocation of Global Citizenship." The 2006 Aquinas Lecture. Australian Catholic University. *Australian eJournal of Theology* Vol. 8, No 1 (2006): 1–19.

—— (ed.) "Global Ethics" *Social Alternatives* Vol. 26, No. 3 (2007).

——. *Ethics: With or Without God*. Melbourne: Mosaic, 2014; Morning Star Publishing, 2014.

——. *Understanding Ethics* 4th ed. Sydney: Federation, 2014.

Price, Robert M. *The Christ-Myth Theory and Its Problems*. Cranford, NJ: The American Atheist Press, 2012.

Reuther, Rosemary Radford. *Gaia and God*. New York, NY: Harper Collins, 1992.

Robinson, John A. T.. *Christian Freedom in a Permissive Society*. London: SCM, 1970.

——. *Honest to God*. London: SCM Press, 1963.

——. *The Human Face of God*. London: SCM, 1973.

——. *Jesus and His Coming: The Emergence of a Doctrine*. London: SCM, 1957.

——. *The New Reformation?* London: SCM, 1965.

——. *Thou Who Art*. London: Continuum, 2006.

——. *Where Three Ways Meet*. London: SCM, 1987.

Rubenstein, Richard L. *After Auschwitz*. Indianapolis, IN: Bobbs-Merrill, 1966.

Scheiermacher, Friedrich. *Christmas Eve: A Dialogue on the Celebration of Christmas*. Edinburgh: T & T Clark, 1890.

——. *On Religion: Speeches to its Cultured Despisers*. New York, NY: Harper Torchbook, 1958.

——. *The Christian Faith*. Edinburgh: T & T Clark, 1928.

Schweitzer, Albert. *The Quest of the Historical Jesus*. London: A & C Black, 1910.

Scott, B. Brandon. *Re-Imagine the World: An Introduction to the Parables*. Santa Rosa, CA: Polebridge, 2001.

Seaburg, Carl (ed.). *The Communion Book*. Boston, MA: Unitarian Universalist Ministers Association, 1993.

Smith, Dennis E. "Messianic Banquet." In *Anchor Yale Bible Dictionary*, edited by David Noel Freedman 4, 788–91. New York, NY: Doubleday, 1992.

—— and Hal E. Taussig. *Many Tables: The Eucharist in the New Testament and Liturgy Today*. Eugene, OR: Wipf and Stock, 2001.

Smith, Huston. *Why Religion Matters: The Fate of the Human Spirit in the Age of Unbelief*. New York, NY: HarperSanFrancisco, 2001.

Smith, John W. H., and Rex A. E. Hunt (eds.). *New Life: Rediscovering Faith. Stories from Progressive Christians*. Melbourne: Mosaic, 2013; Morning Star Publishing, 2014.

Soelle, Dorothee. *The Silent Cry: Mysticism and Resistance*. Minneapolis, MN: Augsburg Fortress Press, 2001.

Sparks, Kenton L. *God's Word in Human Words: An Evangelical Appropriation of Biblical Criticism*. Grand Rapids, MI: Baker Academic Press, 2008.

Spong, John Shelby. *A New Christianity for a New World*. San Francisco, CA: HarperCollins, 2002.

——. *Here I Stand: My Struggle for a Christianity of Integrity, Love, and Equality*. New York, NY: HarperCollins, 2000.

——. *Why Christianity Must Change or Die: A Bishop Speaks to Believers in Exile.* New York, NY: HarperCollins, 1999.

Stevenson, Eric. "Words of Committal". In private circulation, 2013. Used with permission.

Stinson, J. "The Encounter of Progressive Christian Theology with the Language of Prayer and Ritual on Sunday Morning". Westar Institute/ Literacy & Liturgy Seminar. In private circulation, 2006.

Tacey, David. *ReEnchantment: The New Australian Spirituality.* Sydney: HarperCollins, 2000.

Tatum, W. Barnes. *Jesus at the Movies.* 3rd ed. Santa Rosa, CA: Polebridge, 2012.

Taussig, Hal E. *A New New Testament: A Bible for the 21st Century Combining Traditional and Newly Discovered Texts.* Chicago, IL: Houghton Mifflin Harcourt, 2013.

——. *A New Spiritual Home. Progressive Christianity at the Grassroots.* Santa Rosa, CA: Polebridge, 2006.

——, "Grassroots Progressive Christianity: A Quiet Revolution" in *The Fourth R 19,* 3, (2006): 3-8.

Teilhard de Chardin, Pierre. *The Future of Man.* New York, NY: Harper & Row, 1959.

——. *The Phenomenon of Man.* New York, NY: Harper Perennial, 1955.

Tillich, Paul. *The Courage to Be.* London: Collins, 1952.

——. *The Shaking of the Foundations.* Harmondsworth, UK: Penguin Books, 1949.

——. *Systematic Theology.* 3 vols. Welwyn, UK: James Nisbet, 1953–1964.

Treston, Kevin. *Emergence for Life not Fall from Grace.* Melbourne: Mosaic, 2013; Morning Star Publishing, 2014.

Turner, Victor. *The Forest of Symbols: Aspects of Ndembu Ritual.* Ithaca, NY: Cornell University Press, 1967.

Underhill, Everlyn. *Practical Mysticism: A Little Book for Normal People.* New York, NY: E.P. Dutton, 1915.

Uniting in Worship 2. Sydney: Uniting Church Press, 2005.

Verhoeven, Paul. *Jesus of Nazareth*. New York, NY: Seven Stories Press, 2010.

Vogt, Von O. *Modern Worship*. Lowell Institute Lectures 1927. New Haven, CT: Yale University Press, 1927.

Vosper, Gretta. *With or Without God. Why the way we Live is more important that what we Believe.* Toronto. HarperCollins, 2008.

Ward, Keith. *A Vision to Pursue: Beyond the Crisis in Christianity.* London: SCM, 1991.

Watkins, Peter. *An (Un)Common Book of Hours.* eBook: Smashwords, 2013.

Webb, Val. *In Defense of Doubt: An Invitation to Adventure.* St. Louis: Chalice Press, 1995.

——. *Why We're Equal: Introducing Feminist Theology.* St. Louis: Chalice Press, 1999.

——. *John's Message: Good News for the New Millennium.* Nashville, TN: Abingdon Press, 1999.

——. *Florence Nightingale: The Making of a Radical Theologian.* St. Louis: Chalice Press, 2002.

——. *Like Catching Water in a Net: Human Attempts to Describe the Divine.* New York and London: Continuum, 2007.

——. *Stepping Out With the Sacred: Human Attempts to Engage the Divine.* New York and London: Continuum, 2010.

——. *In Defence of Doubt: An Invitation to Adventure.* 2nd. ed. Melbourne: Mosaic Press, 2012; Morning Star Publishing, 2014.

Weir, John E. (ed.). *Collected Poems James K. Baxter.* Wellington: Oxford University Press, 1979.

White, Susan J. *Christian Worship and Technological Change.* Nashville, TN: Abington Press, 1994.

Wiig, R. "Words of Committal". In private circulation, 2013. Used with permission.

—— and D. McKenzie. *Baptism Liturgy.* "God's love, like a …" In private circulation from the authors. 1998. Used with permission.

Williams, Colin W. *John Wesley's Theology Today: A Study of the Wesleyan tradition in the Light of Current Theological Debate.* London:

Epworth, 1960.

Wilson, Barry. *How Jesus Became Christian*. Toronto: Random House Canada, 2008.

Wilson, E. O. *Consilience: The Unity of Knowledge*. New York, NY: Little Brown and Company, 1998.

Wolsey, Roger. *Kissing Fish: Christianity for People Who Don't Like Christianity*. Bloomington, IN: Xlibris, 2011.

World Council of Churches. *Baptism, Eucharist and Ministry*. Geneva: World Council of Churches, 1982.

Index

Made in the USA
San Bernardino, CA
03 November 2016